CONTENTS

easy
Office 2013

Patrice-Anne Rutledge
Sherry Kinkoph Gunter

800 East 96th Street
Indianapolis, Indiana 46240

**PART V
Microsoft
Outlook 2013**

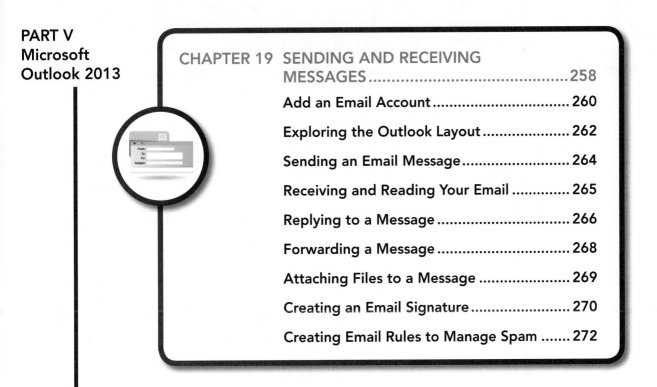

EASY OFFICE 2013

ISBN-13: 978-0-7897-5077-8

ISBN-10: 0-7897-5077-5

Library of Congress Cataloging-in-Publication data is on file and available upon request.

Printed in the United States of America

First Printing: March 2013

TRADEMARKS

WARNING AND DISCLAIMER

BULK SALES

Que Publishing offers excellent discounts on this book when ordered in quantity for bulk purchases or special sales. For more information, please contact

U.S. Corporate and Government Sales
1-800-382-3419
corpsales@pearsontechgroup.com

For sales outside of the U.S., please contact

International Sales
international@pearsoned.com

Editor-in-Chief
Greg Wiegand

Acquisitions Editor
Michelle Newcomb

Development Editor
Charlotte Kughen

Managing Editor
Kristy Hart

Senior Project Editor
Lori Lyons

Indexer
Lisa Stumpf

Technical Editor
Vince Averello

Editorial Assistant
Cindy Teeters

Copy Editor
Apostrophe Editing Services

Interior and Cover Designer
Anne Jones

Senior Compositor
Gloria Schurick

Proofreader
Dan Knott

ABOUT THE AUTHORS

Patrice-Anne Rutledge is a business technology author and consultant who specializes in teaching others to maximize the power of new technologies. Patrice has used—and has trained others to use—Microsoft Office for many years. She is the author of numerous books about Office for Pearson Education, including *PowerPoint 2013 Absolute Beginner's Guide*. She can be reached through her website at www.patricerutledge.com.

Sherry Kinkoph Gunter has written and edited oodles of books over the past 20 years covering a wide variety of computer topics, including Microsoft Office programs, digital photography, and web applications. Her recent titles include *Easy Microsoft Word 2010*, *Craigslist 4 Everyone*, and *Sams Teach Yourself Facebook in 10 Minutes*. Sherry's ongoing quest is to aid users of all levels in the mastering of ever-changing computer technologies, helping users make sense of it all and get the most out of their machines and online experiences.

DEDICATION

To my family, with thanks for their ongoing support and encouragement.

ACKNOWLEDGMENTS

Special thanks to Michelle Newcomb, Charlotte Kughen, Vince Averello, and Lori Lyons for their feedback, suggestions, and attention to detail.

WE WANT TO HEAR FROM YOU!

As the reader of this book, *you* are our most important critic and commentator. We value your opinion and want to know what we're doing right, what we could do better, what areas you'd like to see us publish in, and any other words of wisdom you're willing to pass our way.

We welcome your comments. You can email or write to let us know what you did or didn't like about this book—as well as what we can do to make our books better.

Please note that we cannot help you with technical problems related to the topic of this book.

When you write, please be sure to include this book's title and author as well as your name, email address, and phone number. We will carefully review your comments and share them with the authors and editors who worked on the book.

Email: feedback@quepublishing.com

Mail: Que Publishing
ATTN: Reader Feedback
800 East 96th Street
Indianapolis, IN 46240 USA

READER SERVICES

Visit our website and register this book at informit.com/register for convenient access to any updates, downloads, or errata that might be available for this book.

IT'S AS EASY AS 1-2-3

Each part of this book is made up of a series of short, instructional lessons, designed to help you understand basic information.

 Each step is fully illustrated to show you how it looks onscreen

 Each task includes a series of quick, easy steps designed to guide you through the procedure.

3 Items that you select or click in menus, dialog boxes, tabs, and windows are shown in **bold**.

Tips, notes, and cautions give you a heads-up for any extra information you may need while working through the task.

How to Drag: Point to the starting place or object. Hold down the mouse button (right or left per instructions), move the mouse to the new location, and then release the button.

Click: Click the left mouse button once.

Click & Type: Click once where indicated and begin typing to enter your text or data.

Selection: Highlights the area onscreen discussed in the step or task.

Double-click: Click the left mouse button twice in rapid succession.

Right-click: Click the right mouse button once.

Pointer arrow: Highlights an item on the screen you need to point to or focus on in the step or task.

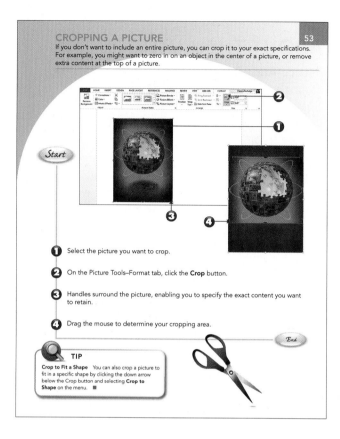

CROPPING A PICTURE

If you don't want to include an entire picture, you can crop it to your exact specifications. For example, you might want to zero in on an object in the center of a picture, or remove extra content at the top of a picture.

1 Select the picture you want to crop.

2 On the Picture Tools–Format tab, click the **Crop** button.

3 Handles surround the picture, enabling you to specify the exact content you want to retain.

4 Drag the mouse to determine your cropping area.

TIP

Crop to Fit a Shape You can also crop a picture to fit in a specific shape by clicking the down arrow below the Crop button and selecting **Crop to Shape** on the menu.

INTRODUCTION TO
EASY OFFICE 2013

Microsoft Office 2013 is the latest version of Microsoft's popular suite of business software applications. Using Office, you can quickly create documents such as letters, reports, and resumes; calculate and analyze data in spreadsheets; design and deliver presentations; send and receive email; and store data in digital notebooks.

The world is becoming increasing mobile, and so is Office 2013. This new version is integrated with SkyDrive, Microsoft's online storage solution. In addition to web-based file-sharing, SkyDrive also gives you access to the Microsoft Web Apps for Word, Excel, PowerPoint, and OneNote. Office 2013 makes it easy to access, edit, and create Office files on the go, using a mobile device such as a tablet or smartphone.

Easy Microsoft Office 2013 is designed to get you up and running on Office as quickly as possible. This book covers five of the most popular Office applications—Word, Excel, PowerPoint, Outlook, and OneNote—and provides visual, step-by-step instructions that help you master tasks with little effort. For now, turn to Chapter 1, "Getting Started with Microsoft Office 2013," to begin exploring this powerful application suite.

WHO THIS BOOK IS FOR

This book is for you if...

- You want to become productive with the latest version of Office as quickly as possible and are short on time.

- You're new to Office and need to learn the basics in an easy-to-understand format.

- You're a visual learner and want to *see* what to do rather than read lengthy paragraphs describing what to do.

HOW THIS BOOK IS ORGANIZED

Easy Microsoft Office 2013 is divided into six parts.

Part I, "Microsoft Office 2013," introduces Office fundamentals, such as navigating applications, using the Ribbon and Backstage view, getting help, and saving and opening files. If you're an experienced computer user but are new to Office, these chapters provide a foundation for using the Office suite. If you've used Office in the past, they can serve as a quick review and introduce you to the new, exciting features of Office 2013.

In Part II, "Microsoft Word 2013," you continue on to one of the most popular Office applications: Microsoft Word. In this section, you learn how to create and format documents, modify page layout, and perform a collaborative review of your documents before you print, publish, or send.

Next, you can start exploring Excel, Office's spreadsheet application. Part III, "Microsoft Excel 2013," shows you how to create and format Excel workbooks and worksheets and introduces you to cell formulas and functions. Finally, you can analyze your worksheet data using visual tools such as charts, PivotTables, and sparklines (mini charts).

Part IV, "Microsoft PowerPoint 2013," shows you how to create eye-catching presentations using PowerPoint's powerful collection of ready-made tools, even if you're design-challenged. You also learn how to edit and format presentations; incorporate audio, video, and animation; and prepare for delivery, either in person or on the Web.

Part V, "Microsoft Outlook 2013," helps you get up and running quickly with Office's email, calendaring, and scheduling tools.

And finally, you explore OneNote, Office's digital notebook application that helps you organize masses of data. Part VI, "Microsoft OneNote 2013," introduces you to OneNote basics, such as creating, enhancing, managing, and sharing notebooks.

Chapter 1

GETTING STARTED WITH MICROSOFT OFFICE 2013

Although Microsoft Office 2013 is intuitive and easy to use, it's worth spending several minutes exploring its interface and navigation tools. The most common of these include the Ribbon, Backstage view, the Quick Access toolbar, the mini toolbar, contextual tabs, and task panes.

If you're upgrading from Office 2007 or 2010, the basic Office interface should be reasonably familiar. There are enhancements to the Ribbon and Backstage view, but these key features still work in much the same way. If you're upgrading from a previous Office version, however, take your time exploring the new ways to use and navigate Office.

The first thing you'll notice when you start most Office 2013 applications is the new start screen that welcomes you. This screen is color-coded: blue for Word, green for Excel, and red for PowerPoint. Outlook and OneNote, however, open directly to the Home tab, bypassing the start screen.

For now, let's start with a quick tour of Microsoft Office 2013.

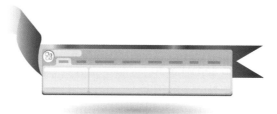

MICROSOFT OFFICE 2013 START SCREEN (WORD)

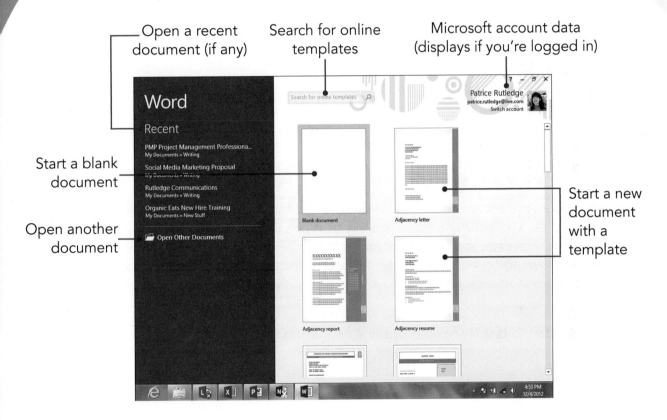

Open a recent document (if any)

Search for online templates

Microsoft account data (displays if you're logged in)

Start a blank document

Open another document

Start a new document with a template

USING THE RIBBON

The *Ribbon*, which replaces the menu structure found in Office 2003 and earlier, provides an easy way to access common commands and buttons using the least amount of space possible. To start, explore some common Ribbon features.

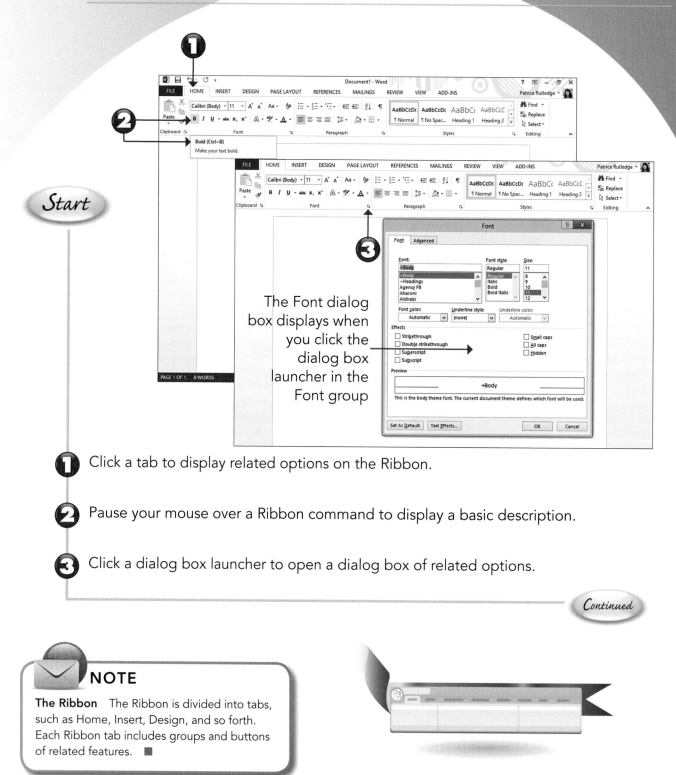

The Font dialog box displays when you click the dialog box launcher in the Font group

Start

1. Click a tab to display related options on the Ribbon.

2. Pause your mouse over a Ribbon command to display a basic description.

3. Click a dialog box launcher to open a dialog box of related options.

Continued

NOTE

The Ribbon The Ribbon is divided into tabs, such as Home, Insert, Design, and so forth. Each Ribbon tab includes groups and buttons of related features. ■

4 Click the **Ribbon Display Options** button to specify your Ribbon display preference: Auto-Hide Ribbon, Show Tabs, or Show Tabs and Commands.

End

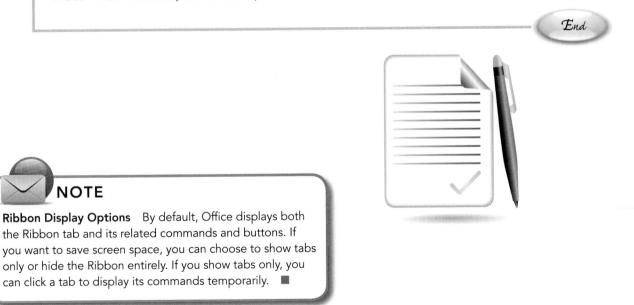

NOTE

Ribbon Display Options By default, Office displays both the Ribbon tab and its related commands and buttons. If you want to save screen space, you can choose to show tabs only or hide the Ribbon entirely. If you show tabs only, you can click a tab to display its commands temporarily. ■

EXPLORING BACKSTAGE VIEW

Backstage view enables you to perform common Office file-related tasks in one place.

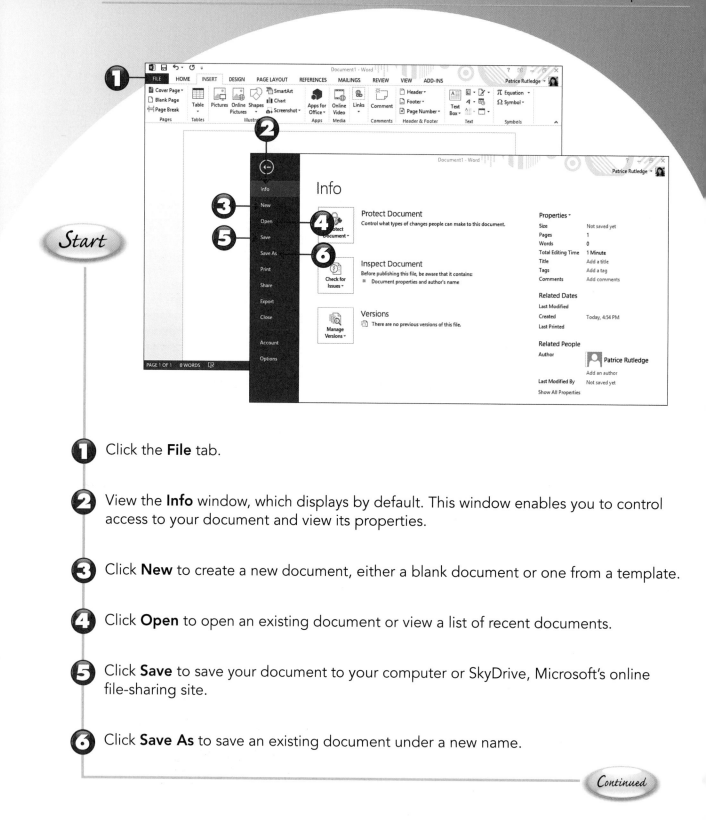

Start

1 Click the **File** tab.

2 View the **Info** window, which displays by default. This window enables you to control access to your document and view its properties.

3 Click **New** to create a new document, either a blank document or one from a template.

4 Click **Open** to open an existing document or view a list of recent documents.

5 Click **Save** to save your document to your computer or SkyDrive, Microsoft's online file-sharing site.

6 Click **Save As** to save an existing document under a new name.

Continued

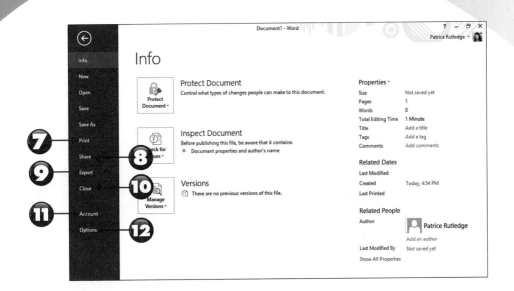

7 Click **Print** to print your document and specify print preferences.

8 Click **Share** to share your document via email, by instant message, or online.

9 Click **Export** to create a PDF/XPS document or change your document's file type.

10 Click **Close** to close your document.

11 Click **Account** to set up or modify your Microsoft account.

12 Click **Options** to access customization options.

End

NOTE

Backstage View Differences   The options available in Backstage view vary by application but are similar to the options shown in this section for Microsoft Word. ∎

USING THE QUICK ACCESS TOOLBAR

The *Quick Access Toolbar* is a small toolbar that displays in the upper-left corner of your screen and is available no matter which Ribbon tab you select.

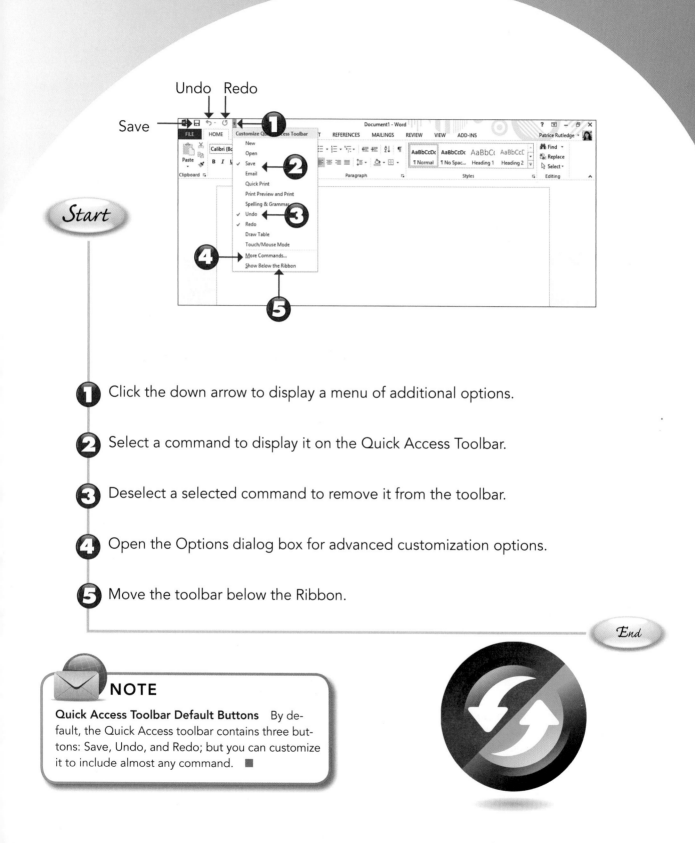

Undo Redo

Save

Start

End

1 Click the down arrow to display a menu of additional options.

2 Select a command to display it on the Quick Access Toolbar.

3 Deselect a selected command to remove it from the toolbar.

4 Open the Options dialog box for advanced customization options.

5 Move the toolbar below the Ribbon.

NOTE

Quick Access Toolbar Default Buttons   By default, the Quick Access toolbar contains three buttons: Save, Undo, and Redo; but you can customize it to include almost any command. ■

USING THE MINI TOOLBAR

The *mini toolbar* is a small contextual toolbar that displays only when you perform specific tasks. For example, when you select text, this toolbar displays with options related to text formatting.

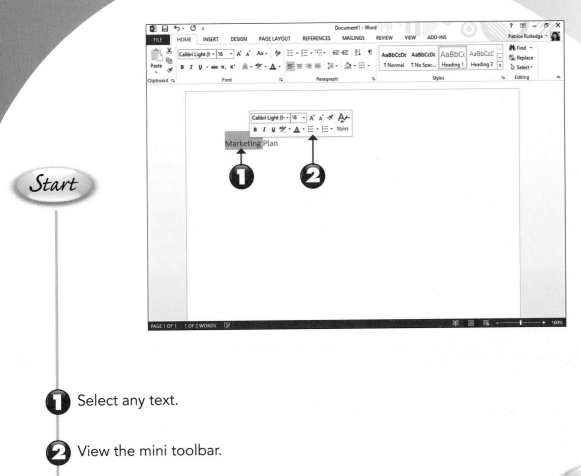

1 Select any text.

2 View the mini toolbar.

End

NOTE

Mini Toolbar Versus the Ribbon Although you can perform the same tasks using the commands on the main Ribbon tab, using the mini toolbar makes these commands available in a more convenient location. ■

TIP

Mini Toolbar Buttons Descriptions Pause your mouse over a mini toolbar button to view its description. ■

USING CONTEXTUAL TABS

Although the main tabs always display on the Ribbon, Office also includes several contextual Ribbon tabs that appear only when you perform specific tasks. For example, take a look at the Drawing Tools–Format tab, which displays only when you select a shape.

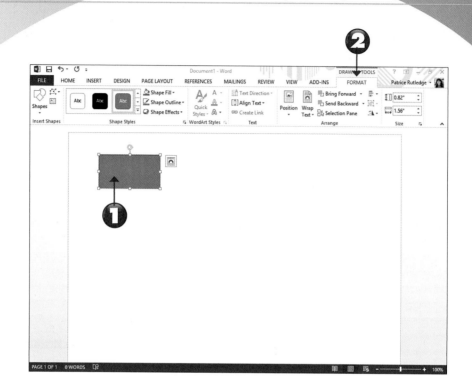

Start

 Select a shape. (You can insert one by clicking the Shapes button on the Insert tab as described in Chapter 5, "Working with Shapes, SmartArt, and Screenshots.")

2 Click the **Drawing Tools–Format** tab to display options that are specific to working with shapes.

End

NOTE

Contextual Tab Examples Some examples of contextual tabs include the following: the Picture Tools–Format tab displays when you select a picture; the Drawing Tools–Format tab displays when you select a shape; and the Chart Tools–Design and Chart Tools–Format tabs display when you select a chart. ■

NOTE

Where Did It Go? A contextual tab remains visible as long as the related object is selected. When you click elsewhere, it disappears. ■

USING TASK PANES

A *task pane* is a window that enables you to perform common tasks without covering your document (such as a dialog box does). Microsoft has converted many dialog boxes to task panes in Office 2013. For example, look at the Format Shape pane.

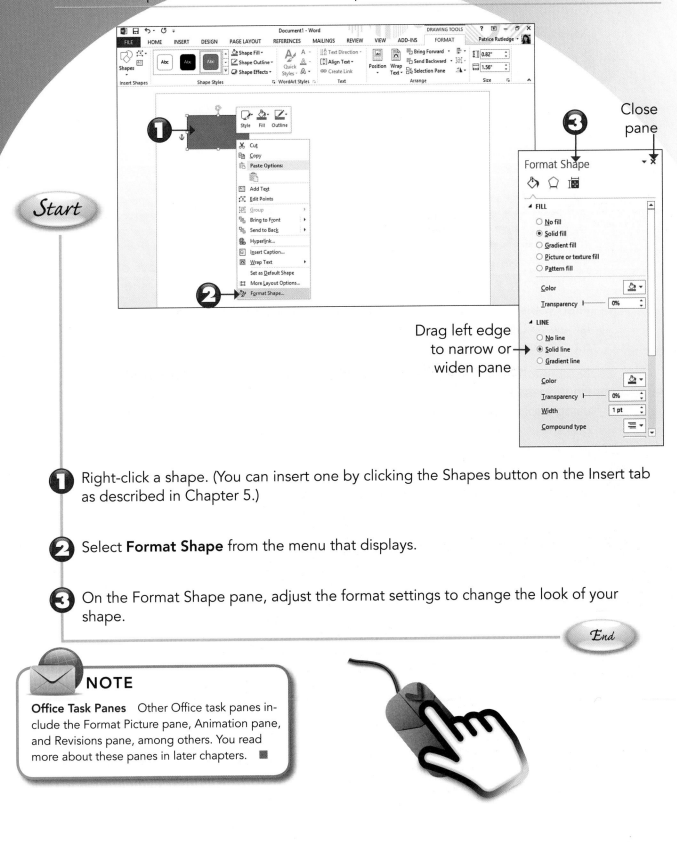

Close pane

Drag left edge to narrow or widen pane

Start

1. Right-click a shape. (You can insert one by clicking the Shapes button on the Insert tab as described in Chapter 5.)

2. Select **Format Shape** from the menu that displays.

3. On the Format Shape pane, adjust the format settings to change the look of your shape.

End

NOTE

Office Task Panes Other Office task panes include the Format Picture pane, Animation pane, and Revisions pane, among others. You read more about these panes in later chapters.

Chapter 2

WORKING WITH OFFICE APPLICATIONS

Spending some time mastering the basics of Office applications pays off in the long run, particularly if you're new to Office or could use a refresher.

First, you should set up Office to connect with your Microsoft account. This is new to Office 2013 and helps you work in today's increasingly connected, mobile world.

Next, learn how to perform Office's most common tasks: opening, saving, printing, sharing, and closing files as well as cutting, copying, and pasting using clipboard functionality. Although these should be familiar if you're upgrading, Office 2013 does include some changes and new features.

Finally, spend a few minutes customizing Office defaults to suit your own work style and preferences.

GETTING HELP

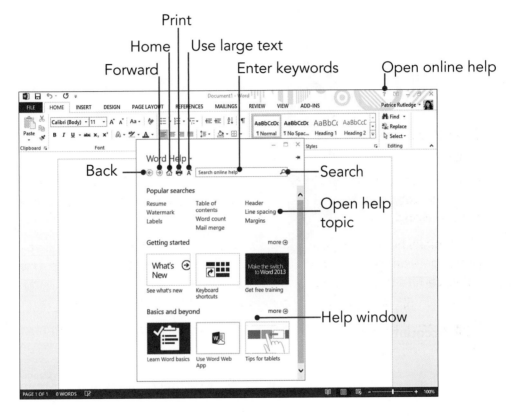

Print

Home | Use large text

Forward | Enter keywords

Open online help

Back — Search

Open help topic

Help window

The *Account window* is where you set up your Microsoft account and connected services, which are both important for taking full advantage of Office 2013. When you first start using this new version of Office, be sure to take a few minutes to handle this important task.

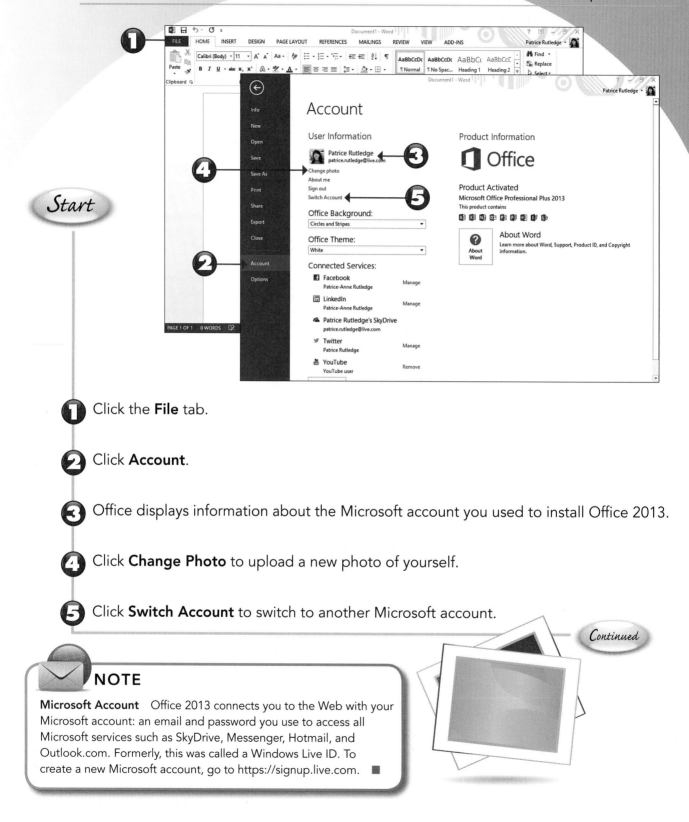

Start

Continued

1. Click the **File** tab.

2. Click **Account**.

3. Office displays information about the Microsoft account you used to install Office 2013.

4. Click **Change Photo** to upload a new photo of yourself.

5. Click **Switch Account** to switch to another Microsoft account.

NOTE

Microsoft Account   Office 2013 connects you to the Web with your Microsoft account: an email and password you use to access all Microsoft services such as SkyDrive, Messenger, Hotmail, and Outlook.com. Formerly, this was called a Windows Live ID. To create a new Microsoft account, go to https://signup.live.com. ∎

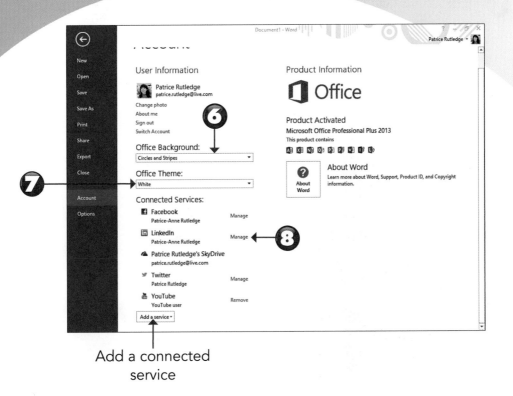

Add a connected
service

6 Select an Office background. The default is Circles and Stripes, but you can also select another option, including Clouds, Straws, or no background.

7 Select an Office theme: White (the default), Light Gray, or Dark Gray.

8 Specify the connected services you want to use with Office.

End

 **NOTE**

Office Theme The Office theme controls the appearance of the Office interface, not the appearance of any documents you create. ■

NOTE

Connected Services The Account window displays the services you've already connected with. (Office finds some services automatically based on your Microsoft account email address.) Click the **Add a Service** button to add more services, including Flickr, YouTube, Office 365 SharePoint, SkyDrive, Facebook, LinkedIn, and Twitter. See "Sharing a File" later in this chapter to learn how to share Office files on the social sites you connect to. ■

You can easily find and open existing files in Microsoft Office.

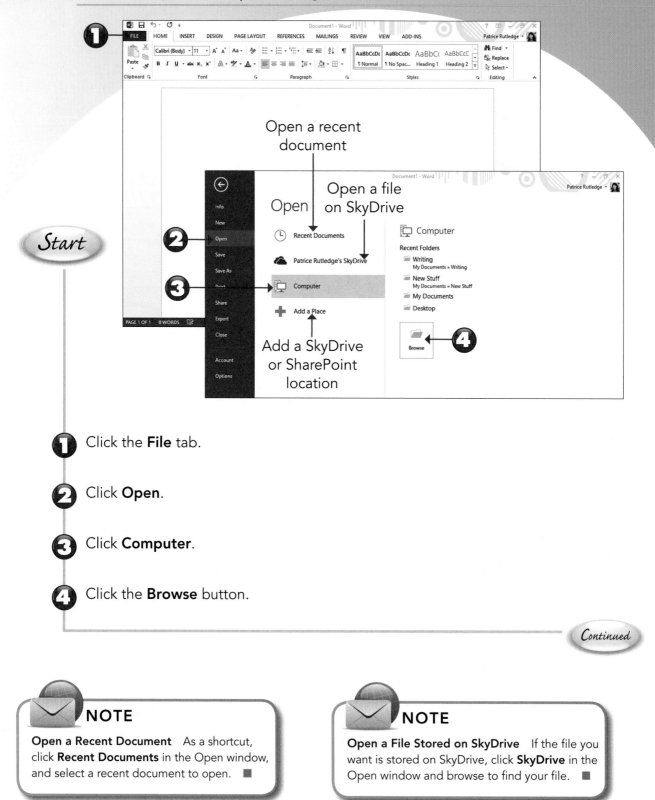

Open a recent document

Open a file on SkyDrive

Add a SkyDrive or SharePoint location

Start

1 Click the **File** tab.

2 Click **Open**.

3 Click **Computer**.

4 Click the **Browse** button.

Continued

NOTE

Open a Recent Document As a shortcut, click **Recent Documents** in the Open window, and select a recent document to open. ■

NOTE

Open a File Stored on SkyDrive If the file you want is stored on SkyDrive, click **SkyDrive** in the Open window and browse to find your file. ■

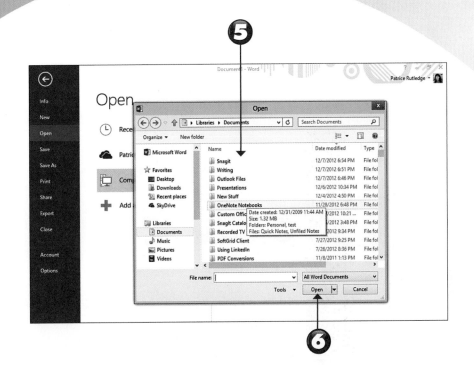

 In the Open dialog box, navigate to the file you want to open.

Click the **Open** button.

End

TIP

Rename a File   To rename a file in the Open dialog box, right-click it, and select **Rename** from the menu. To delete a file, right-click it, and select Delete from the menu. ■

TIP

File-Opening Option   You can also open a file by double-clicking its name in Windows Explorer or by pressing Ctrl+O to display the Open dialog box directly. ■

USING THE CLIPBOARD TO CUT, COPY, AND PASTE

Using the options in the Clipboard group on the Home tab, you can cut, copy, and paste objects. In Office, an *object* refers to any of the components you include in your documents, such as text, shapes, pictures, text boxes, placeholders, SmartArt, charts, WordArt, and so forth.

Display paste options

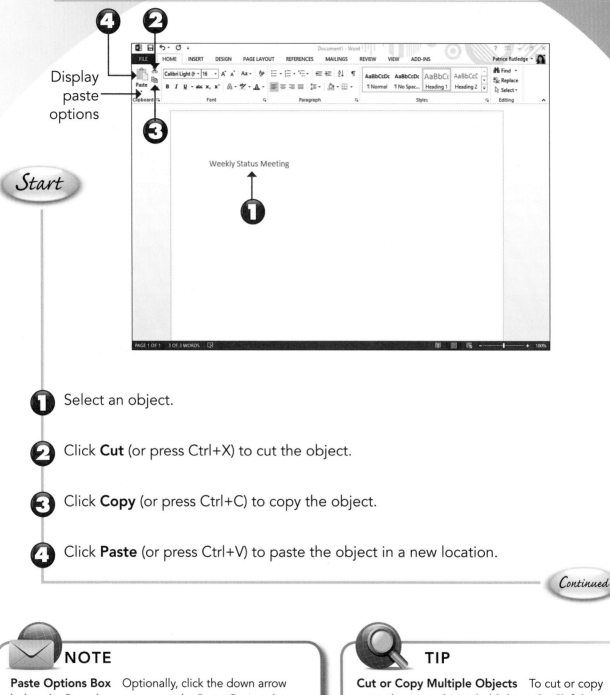

Start

1 Select an object.

2 Click **Cut** (or press Ctrl+X) to cut the object.

3 Click **Copy** (or press Ctrl+C) to copy the object.

4 Click **Paste** (or press Ctrl+V) to paste the object in a new location.

Continued

NOTE

Paste Options Box Optionally, click the down arrow below the Paste button to open the Paste Options box. Pause your mouse over each option button to preview the pasted object. Options include Keep Source Formatting, Use Destination Theme, Picture (convert object to picture; not available with basic text), or Keep Text Only. ■

TIP

Cut or Copy Multiple Objects To cut or copy more than one object, hold down the Shift key while selecting objects, or drag a selection box around all the objects with the mouse. If the objects aren't contiguous, hold down the Ctrl key. ■

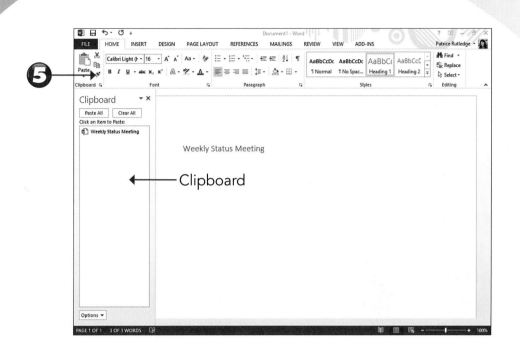

Clipboard

Click **Format Painter** to copy the attributes of one object and apply them to another object you select.

End

TIP

Format Painter The Format Painter is a timesaving tool if you want to reuse formatting you've applied to an object. For example, if you select an object with 3-D effects, click the **Format Painter** button, and then select another object so that new object gets the same 3-D effects. ■

NOTE

The Clipboard When you copy an object, it displays on the Clipboard. To view the Clipboard, click the down arrow to the right of the Clipboard group on the Home tab to open the Clipboard pane. You can also select which item to paste on this pane. ■

Saving files as you work is a good practice and a good way to avoid losing critical data. In this section, you find out how to save a file for the first time.

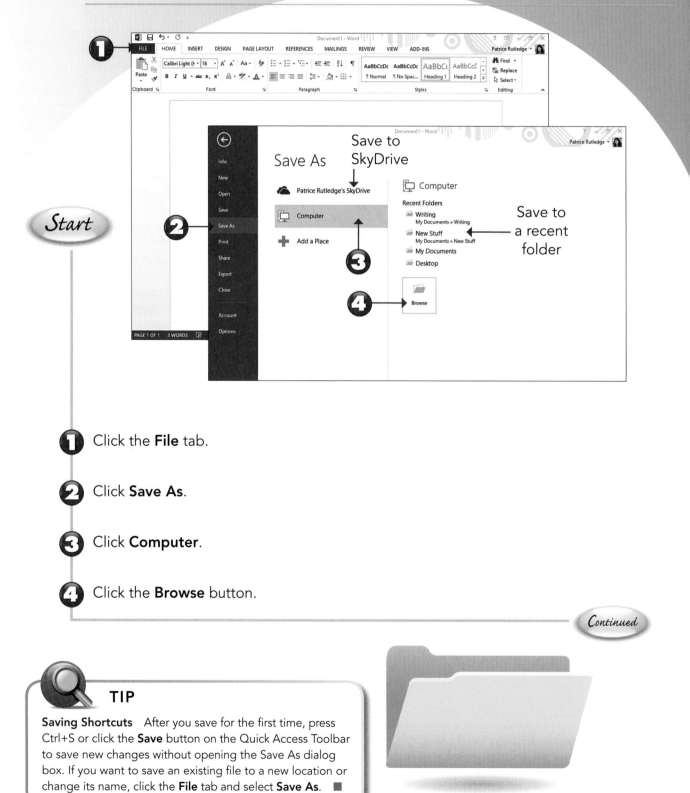

Save to SkyDrive

Save to a recent folder

Start

1 Click the **File** tab.

2 Click **Save As**.

3 Click **Computer**.

4 Click the **Browse** button.

Continued

TIP

Saving Shortcuts After you save for the first time, press Ctrl+S or click the **Save** button on the Quick Access Toolbar to save new changes without opening the Save As dialog box. If you want to save an existing file to a new location or change its name, click the **File** tab and select **Save As**. ■

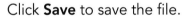

Save As

5 Type a filename.

6 Select a file format from the Save as Type drop-down list if you don't want to save in the default format.

7 Click **Save** to save the file.

End

TIP

Recent Folders Optionally, you can save time by selecting one of the options in the Recent Folders list. If you often save to the same folder, pause your mouse over that folder name, and click the **Pin This Item to the List** icon to ensure that this folder is always at the top of the list for easy convenience. ∎

TIP

Save to SkyDrive You can also save to Sky-Drive (Microsoft's online storage and file-sharing solution) from the Save As window. On the left side of the window, click **SkyDrive**, click the **Browse** button, and select a folder. ∎

SAVING AS A PDF OR AN XPS DOCUMENT

Office enables you to save a file directly as a PDF or an XPS document without requiring an add-in.

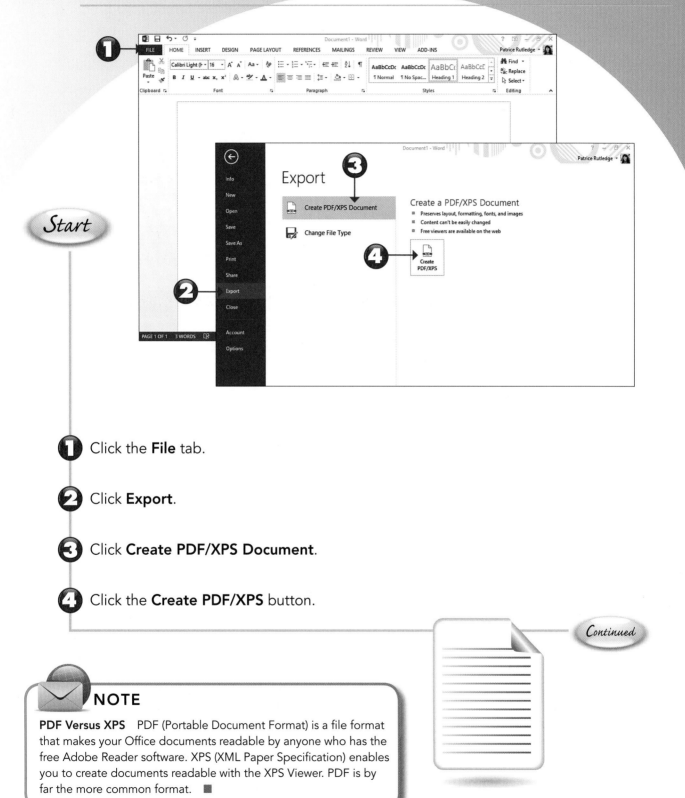

Start

1 Click the **File** tab.

2 Click **Export**.

3 Click **Create PDF/XPS Document**.

4 Click the **Create PDF/XPS** button.

Continued

NOTE

PDF Versus XPS PDF (Portable Document Format) is a file format that makes your Office documents readable by anyone who has the free Adobe Reader software. XPS (XML Paper Specification) enables you to create documents readable with the XPS Viewer. PDF is by far the more common format. ■

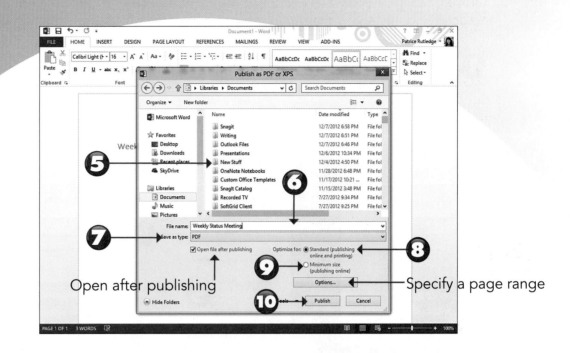

Open after publishing

Specify a page range

5 Select the folder in which to save your document.

6 Type a filename.

7 Select either PDF or XPS Document.

8 Select **Standard** to create a document that's suitable for both online viewing and printing.

9 Select **Minimum Size** if you just want to view online.

10 Click the **Publish** button to create your document.

End

TIP

Save First   Be sure to save your file in your Office application before you save as PDF or XPS documents. ■

SHARING A FILE

Office offers numerous ways to share with others, including several new to Office 2013. You can find numerous sharing options in the Share window in Backstage view.

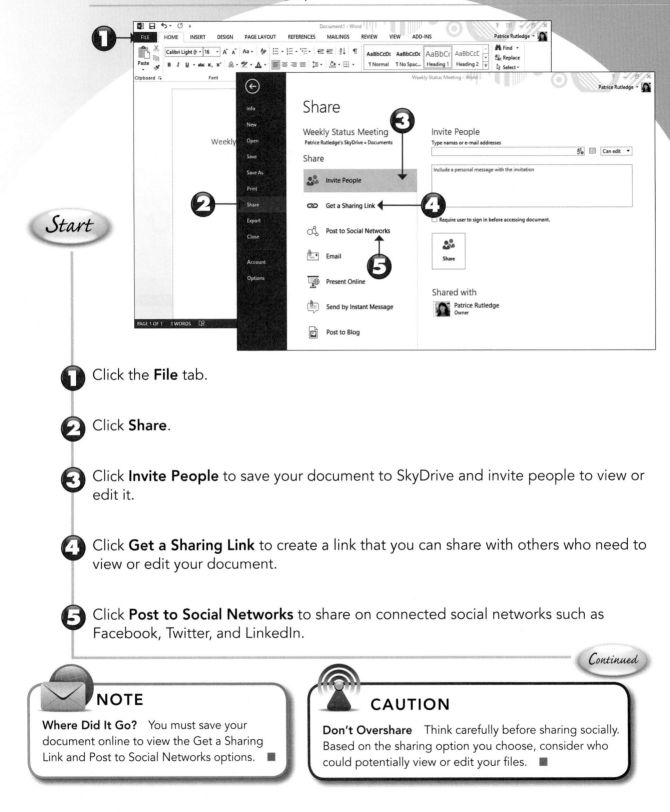

Start

1. Click the **File** tab.

2. Click **Share**.

3. Click **Invite People** to save your document to SkyDrive and invite people to view or edit it.

4. Click **Get a Sharing Link** to create a link that you can share with others who need to view or edit your document.

5. Click **Post to Social Networks** to share on connected social networks such as Facebook, Twitter, and LinkedIn.

Continued

NOTE

Where Did It Go? You must save your document online to view the Get a Sharing Link and Post to Social Networks options. ■

CAUTION

Don't Overshare Think carefully before sharing socially. Based on the sharing option you choose, consider who could potentially view or edit your files. ■

6 Click **Email** to share via email.

7 Click **Present Online** to start an online presentation.

8 Click **Send by Instant Message** to send a link via IM.

End

NOTE

Email Sharing Options Office offers several ways to share via email. You can send as an attachment, send a link, send as a PDF, send as an XPS, or send as an Internet fax. ■

NOTE

Share Window Depending on the application you use, the Share window might have other options. For example, Word enables you to post a document to your blog, and PowerPoint lets you publish slides online. ■

PRINTING A FILE

The Print window simplifies printing Office files. Although the specific printing options available in this window vary by application, they all follow the same basic steps. In this example, you explore the Print window in Microsoft Word.

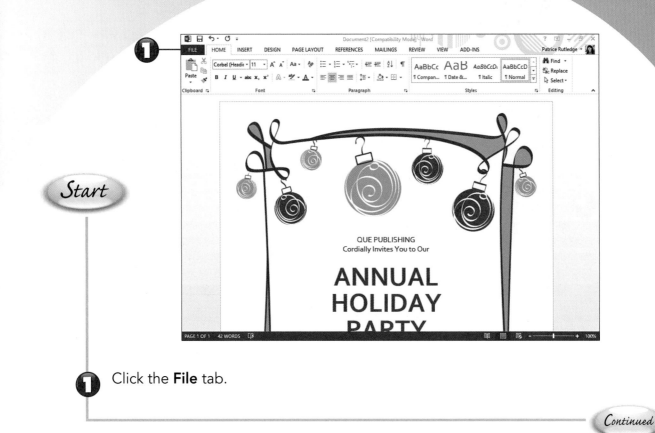

Start

1 Click the **File** tab.

Continued

TIP

Consider a greener alternative to distributing multiple printed copies. Two good options: Save as a PDF or post on SkyDrive. ■

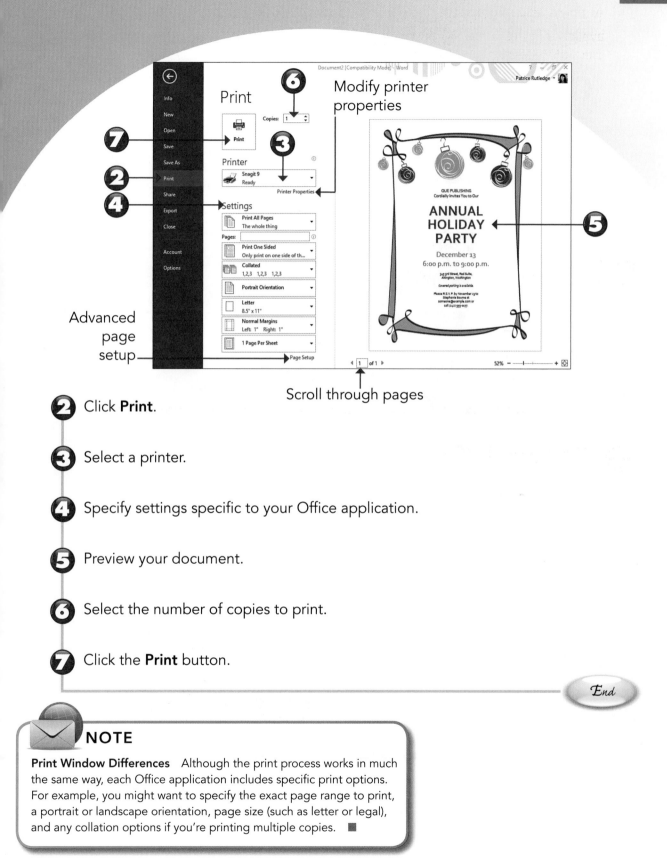

2 Click **Print**.

3 Select a printer.

4 Specify settings specific to your Office application.

5 Preview your document.

6 Select the number of copies to print.

7 Click the **Print** button.

End

NOTE

Print Window Differences Although the print process works in much the same way, each Office application includes specific print options. For example, you might want to specify the exact page range to print, a portrait or landscape orientation, page size (such as letter or legal), and any collation options if you're printing multiple copies. ■

CLOSING A FILE

At times, you might want to close a file without exiting an application. This is particularly useful if you have many files open and want to save memory.

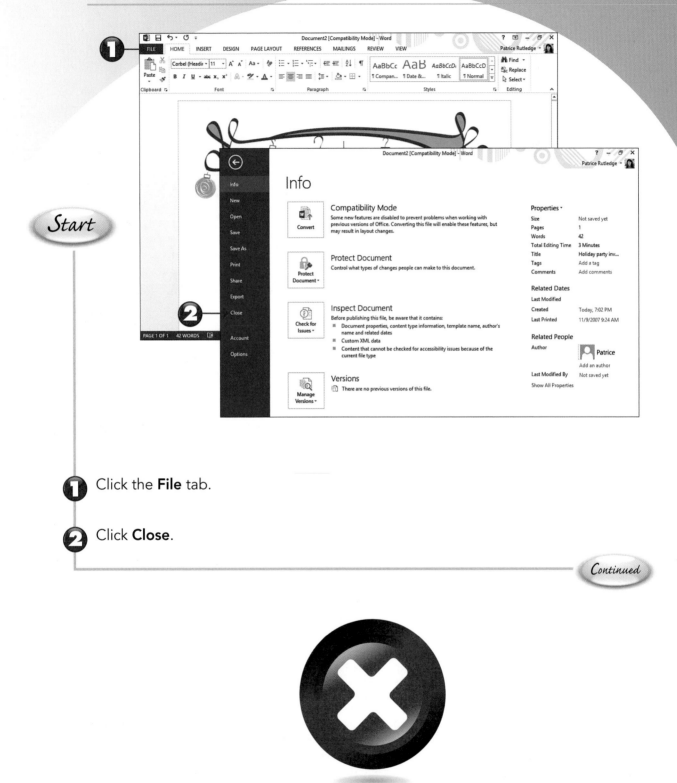

Start

1 Click the **File** tab.

2 Click **Close**.

Continued

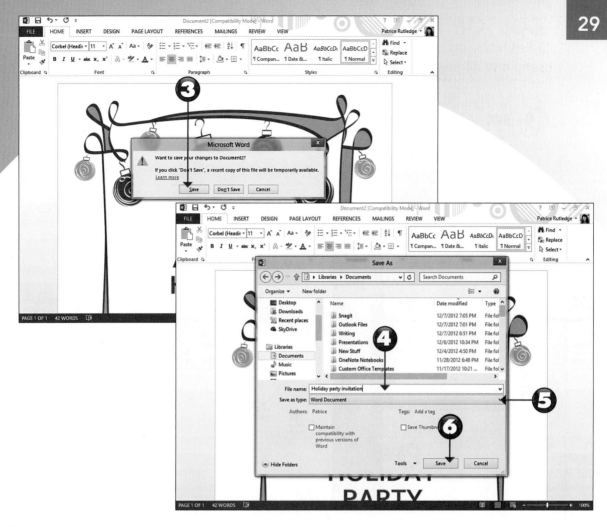

③ Click **Save** to open the Save As dialog box.

④ Type a filename.

⑤ Select a file format from the Save as Type drop-down list if you don't want to save in the default format.

⑥ Click **Save** to save and close the file.

End

NOTE

Previously Saved Files If you've already saved your file, Office doesn't prompt you to do so, and you don't need to complete steps 4 through 6. ■

NOTE

File Closing Options You can also click the Close (**x**) button in the upper-right corner of the screen to close an open file. Note, however, that if this is the only file you have open, this action also closes the application. Optionally, pressing Ctrl+W closes the current file without closing the application. ■

CUSTOMIZING OFFICE

The Options dialog box enables you to customize Office applications to suit your work style and needs.

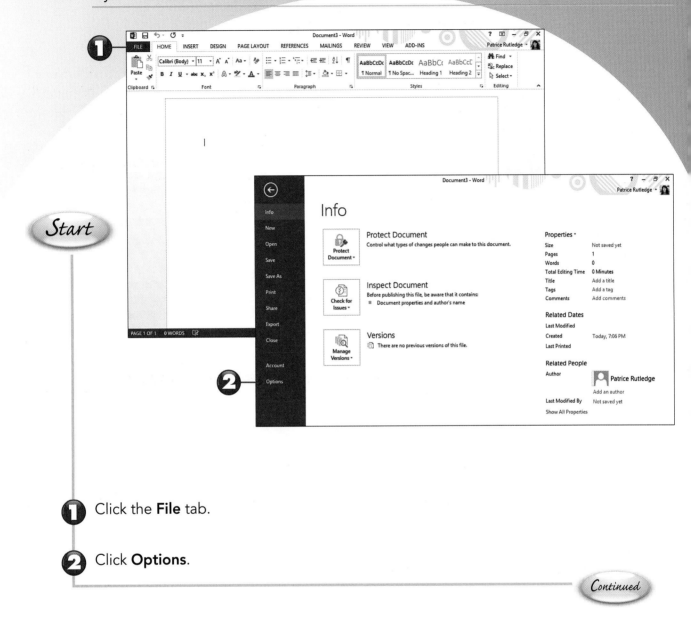

1 Click the **File** tab.

2 Click **Options**.

Continued

TIP

Don't Overlook Customization Although all the available options might seem overwhelming at first, it's worth it to spend a few minutes reviewing the tabs in the Options dialog box to verify which of the defaults you want to change, if any. ■

NOTE

Options Dialog Box Differences Each Office application has a unique Options dialog box, even though most of the settings are common to all applications. In this example, you view the Word Options dialog box. ■

Customize user interface

Specify Word display options

Set up AutoCorrect and spelling

Specify clipboard, chart, display, and print options

Choose editing language

Customize save options

Customize Quick Access Toolbar

Customize Ribbons tabs

Manage Office add-in programs

Learn about privacy

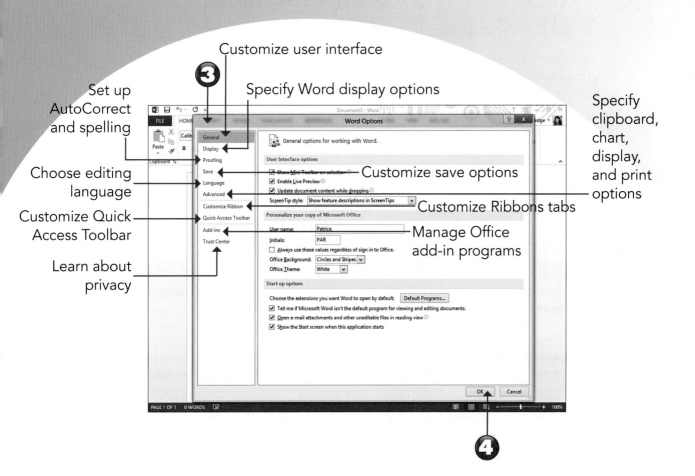

3 Review each tab in the Options dialog box, and make any changes to the default settings.

4 Click **OK** when you finish customizing.

End

NOTE

One Setting for All Apps After you set an option in one Office application, that setting carries over to all the other applications as well. ■

Chapter 3

WORKING WITH TEXT

Adding text in an Office application is easy; just start typing. If the default text formatting doesn't suit your needs, however, Office also offers numerous text formatting and customization options.

The Home tab in Word, PowerPoint, and Excel is "home" to a solid collection of text-formatting tools, giving you the option to select a font style and size, change text color, or apply bold, italic, and underlining to your text.

You can also align text, use WordArt to create sophisticated text objects, search for and replace text, and use the Font dialog box for more advanced formatting.

Finally, you can fix any spelling errors by performing a spell check—which you need to do on every Office document.

FORMATTING TEXT ON THE HOME TAB (WORD)

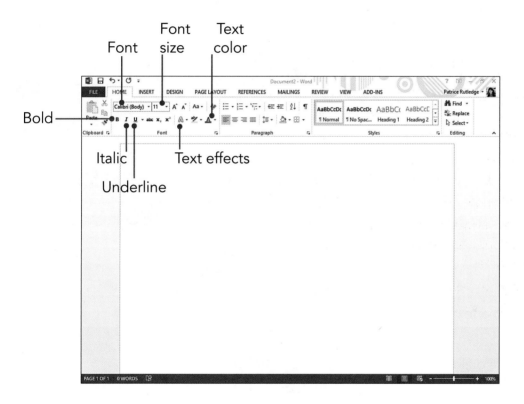

Font

Font size

Text color

Bold

Italic

Underline

Text effects

The Font dialog box offers some advanced formatting options not available on the Home tab.

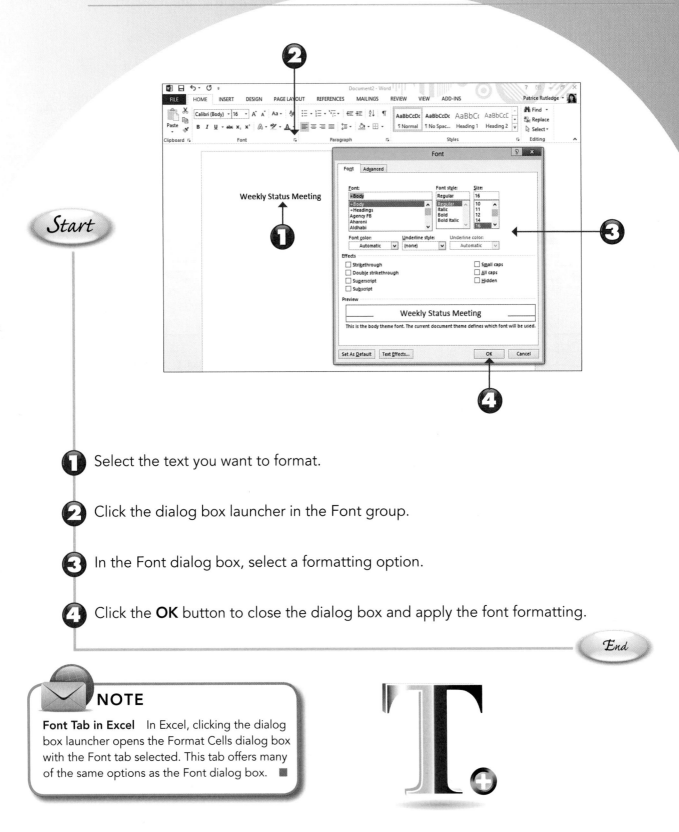

1 Select the text you want to format.

2 Click the dialog box launcher in the Font group.

3 In the Font dialog box, select a formatting option.

4 Click the **OK** button to close the dialog box and apply the font formatting.

End

NOTE

Font Tab in Excel In Excel, clicking the dialog box launcher opens the Format Cells dialog box with the Font tab selected. This tab offers many of the same options as the Font dialog box. ■

You can quickly align text using buttons on the Home tab.

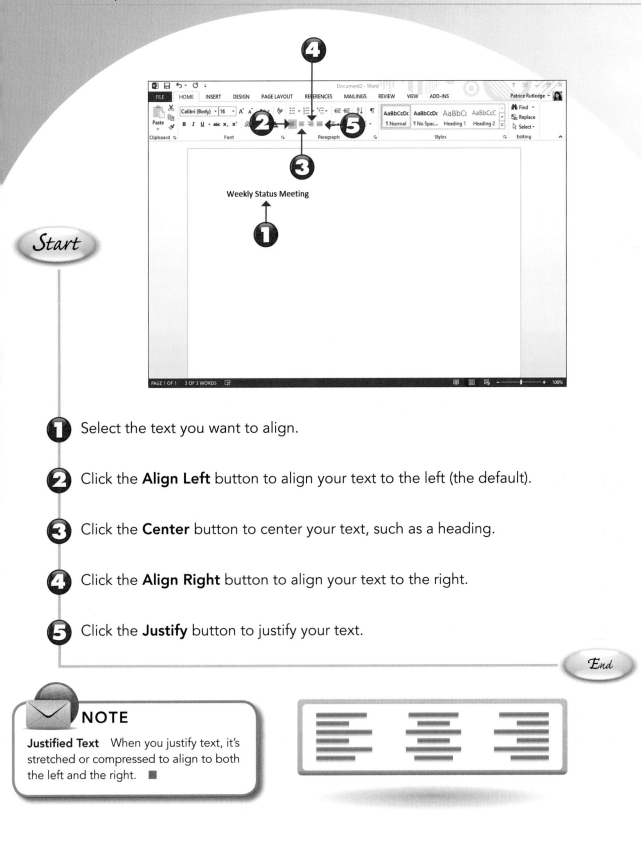

Select the text you want to align.

Click the **Align Left** button to align your text to the left (the default).

Click the **Center** button to center your text, such as a heading.

Click the **Align Right** button to align your text to the right.

Click the **Justify** button to justify your text.

NOTE

Justified Text When you justify text, it's stretched or compressed to align to both the left and the right. ■

FINDING AND REPLACING TEXT

At times, you might need to change a word or phrase that's used throughout a document. The Find and Replace dialog box makes it easy to replace text, especially in long documents.

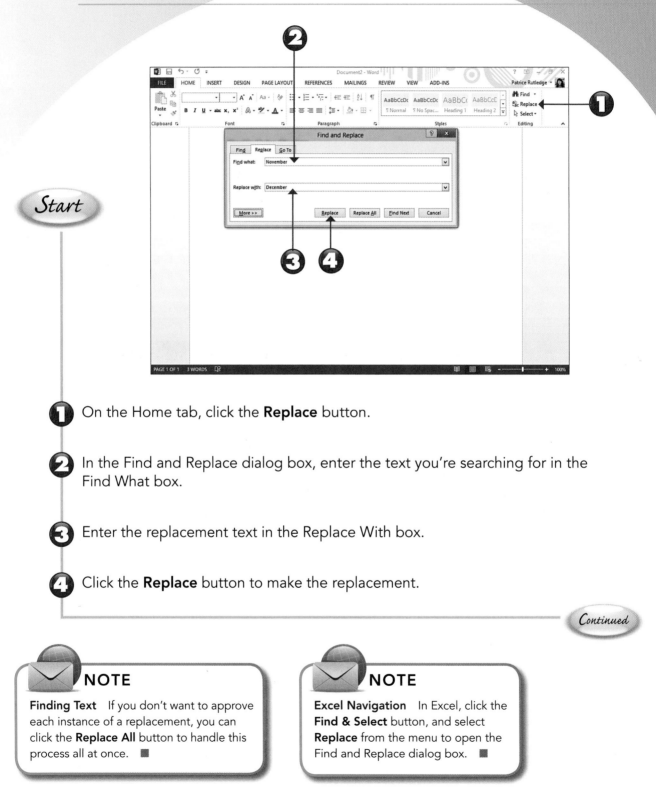

Start

① On the Home tab, click the **Replace** button.

② In the Find and Replace dialog box, enter the text you're searching for in the Find What box.

③ Enter the replacement text in the Replace With box.

④ Click the **Replace** button to make the replacement.

Continued

NOTE

Finding Text If you don't want to approve each instance of a replacement, you can click the **Replace All** button to handle this process all at once. ■

NOTE

Excel Navigation In Excel, click the **Find & Select** button, and select **Replace** from the menu to open the Find and Replace dialog box. ■

5 Office notifies you when the process is finished. Click **OK** to close the notification.

6 Click the **Close** button to close the Find and Replace dialog box.

End

NOTE

Finding Text Just want to find specific text rather than replace it? Enter the text in the Find What box, and click the **Find Next** button. You can also click the **Find** button on the Home tab to perform a search. ■

NOTE

More Options Click the **More** button to display more find-and-replace options. For example, you might want to replace only text with matching case or search only for whole words. ■

INSERTING WORDART

WordArt enables you to create special text effects such as shadowed, rotated, stretched, and multicolored text.

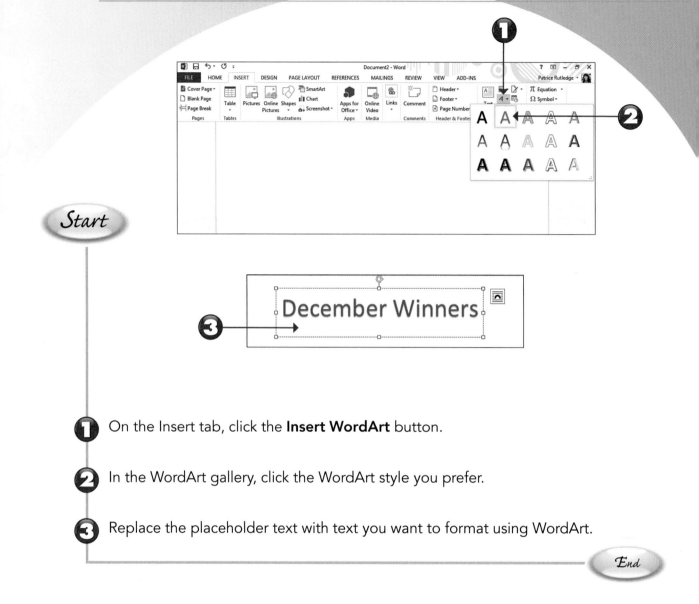

On the Insert tab, click the **Insert WordArt** button.

In the WordArt gallery, click the WordArt style you prefer.

Replace the placeholder text with text you want to format using WordArt.

NOTE

WordArt Navigation This example demonstrates adding WordArt in Microsoft Word. In PowerPoint, click the **Word-Art** button on the Insert tab. In Excel, click the **Text** button on the Insert tab, and select **WordArt** from the menu. ■

Office offers a wide selection of formatting options for WordArt. You can apply a Quick Style, gradients, textures, bevels, rotations, and more.

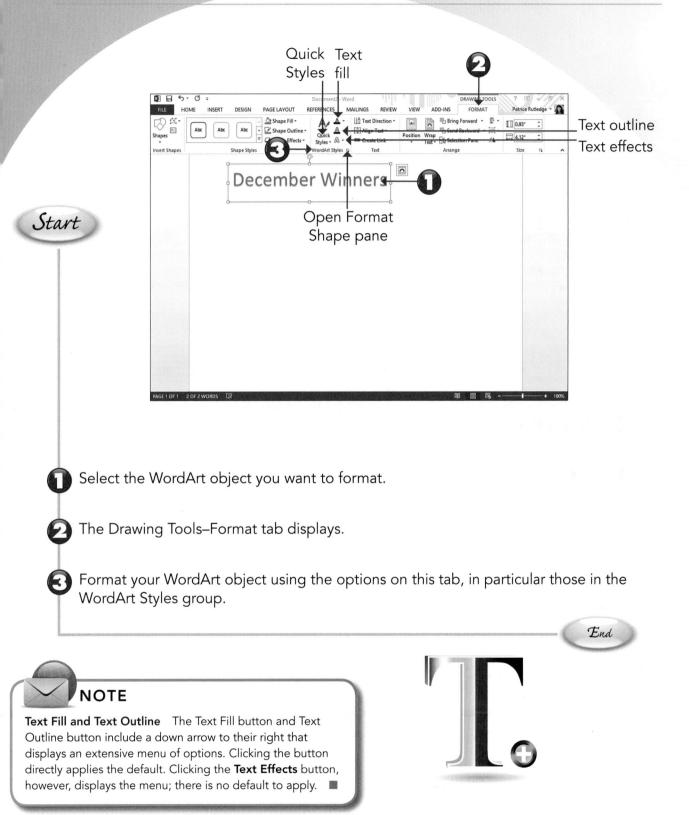

Quick Text
Styles fill

Text outline
Text effects

December Winners

Open Format
Shape pane

Start

1. Select the WordArt object you want to format.

2. The Drawing Tools–Format tab displays.

3. Format your WordArt object using the options on this tab, in particular those in the WordArt Styles group.

End

NOTE

Text Fill and Text Outline The Text Fill button and Text Outline button include a down arrow to their right that displays an extensive menu of options. Clicking the button directly applies the default. Clicking the **Text Effects** button, however, displays the menu; there is no default to apply. ∎

CHECKING SPELLING

Creating quality, error-free, and easy-to-read content is a natural objective when you use an Office application. Fortunately, Office offers a spelling checker to help eliminate spelling errors. You can also spell check your entire document at once.

Suspected misspelling

Start

Continued

1. On the Review tab, click the **Spelling & Grammar** button. (In Excel and PowerPoint, this is called the Spelling button.)

2. The Spelling pane opens, and the spell checker starts examining your document.

3. Select the correct spelling, and click the **Change** button.

4. Click the **Ignore** button if the suspected misspelling isn't an error.

5. Click the **Add** button to add the word as-is to the dictionary.

NOTE

No Spelling Errors   If your document contains no errors, Office displays a dialog box informing you of this and doesn't open the Spelling pane. ◼

TIP

Change or Ignore All   To save time, you can click either the **Change All** button or **Ignore All** button to resolve all instances of the suspected error at once. ◼

 Office notifies you when the spelling checker is finished. Click **OK** to close the notification.

End

CAUTION

Spelling Checker Limitations Keep in mind that although an automated tool can help you catch errors, it isn't foolproof and doesn't take the place of thorough proofreading by a person. ■

NOTE

Spelling Options By default, Office checks spelling as you type and displays a red squiggly line under all suspected misspellings. To modify the default spell-checking options, click the **File** tab, select **Options** in Backstage view, and click **Proofing**. ■

Chapter 4

WORKING WITH PICTURES

Microsoft Office offers several ways to enliven your documents with pictures, including both illustrations and photographs. You can insert a picture from your computer or network location or insert online pictures from the Office.com clip art collection, your SkyDrive account, or an external site such as Flickr.

In addition, Office provides a variety of customization and formatting options, including color correction, artistic effects, picture styles, borders, and much more.

You can insert and modify pictures in Word, PowerPoint, and Excel. You can also insert pictures in OneNote and Outlook, but you can't modify them because these applications don't include the Picture Tools–Format tab.

PICTURE TOOLS–FORMAT TAB

Change brightness/
contrast

Compress
picture

Change
picture

Apply
border

Change
saturation/
tone

Crop
picture

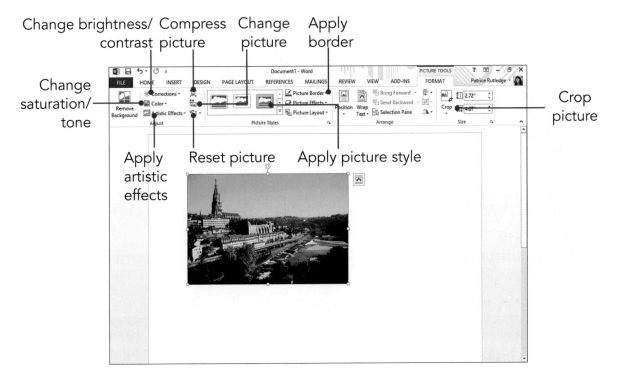

Apply
artistic
effects

Reset picture

Apply picture style

INSERTING A PICTURE FROM YOUR COMPUTER

Office makes it easy to insert a picture from your computer or a network location.

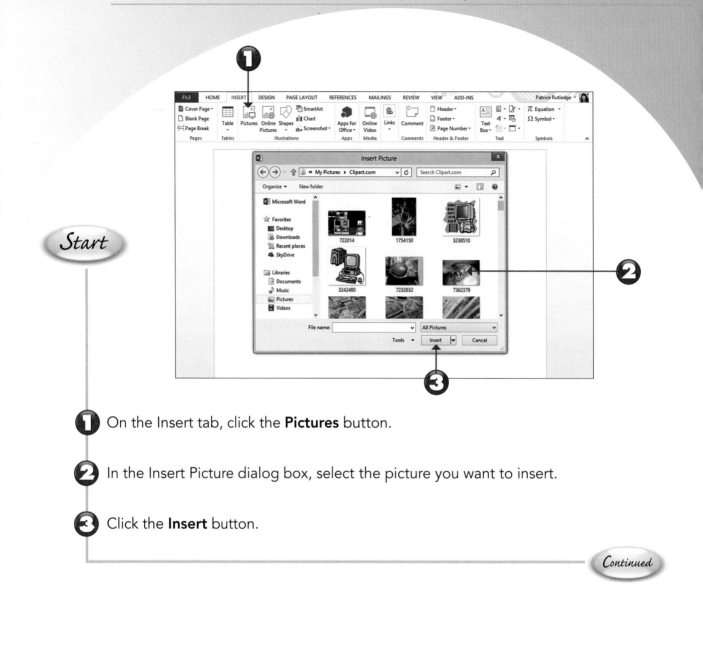

Start

1. On the Insert tab, click the **Pictures** button.

2. In the Insert Picture dialog box, select the picture you want to insert.

3. Click the **Insert** button.

Continued

NOTE

Picture File Types   Office works with two basic types of pictures. *Bitmap* pictures are composed of pixels (tiny dots of color), such as photos from a digital camera. Common bitmap file formats include .bmp, .gif, .jpg, .png, and .tif. *Vector* pictures are composed of points, lines, and curves and are popular for pictures you need to modify and resize such as logos. Common vector file formats include .eps and .wmf. ■

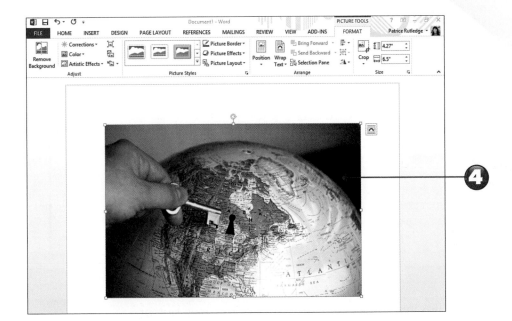

4 Office inserts the picture.

End

 TIP

Select Multiple Pictures To select multiple pictures, hold down the **Shift** key as you select. If the pictures aren't contiguous, hold down the **Ctrl** key. ■

 **TIP**

Excel Navigation In Excel, depending on your screen size and resolution, you might have to click the **Illustrations** button on the Insert tab and select **Pictures** from the menu. ■

Office.com offers a vast collection of royalty-free pictures, illustrations, and photos that you can insert in your Office documents.

Start

1️⃣ On the Insert tab, click the **Online Pictures** button.

2️⃣ In the Insert Pictures dialog box, enter a keyword or keywords in the Search Office.com field, and then click the **Search** button.

Continued

TIP

Excel Navigation In Excel, depending on your screen size and resolution, you might have to click the **Illustrations** button on the Insert tab, and select **Online Pictures** from the menu. ∎

NOTE

Online Picture Options From the Insert Pictures dialog box, you can also insert pictures from your SkyDrive account and other locations on the Web, such as Bing Image Search and Flickr. ∎

Return to initial
dialog box

Revise
keywords

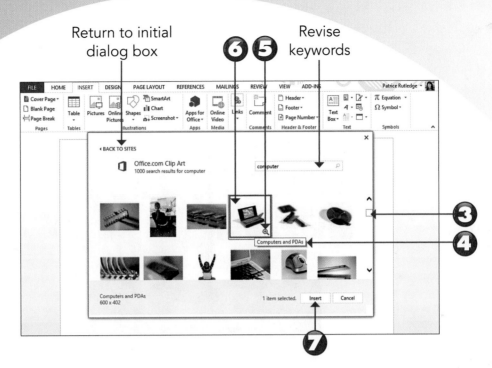

3 Scroll down the right side of the dialog box to view all results that match your keywords.

4 Pause your mouse over a picture to display a description.

5 Click the **View Larger** button to enlarge a picture.

6 Select one or more pictures from the matching results.

7 Click the **Insert** button to insert the picture.

End

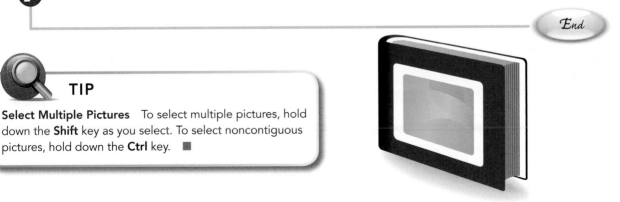

TIP

Select Multiple Pictures To select multiple pictures, hold down the **Shift** key as you select. To select noncontiguous pictures, hold down the **Ctrl** key. ■

ENHANCING A PICTURE

When you select a picture, the Picture Tools–Format tab displays. The Adjust group on this tab offers numerous picture enhancement options.

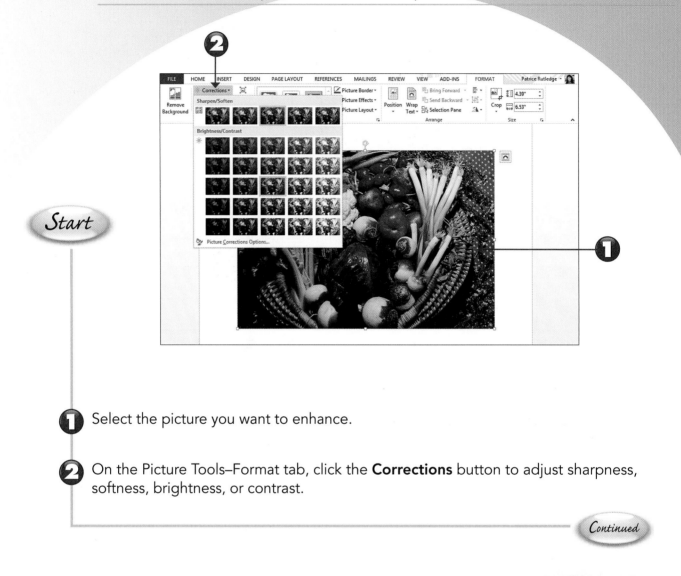

Start

1 Select the picture you want to enhance.

2 On the Picture Tools–Format tab, click the **Corrections** button to adjust sharpness, softness, brightness, or contrast.

Continued

NOTE

Other Picture Enhancements The Adjust group on the Picture Tools–Format tab also enables you to remove picture backgrounds, compress a picture to reduce its size, change to a different picture, or reset a picture after changing it. ■

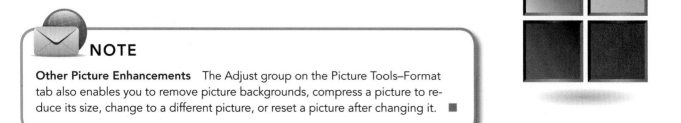

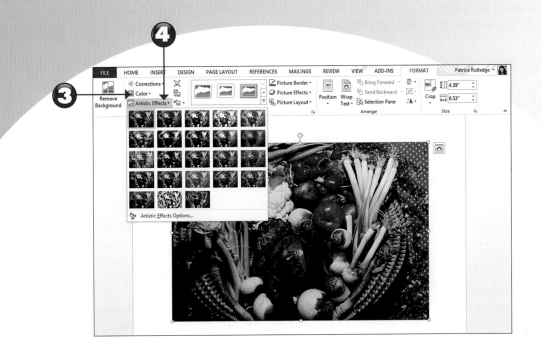

3 Click the **Color** button to modify color saturation and color tone or to recolor your picture.

4 Click **Artistic Effects** to apply artistic effects such as Pencil Sketch, Mosaic Bubbles, or Paint Brush.

End

CAUTION

Don't Overdo Enhancements Although the tools in the Adjust group give you many creative options for modifying your pictures, be careful not to overdo it and make your picture unrecognizable. ■

APPLYING A PICTURE STYLE

To enliven a picture, consider using a picture style. For example, you might apply a rotated white border or a soft-edge oval shape to your picture.

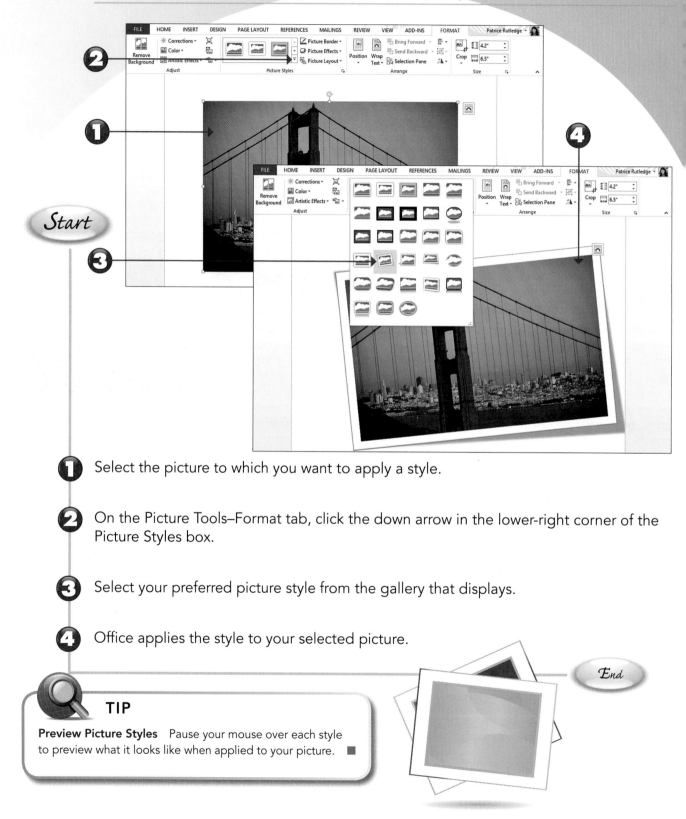

1. Select the picture to which you want to apply a style.

2. On the Picture Tools–Format tab, click the down arrow in the lower-right corner of the Picture Styles box.

3. Select your preferred picture style from the gallery that displays.

4. Office applies the style to your selected picture.

TIP

Preview Picture Styles Pause your mouse over each style to preview what it looks like when applied to your picture. ■

APPLYING A PICTURE BORDER

Applying a simple border to your picture can give it a professional look and distinguish it from a background of a similar color.

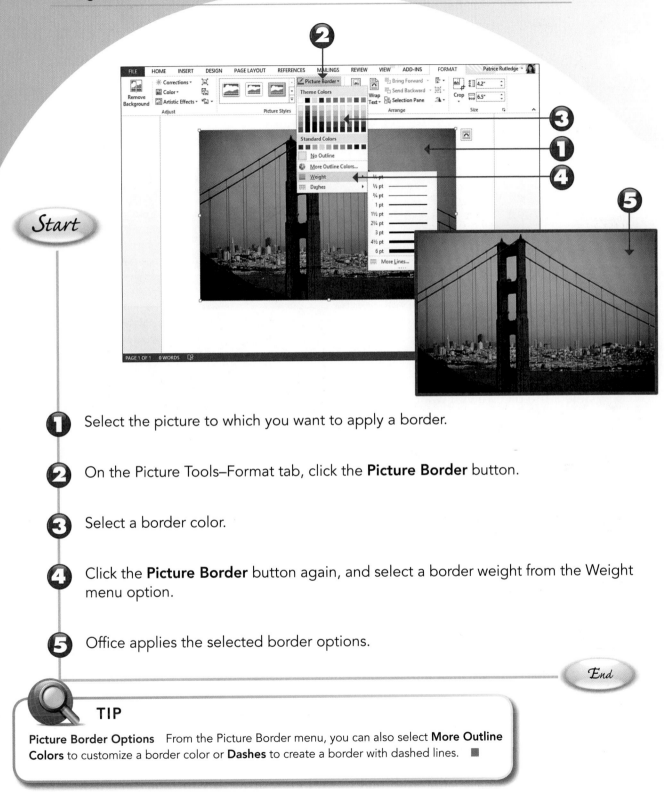

1. Select the picture to which you want to apply a border.

2. On the Picture Tools–Format tab, click the **Picture Border** button.

3. Select a border color.

4. Click the **Picture Border** button again, and select a border weight from the Weight menu option.

5. Office applies the selected border options.

TIP

Picture Border Options From the Picture Border menu, you can also select **More Outline Colors** to customize a border color or **Dashes** to create a border with dashed lines. ■

RESIZING A PICTURE

If your picture is either too large or too small, you can resize it easily by dragging a corner with your mouse.

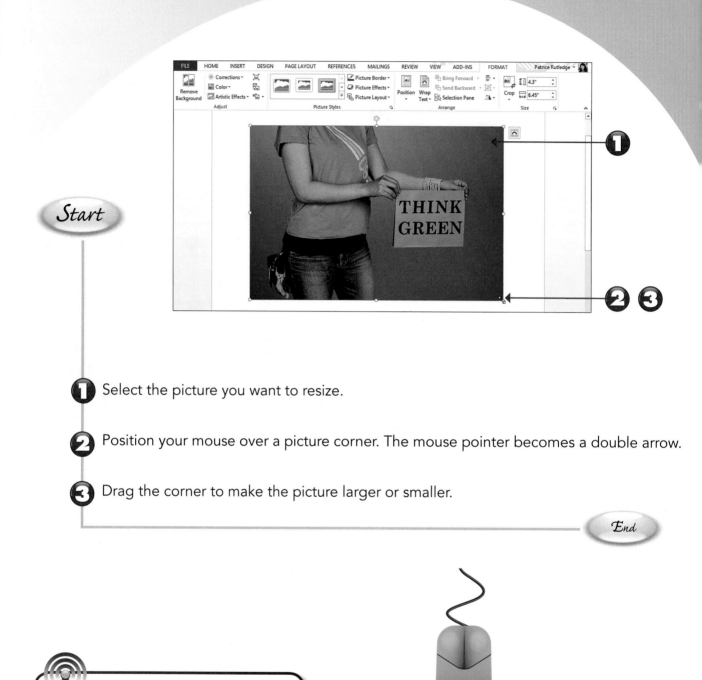

Start

1. Select the picture you want to resize.

2. Position your mouse over a picture corner. The mouse pointer becomes a double arrow.

3. Drag the corner to make the picture larger or smaller.

End

CAUTION

Be sure to drag a picture corner to size the picture proportionally. If you drag a picture on its side, you'll distort it. ■

If you don't want to include an entire picture, you can crop it to your exact specifications. For example, you might want to zero in on an object in the center of a picture, or remove extra content at the top of a picture.

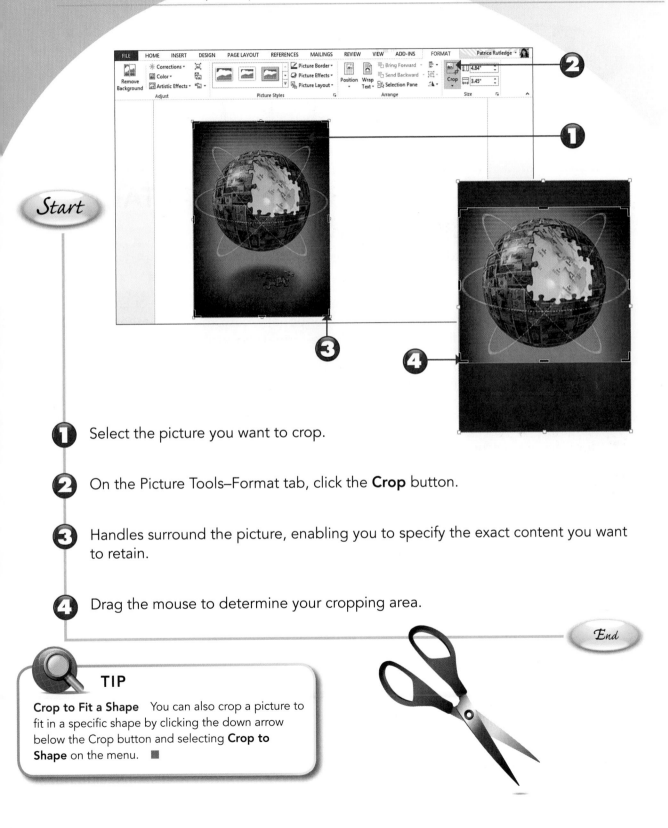

Start

1 Select the picture you want to crop.

2 On the Picture Tools–Format tab, click the **Crop** button.

3 Handles surround the picture, enabling you to specify the exact content you want to retain.

4 Drag the mouse to determine your cropping area.

End

TIP

Crop to Fit a Shape   You can also crop a picture to fit in a specific shape by clicking the down arrow below the Crop button and selecting **Crop to Shape** on the menu. ■

Chapter 5

WORKING WITH SHAPES, SMARTART, AND SCREENSHOTS

Office makes it easy to enhance your documents with shapes, SmartArt, and screenshots.

A *shape* is an object, such as a line, arrow, rectangle, circle, square, or callout. You can quickly insert a basic shape and, optionally, customize it to meet your exact needs using Office's numerous shape-formatting tools.

SmartArt takes the power and flexibility of shapes one step further. SmartArt enables you to combine shapes and text to create informative lists, matrices, pyramids, and more.

Finally, Office gives you the option of inserting *screenshots* without the need for a screen-capture tool. For example, you might want to capture something from another Office application or from an external website.

You can insert and modify shapes, SmartArt, and screenshots in Word, PowerPoint, and Excel.

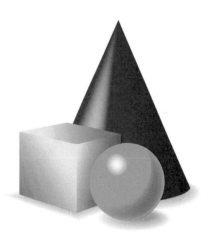

INSERT TAB

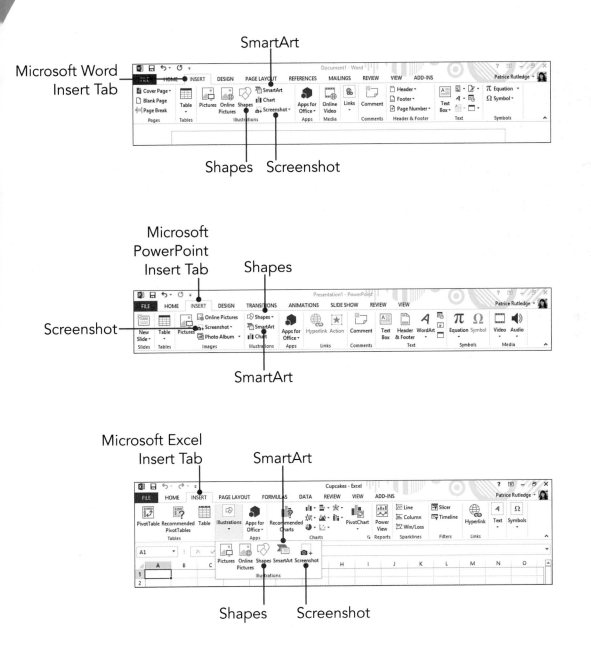

INSERTING A SHAPE

Office offers dozens of ready-made shapes for you to use.

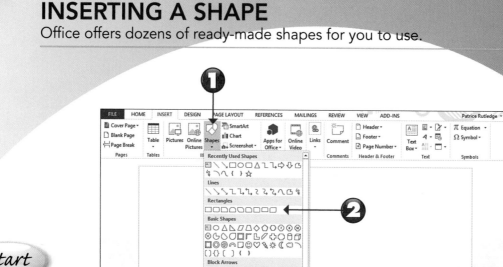

1 On the Insert tab, click the **Shapes** button.

2 From the gallery, select the shape you want to insert.

Continued

---

TIP

Excel Navigation In Excel, depending on your screen size and resolution, you might have to click the **Illustrations** button on the Insert tab, and select **Shapes** from the menu. ■

NOTE

Shape Options Shape options include lines, rectangles, arrows, equations, flowcharts, stars, banners, callouts, and basic shapes such as ovals, triangles, diamonds, and more. ■

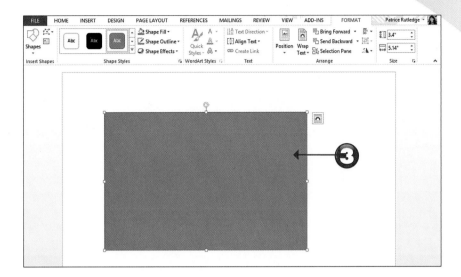

 Click where you want the shape to appear, and then drag until the shape is the size you want.

End

FORMATTING A SHAPE

When you select a shape, the contextual Drawing Tools–Format tab appears. This tab offers numerous options for shape formatting and enhancement, which you explore in this section.

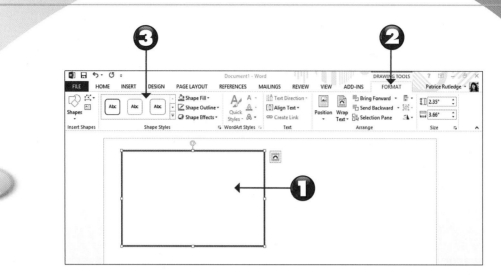

Start

1 Select the shape you want to format.

2 The Drawing Tools–Format tab displays.

3 Select a **Shape Style** to apply a gradient or shaded fill to your shape.

Continued

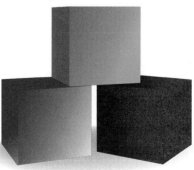

NOTE

Drawing Tools–Format Tab Differences The Drawing Tools–Format tab in each Office application has slight differences. If your application doesn't match the figure in this book exactly, pause your mouse over the Ribbon tab buttons to find the right option. ■

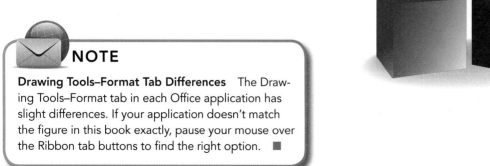

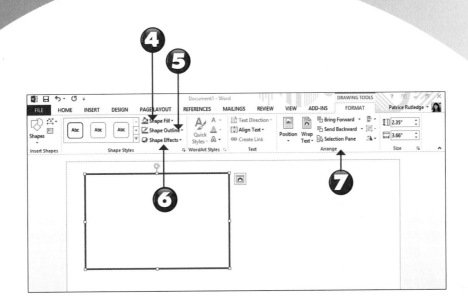

4 Click the **Shape Fill** button to change the shapes color or apply other gradient or texture effects.

5 Click the **Shape Outline** button to apply a shape border.

6 Click the **Shape Effects** button to apply a shadow, reflection, glow, or other special effect.

7 Select an option in the Arrange group to position, group, rotate, or align a shape.

End

TIP

Format Shape Pane You can use the Format Shape pane to apply numerous formatting changes from one place. To open this pane, right-click a shape, and choose **Format Shape** from the menu that displays. ■

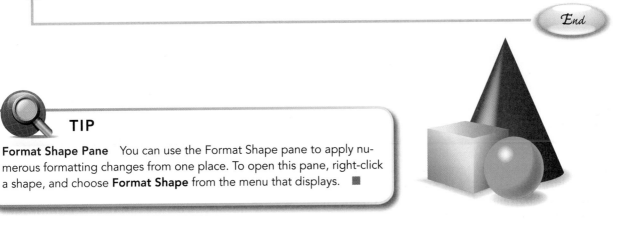

INSERTING A SMARTART GRAPHIC

SmartArt offers a unique opportunity to present content, such as an organization chart or a process, in a way that makes the most of Office's sophisticated design features.

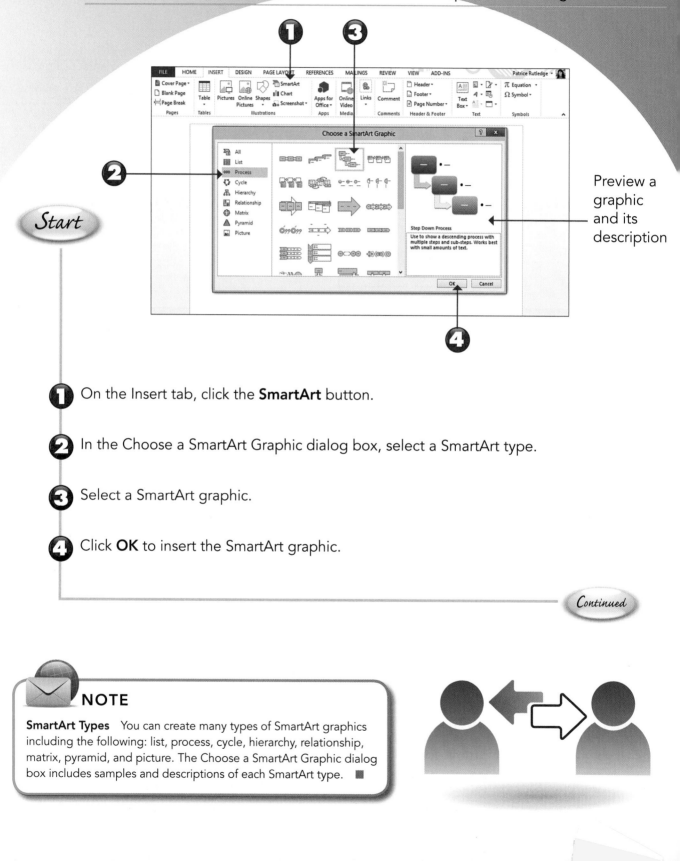

Preview a graphic and its description

Start

1 On the Insert tab, click the **SmartArt** button.

2 In the Choose a SmartArt Graphic dialog box, select a SmartArt type.

3 Select a SmartArt graphic.

4 Click **OK** to insert the SmartArt graphic.

Continued

NOTE

SmartArt Types   You can create many types of SmartArt graphics including the following: list, process, cycle, hierarchy, relationship, matrix, pyramid, and picture. The Choose a SmartArt Graphic dialog box includes samples and descriptions of each SmartArt type. ∎

SmartArt
Tools-Design tab

SmartArt
Tools-Format tab

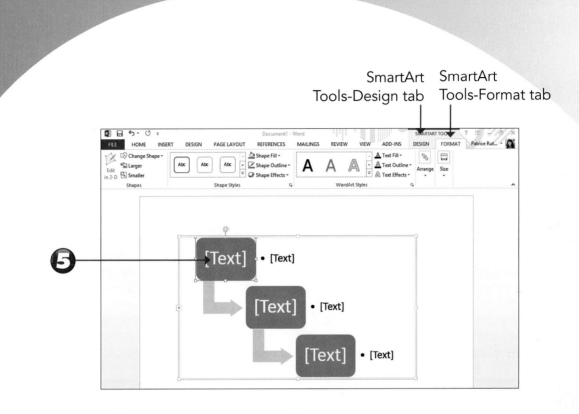

 Enter your text in the placeholders.

INSERTING A SCREENSHOT

Rather than using an external application to take screenshots, Office offers its own screen-capture tool.

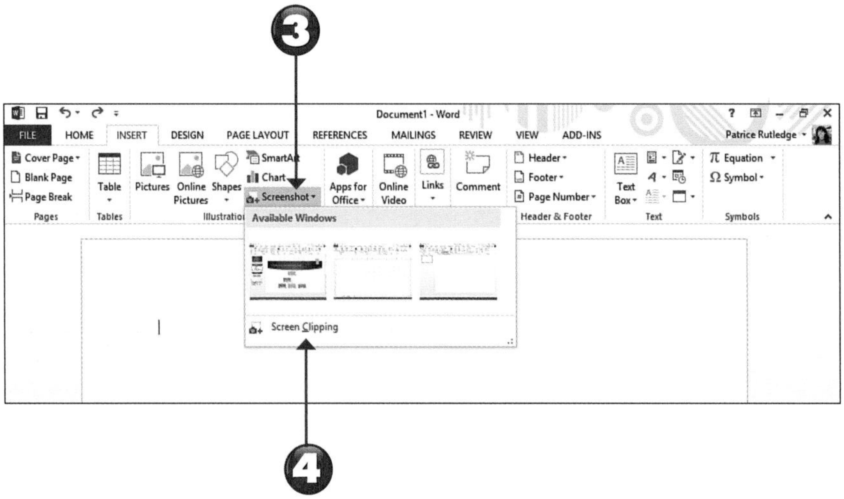

Start

1. Open the application from which you want to take a screenshot.

2. Open the Office document where you want to place the screenshot.

3. On the Insert tab, click the **Screenshot** button.

4. Click **Screen Clipping**.

Continued

TIP

Insert the Entire Window If you want to insert a screenshot of the entire window, select that window from the list that displays. ■

5 Select the area you want to include in your document using your mouse pointer (which now appears as a crosshair).

6 Release the mouse to insert the screenshot.

End

NOTE

Screen Clippings Selecting Screen Clipping minimizes your Office application and displays other open applications and the desktop with a white semi-transparent layer. ◼

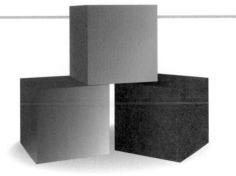

Chapter 6

USING MICROSOFT OFFICE ON THE WEB AND MOBILE DEVICES

Even if you're away from the computer where you installed Office 2013—or away from any computer, for that matter—you can still access your Office files.

To get started, explore SkyDrive, Microsoft's online storage and file-sharing solution. You can store and share files on SkyDrive directly from your Office applications and then access them anywhere you have Internet access. SkyDrive also offers the Office Web Apps for Word, PowerPoint, Excel, and OneNote, which enable you to create and edit files remotely.

EXPLORING SKYDRIVE

Return to SkyDrive
Home page

Get
help

More options

View
thumbnails

Open
folder

View
details

Space
available

Empty recycle bin

Buy more
space

GETTING STARTED WITH SKYDRIVE

SkyDrive offers several gigabytes of free online storage that you can use to collaborate with colleagues anywhere in the world using a PC, Mac, or mobile device (such as smartphone, iPad, or other tablet).

Start

1. Navigate to http://skydrive.com.

2. Enter your Microsoft account username.

3. Enter your password.

4. Click **Sign In**.

End

NOTE

SkyDrive Basics SkyDrive requires a free Microsoft account to access. If you have an existing account with another Microsoft application such as Hotmail or Messenger, you already have an account. If you don't, you can sign up for a free account when you access SkyDrive. ■

Just like on your computer, you store SkyDrive files in folders. You can add files to SkyDrive default folders, or create your own.

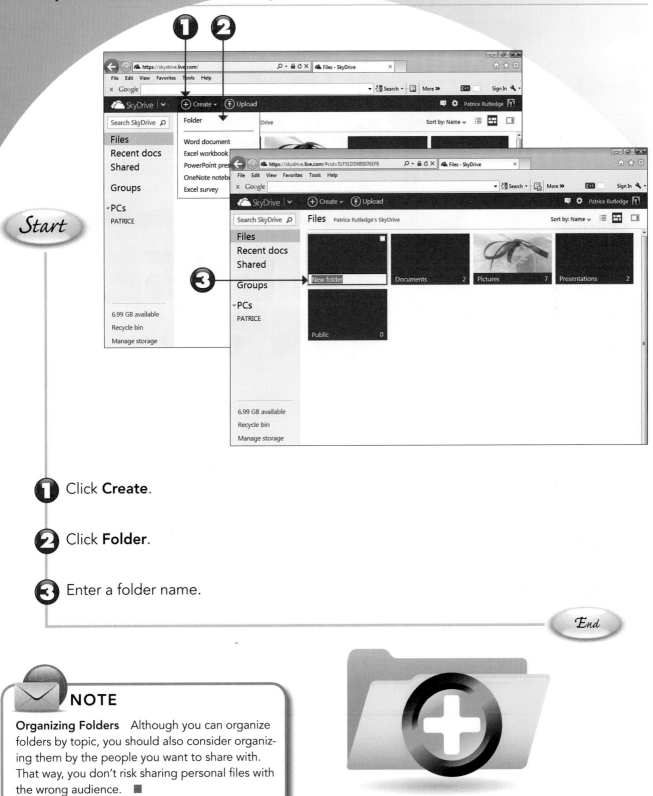

Start

1 Click **Create**.

2 Click **Folder**.

3 Enter a folder name.

End

NOTE

Organizing Folders Although you can organize folders by topic, you should also consider organizing them by the people you want to share with. That way, you don't risk sharing personal files with the wrong audience. ◼

MANAGING FOLDERS

SkyDrive makes it easy to manage your folders, including the capability to share, delete, and move them.

Start

1 Click a folder to open it.

2 SkyDrive displays the files it contains.

3 Click **Share Folder** to share this folder with other users.

Continued

CAUTION

Sharing Folders Consider carefully who should have access to specific content before sharing it. ■

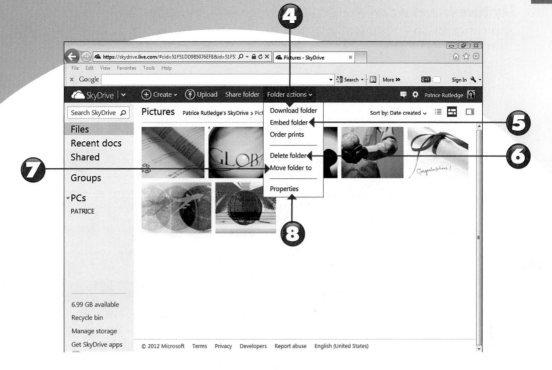

4 Select **Download Folder** from the Folder Actions drop-down menu to download this folder to your computer.

5 Select **Embed Folder** from the Folder Actions drop-down menu to embed this folder on a blog or web page.

6 Select **Delete Folder** from the Folder Actions drop-down menu to delete this folder.

7 Select **Move Folder To** from the Folder Actions drop-down menu to move this folder to another location on SkyDrive.

8 Select **Properties** from the Folder Actions drop-down menu to view folder properties.

End

NOTE

File Actions To manage a file in a folder, right-click it, and select from a menu of options. For example, you can open, rename, and so forth. ∎

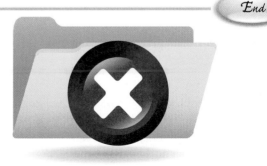

UPLOADING FILES TO SKYDRIVE

Although you can save your Office files to SkyDrive directly from an Office application, you can also do so manually.

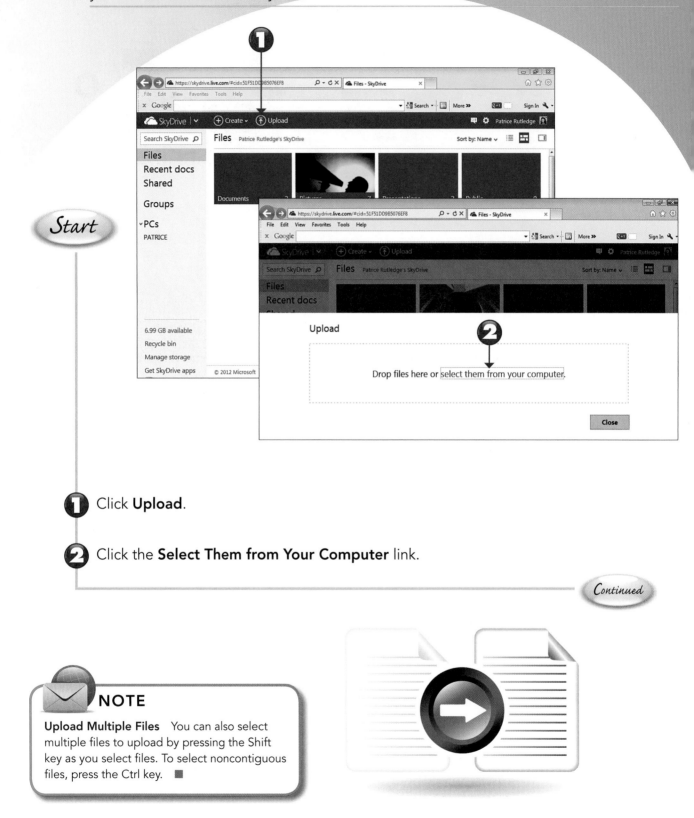

Start

1 Click **Upload**.

2 Click the **Select Them from Your Computer** link.

Continued

NOTE

Upload Multiple Files You can also select multiple files to upload by pressing the Shift key as you select files. To select noncontiguous files, press the Ctrl key. ■

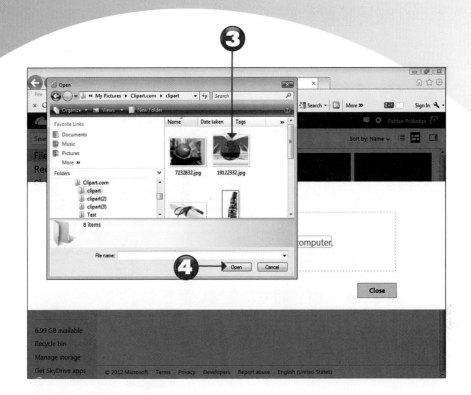

3 Select the file you want to upload.

4 Click the **Open** button to upload and return to SkyDrive.

End

TIP

Upload Many Types of Files Uploading files to SkyDrive isn't limited to files you create in Office. You can also store any other files on SkyDrive, such as photos, PDFs, and so forth. ∎

CREATING A NEW FILE IN SKYDRIVE

Another option is to create a new file directly in SkyDrive. In this example, you create a new PowerPoint presentation.

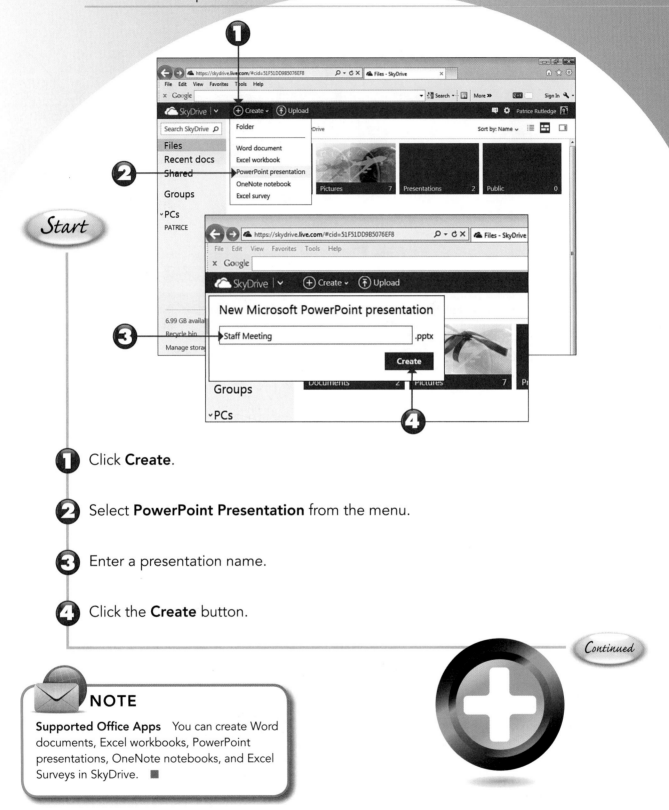

Start

1 Click **Create**.

2 Select **PowerPoint Presentation** from the menu.

3 Enter a presentation name.

4 Click the **Create** button.

Continued

NOTE

Supported Office Apps You can create Word documents, Excel workbooks, PowerPoint presentations, OneNote notebooks, and Excel Surveys in SkyDrive. ■

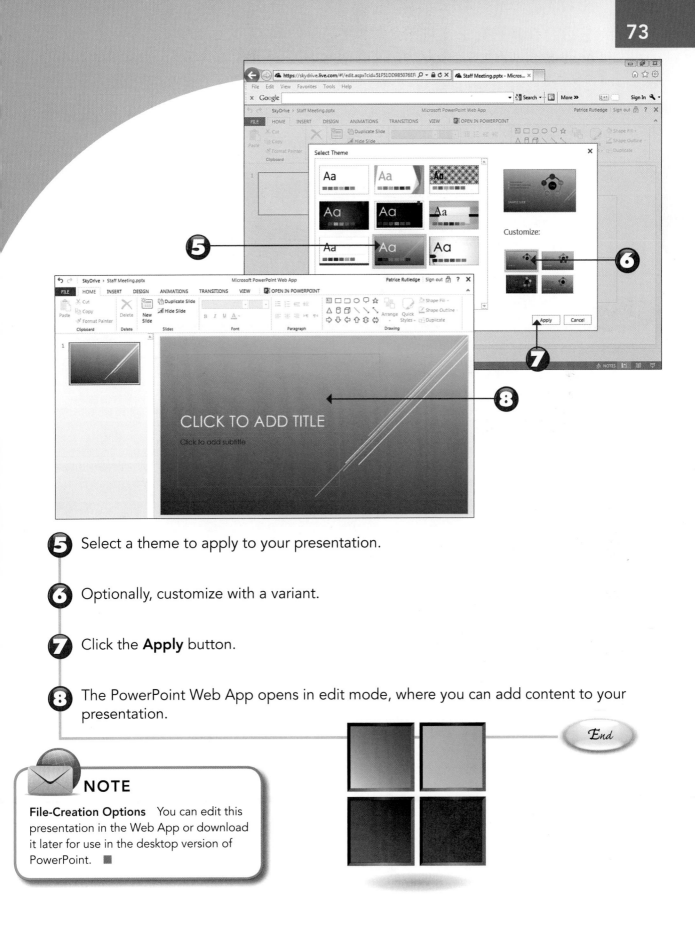

5 Select a theme to apply to your presentation.

6 Optionally, customize with a variant.

7 Click the **Apply** button.

8 The PowerPoint Web App opens in edit mode, where you can add content to your presentation.

End

NOTE

File-Creation Options You can edit this presentation in the Web App or download it later for use in the desktop version of PowerPoint. ■

EDITING A FILE IN SKYDRIVE

You can edit Word, Excel, PowerPoint, and OneNote files that you create or store in SkyDrive using its associated Web App. As an example, edit a Word document in the Word Web App.

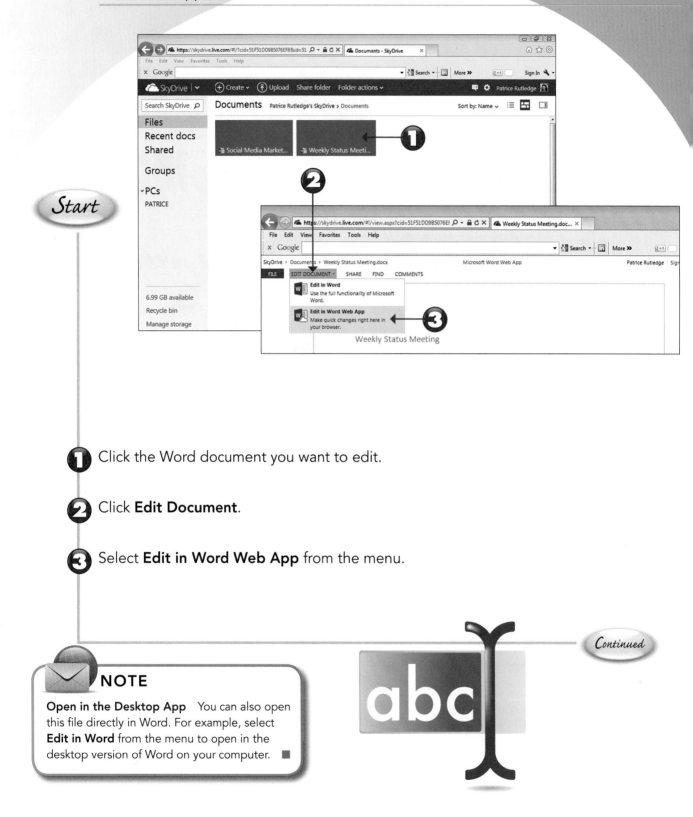

Start

1. Click the Word document you want to edit.

2. Click **Edit Document**.

3. Select **Edit in Word Web App** from the menu.

Continued

NOTE

Open in the Desktop App You can also open this file directly in Word. For example, select **Edit in Word** from the menu to open in the desktop version of Word on your computer. ∎

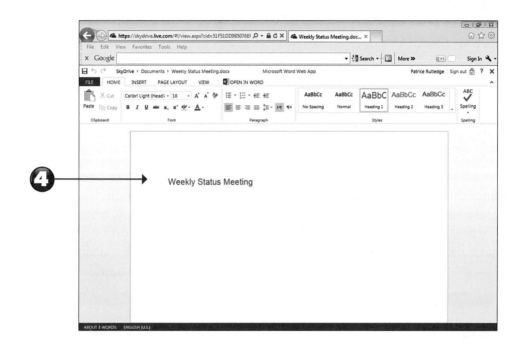

4 Edit your document as you would in the desktop version of Word.

NOTE

Editing in the Web App The commands and buttons on these tabs function in much the same way as they do in the desktop version of Word. The main difference is that you can perform the commands online on a computer that doesn't have Word installed. ■

NOTE

Where's the Save Button? The PowerPoint Web App doesn't have a Save button because it saves your changes automatically. ■

Chapter 7

CREATING A DOCUMENT IN MICROSOFT WORD

Microsoft Word is considered the workhorse of the Office suite and the leading champion among word processing software worldwide. It's the go-to program for any document-creation tasks that come your way, from memos and letters to reports and research papers. In this chapter, you find out how to make new documents using templates and apply basic formatting options.

NAVIGATING THE WORD PROGRAM SCREEN

Use Formatting tools to change the appearance of text

The document name appears in the Title Bar

Find shortcuts to common tools in the Quick Access Toolbar

The Program Window Controls manage the window size

Use the Ribbon to access commands

Use the Work Area to build your document

Use the Scroll Bar to move around the document

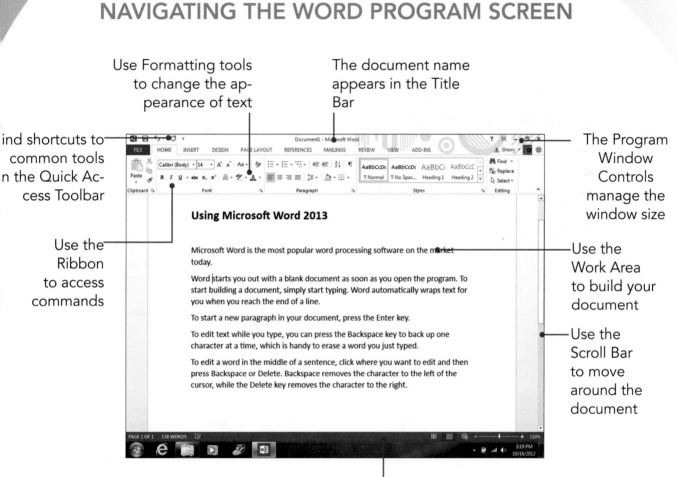

The Status Bar shows current page count, word count, and more

STARTING A BLANK DOCUMENT

When you first open Microsoft Word, it lists several templates you can use to create a new document. The blank document, which is the default choice, is just as the name implies—an empty document waiting for you to add your own text and formatting.

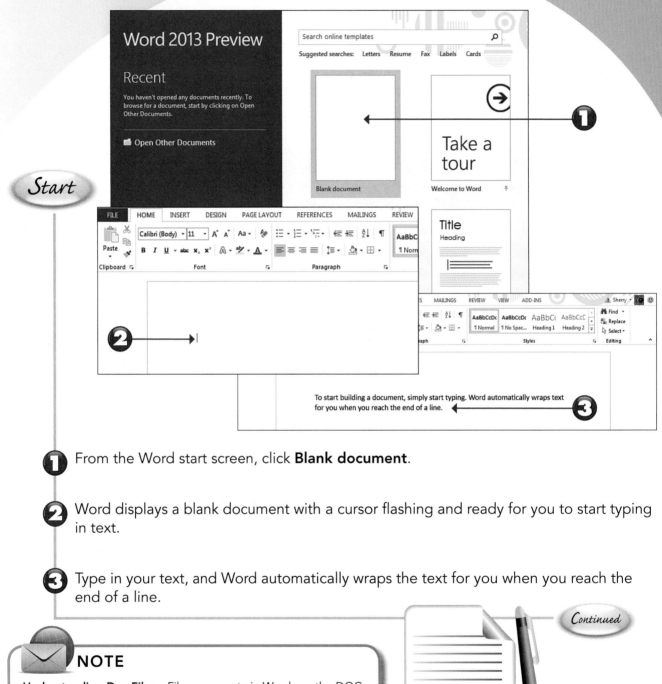

1 From the Word start screen, click **Blank document**.

2 Word displays a blank document with a cursor flashing and ready for you to start typing in text.

3 Type in your text, and Word automatically wraps the text for you when you reach the end of a line.

Continued

NOTE

Understanding Doc Files   Files you create in Word use the DOC file type, which adds a .doc file extension to the filename, unless you choose to save them in another file format. The default DOCX format assigned in Word is backward compatible, which means older versions of Word can still read the file. ■

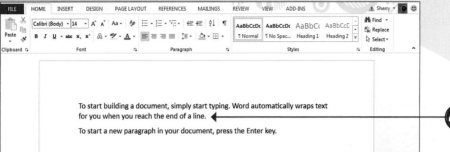

To start building a document, simply start typing. Word automatically wraps text for you when you reach the end of a line.

To start a new paragraph in your document, press the Enter key.

4

To start building a document, simply start typing. Word automatically wraps text for you when you reach the end of a line.

To start a new paragraph in your document, press the Enter key.

To edit text while you type, you can press the Backspace key to back up one character at a time, which is handy to erase a word you just typ

5

To start building a document, simply start typing. Word automatically wraps text for you when you reach the end of a line.

To start a new paragraph in your document, press the Enter key.

To edit text while you type, you can press the Backspace key to back up one character at a time, which is handy to erase a word you just typed.

To edit a word in the middle of a sentence, click where you want to edit and then press Backspace or Delete. Backspace removes the character to the left of the cursor, while the Delete key removes the character to the right.

6

4 Press **Enter** when you want to start a new paragraph.

5 To remove a character while typing, press the **Backspace** key.

6 To edit a word in the middle of a sentence, click where you want to edit, and press **Backspace** to remove characters to the left of the cursor, or press **Delete** to remove characters to the right.

End

TIP

Save It!   To save your work, click the **Save** icon on the Quick Access toolbar. You can also click the **File** tab and choose **Save**. Word prompts you to choose a location for the document, such as storing it online, on your computer, or at another location. ■

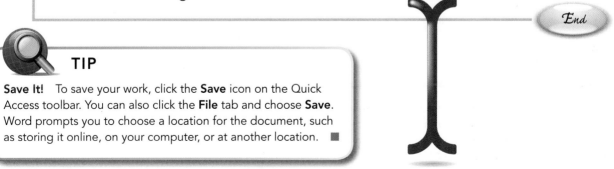

STARTING A NEW DOCUMENT

You can start a new document file any time you need one, even when other files are open. You can choose to base the new document on the default blank document or on a specific template.

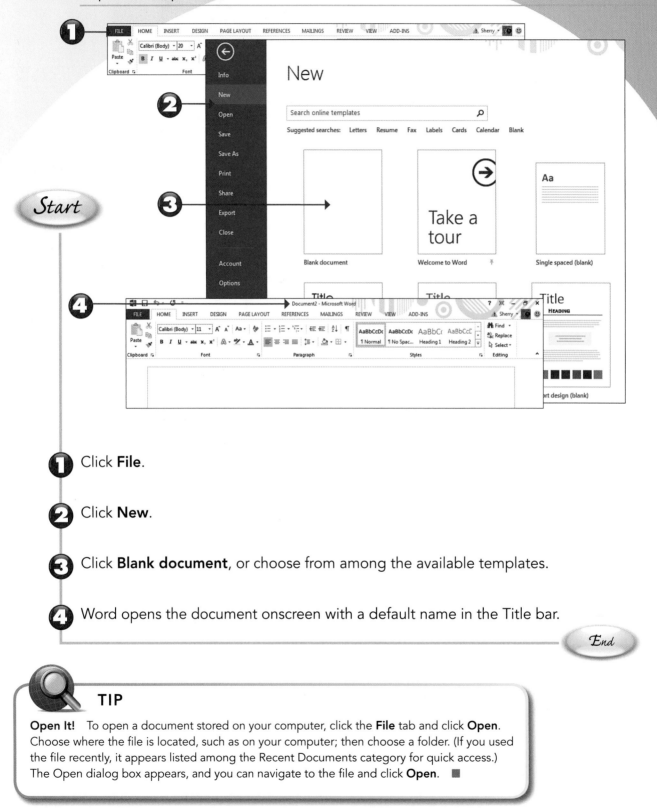

1. Click **File**.

2. Click **New**.

3. Click **Blank document**, or choose from among the available templates.

4. Word opens the document onscreen with a default name in the Title bar.

Start

End

TIP

Open It!   To open a document stored on your computer, click the **File** tab and click **Open**. Choose where the file is located, such as on your computer; then choose a folder. (If you used the file recently, it appears listed among the Recent Documents category for quick access.) The Open dialog box appears, and you can navigate to the file and click **Open**. ■

As you build your document, you can select text to perform various tasks, such as applying formatting, moving and copying text, or deleting text. You can select a single character, word, sentence, paragraph, or the entire document. You can use a mouse-clicking method to select text, or you can click and drag across the words you want to select.

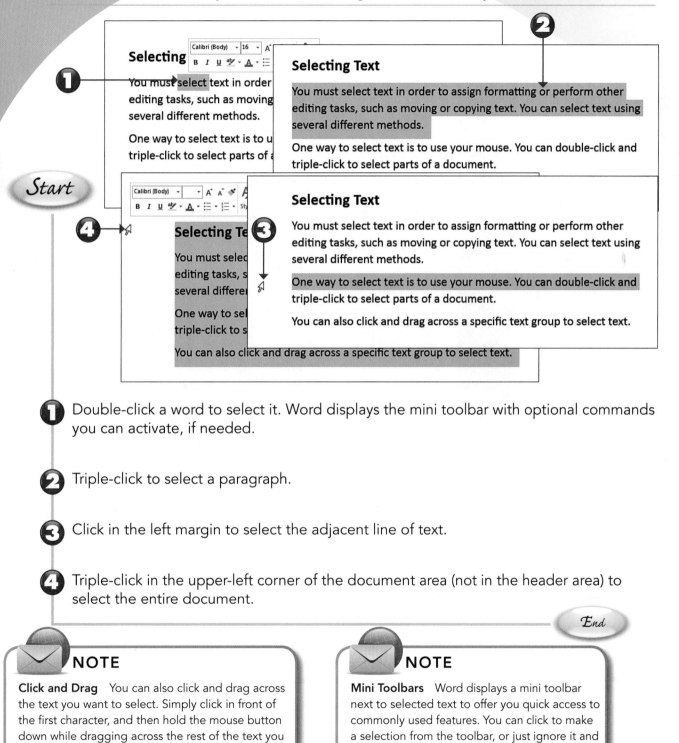

1 Double-click a word to select it. Word displays the mini toolbar with optional commands you can activate, if needed.

2 Triple-click to select a paragraph.

3 Click in the left margin to select the adjacent line of text.

4 Triple-click in the upper-left corner of the document area (not in the header area) to select the entire document.

NOTE

Click and Drag You can also click and drag across the text you want to select. Simply click in front of the first character, and then hold the mouse button down while dragging across the rest of the text you want to include in the selection. ■

NOTE

Mini Toolbars Word displays a mini toolbar next to selected text to offer you quick access to commonly used features. You can click to make a selection from the toolbar, or just ignore it and keep working—it eventually disappears. ■

CREATING A DOCUMENT FROM A TEMPLATE

Templates are the underlying structure for a document, a fill-in-the blanks skeleton to help you build files. You can find ready-made templates in Word to help you create letters, memos, labels, and more. Templates offer preset formatting and styles—all you need to do is add your own text. Even the blank document, for example, is a template, but just an empty one.

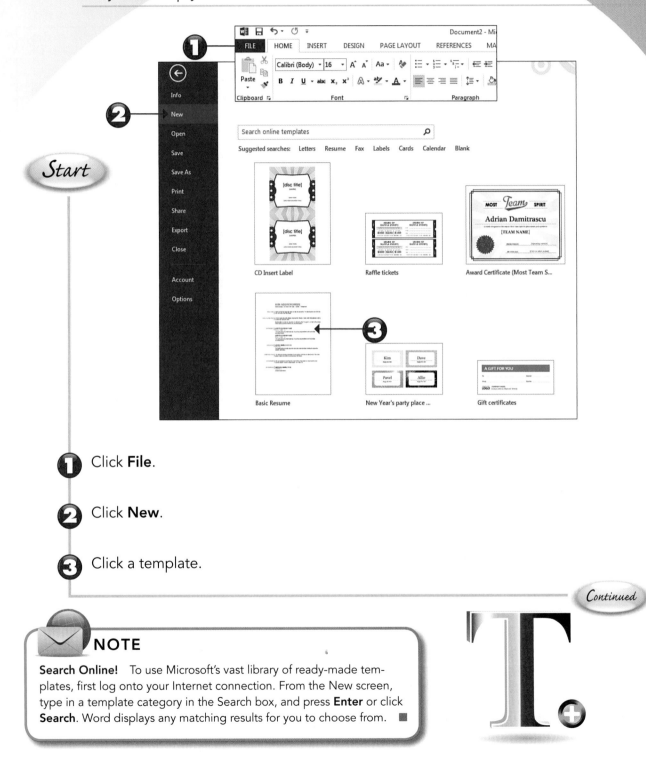

Start

1 Click **File**.

2 Click **New**.

3 Click a template.

Continued

NOTE

Search Online! To use Microsoft's vast library of ready-made templates, first log onto your Internet connection. From the New screen, type in a template category in the Search box, and press **Enter** or click **Search**. Word displays any matching results for you to choose from. ■

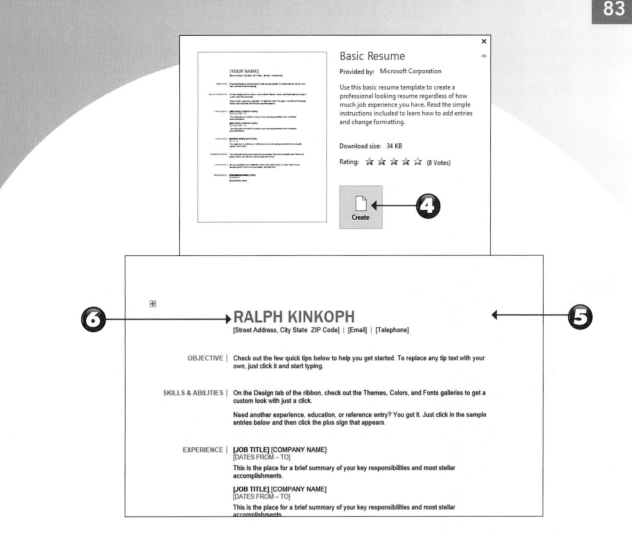

4 Click **Create**.

5 Word opens the template.

6 Click the placeholder text you want to replace, and type in your own text.

End

TIP

Make Your Own Template You can turn any document into a template to reuse. Click the Ribbon's **File** tab and click **Save As**. Choose a location for the file; then in the Save As dialog box, choose **Word Template** from the **Save as Type** drop-down list.

CREATING BULLET AND NUMBER LISTS

You can use Word's bulleting and numbering features to present polished lists or draw attention to important text. A bulleted list inserts bullets or circles in front of each listed item, whereas a numbered list inserts numbers. You can customize the style of your bullets and numbers to create the right effect.

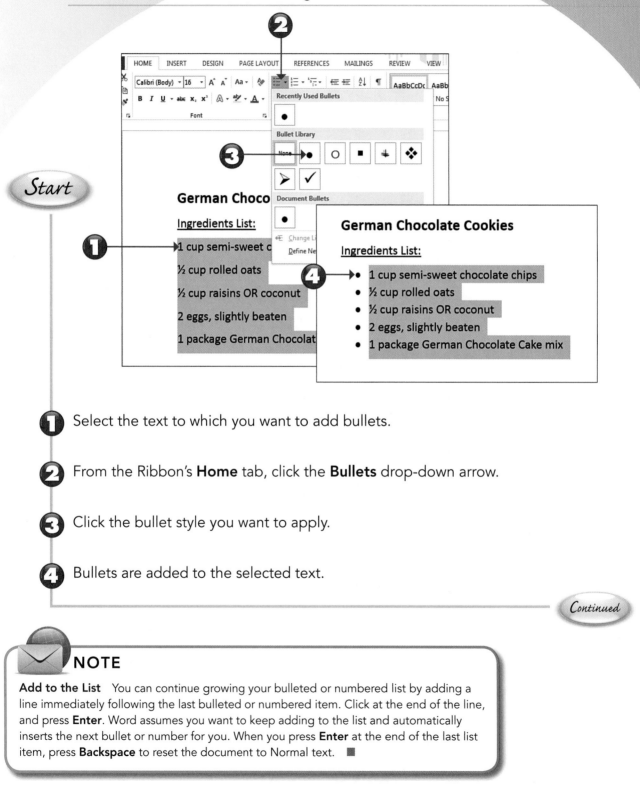

1 Select the text to which you want to add bullets.

2 From the Ribbon's **Home** tab, click the **Bullets** drop-down arrow.

3 Click the bullet style you want to apply.

4 Bullets are added to the selected text.

Continued

NOTE

Add to the List   You can continue growing your bulleted or numbered list by adding a line immediately following the last bulleted or numbered item. Click at the end of the line, and press **Enter**. Word assumes you want to keep adding to the list and automatically inserts the next bullet or number for you. When you press **Enter** at the end of the last list item, press **Backspace** to reset the document to Normal text. ∎

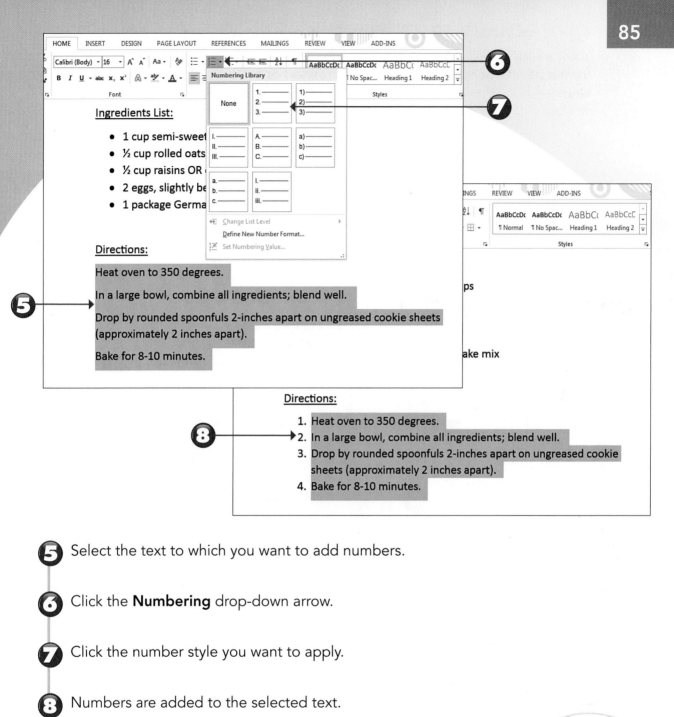

5 Select the text to which you want to add numbers.

6 Click the **Numbering** drop-down arrow.

7 Click the number style you want to apply.

8 Numbers are added to the selected text.

End

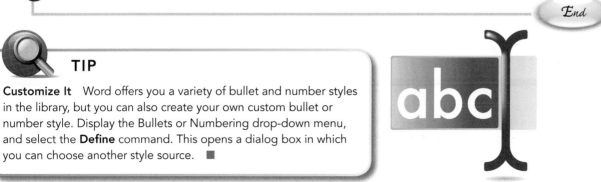

TIP

Customize It   Word offers you a variety of bullet and number styles in the library, but you can also create your own custom bullet or number style. Display the Bullets or Numbering drop-down menu, and select the **Define** command. This opens a dialog box in which you can choose another style source. ■

You can apply color to your Word text through Font Color formatting. You can choose from a palette of colors that are theme-related or from Word's Standard Colors. Always keep legibility in mind when choosing font colors.

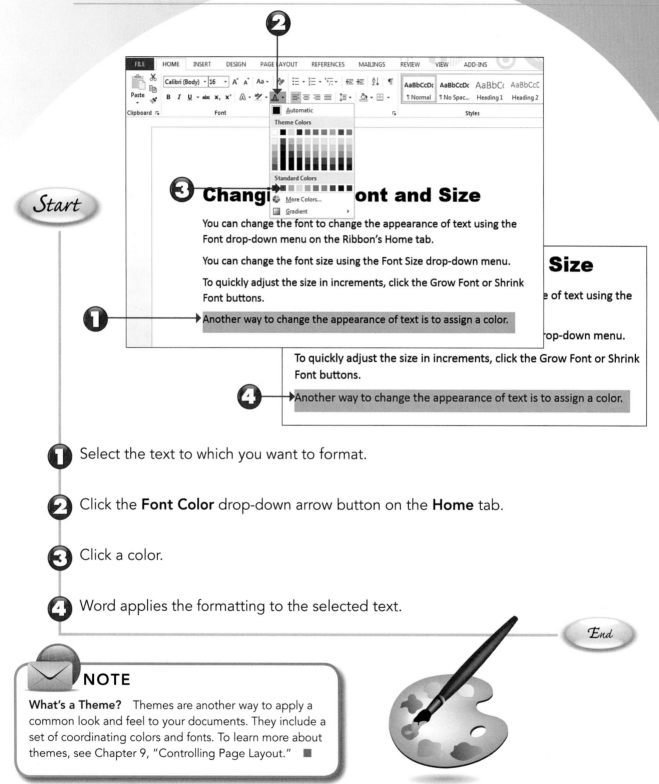

Start

Changing Font and Size

You can change the font to change the appearance of text using the Font drop-down menu on the Ribbon's Home tab.

You can change the font size using the Font Size drop-down menu.

To quickly adjust the size in increments, click the Grow Font or Shrink Font buttons.

Another way to change the appearance of text is to assign a color.

Size

...e of text using the

...rop-down menu.

To quickly adjust the size in increments, click the Grow Font or Shrink Font buttons.

Another way to change the appearance of text is to assign a color.

1 Select the text to which you want to format.

2 Click the **Font Color** drop-down arrow button on the **Home** tab.

3 Click a color.

4 Word applies the formatting to the selected text.

End

NOTE

What's a Theme?   Themes are another way to apply a common look and feel to your documents. They include a set of coordinating colors and fonts. To learn more about themes, see Chapter 9, "Controlling Page Layout." ■

You can use Word's Quick Styles to quickly and easily apply preset formatting to your document text. You can use the Quick Styles gallery—a pop-up menu on the Ribbon's Home tab—to preview a style before you apply it.

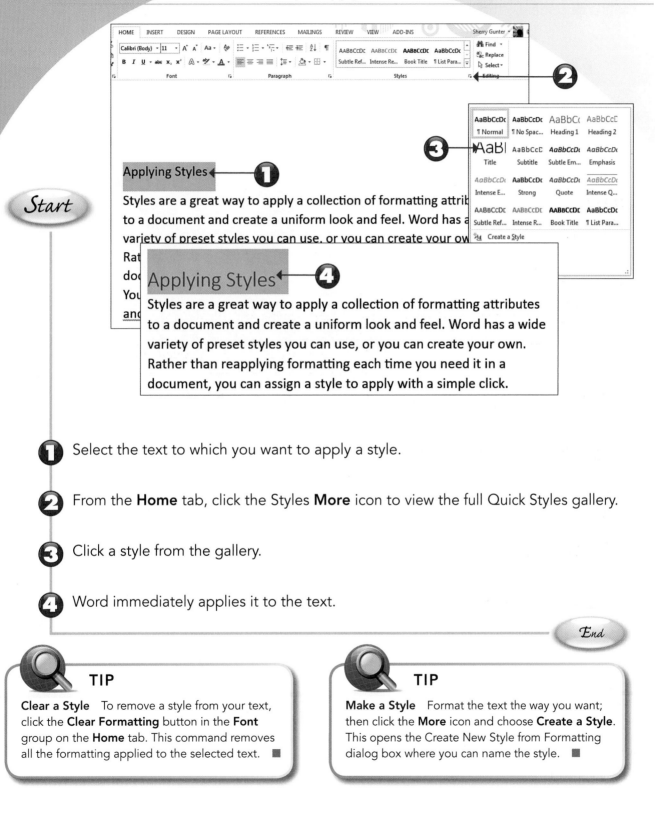

1 Select the text to which you want to apply a style.

2 From the **Home** tab, click the Styles **More** icon to view the full Quick Styles gallery.

3 Click a style from the gallery.

4 Word immediately applies it to the text.

TIP

Clear a Style To remove a style from your text, click the **Clear Formatting** button in the **Font** group on the **Home** tab. This command removes all the formatting applied to the selected text. ■

TIP

Make a Style Format the text the way you want; then click the **More** icon and choose **Create a Style**. This opens the Create New Style from Formatting dialog box where you can name the style. ■

ADDING QUICK PARTS

Word's Quick Parts offers you dozens of premade content elements, called building blocks, you can insert into your documents. Building blocks include text boxes, tables, page numbers, and more. Reusable Quick Parts elements make it easy to build your documents, and you can add your own custom quick parts to the mix.

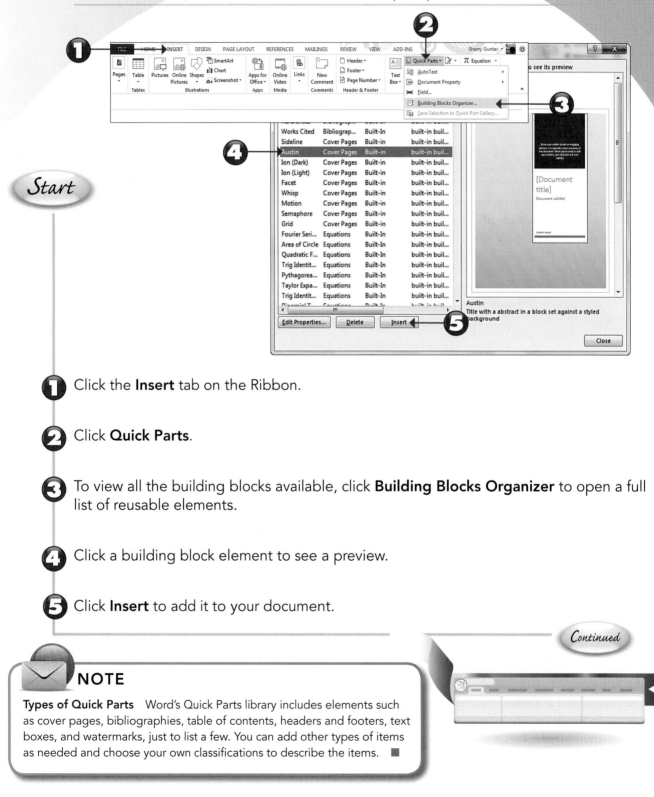

Start

Continued

1. Click the **Insert** tab on the Ribbon.

2. Click **Quick Parts**.

3. To view all the building blocks available, click **Building Blocks Organizer** to open a full list of reusable elements.

4. Click a building block element to see a preview.

5. Click **Insert** to add it to your document.

NOTE

Types of Quick Parts Word's Quick Parts library includes elements such as cover pages, bibliographies, table of contents, headers and footers, text boxes, and watermarks, just to list a few. You can add other types of items as needed and choose your own classifications to describe the items. ■

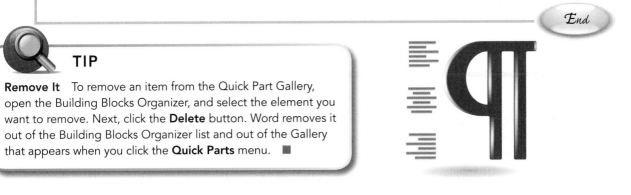

6 To turn text into a building block, first select the text in the document.

7 Click **Quick Parts**.

8 Click **Save Selection to Quick Part Gallery**.

9 Fill out any details you want to save along with the text element, and click **OK**.

10 Word displays the text in the gallery the next time you click Quick Parts.

End

TIP

Remove It To remove an item from the Quick Part Gallery, open the Building Blocks Organizer, and select the element you want to remove. Next, click the **Delete** button. Word removes it out of the Building Blocks Organizer list and out of the Gallery that appears when you click the **Quick Parts** menu. ■

CREATING A TABLE

You can use tables in Word to present information in an organized fashion. Tables are composed of intersecting columns and rows that form cells, which hold data.

Start

1 Click the **Insert** tab on the Ribbon.

2 Click **Table**.

3 Click and drag across the number of columns and rows you want to create.

4 Word immediately inserts the table, and you can start typing in text in each cell.

End

TIP

Navigating Tables You can press the **Tab** key to move from cell to cell in a table. You can press **Shift+Tab** to move back to the previous cell. ■

NOTE

New Tabs When working with tables, two new tabs appear on the Ribbon under the category of Table Tools: **Design** and **Layout**. They both offer special tools and features for working with tables. ■

TIP

Selecting Rows and Columns You can select cells, rows, and columns to perform edits to the table data, such as apply formatting. To select a cell, click the top-left edge of the cell. To select a table row, simply click the far-left edge of the row. To select a column, click the top edge of the column. To select the entire table, click the top-left corner of the table. ■

Word installs with several preset tables you can instantly insert, called Quick Tables.
You can use Quick Tables to insert calendars, tabular lists, and other common table designs.

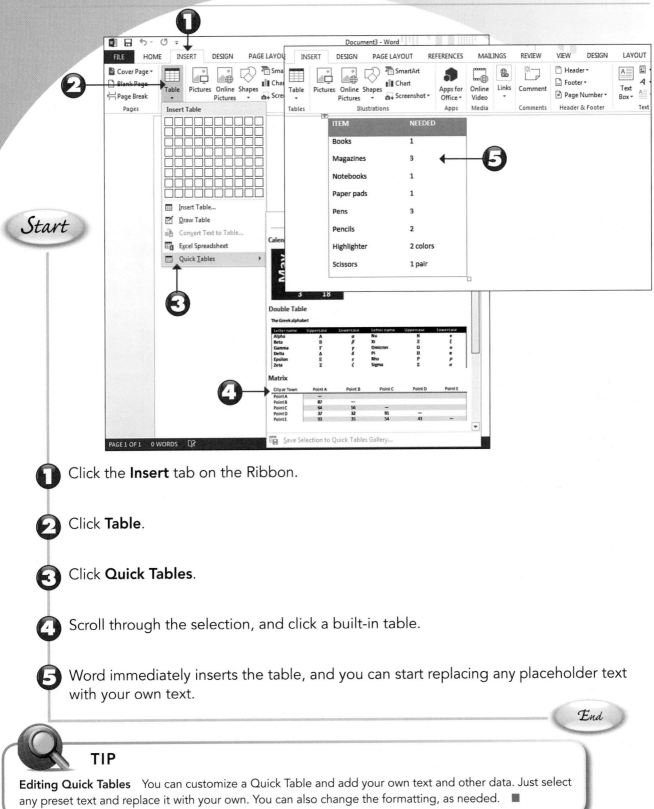

Start

1 Click the **Insert** tab on the Ribbon.

2 Click **Table**.

3 Click **Quick Tables**.

4 Scroll through the selection, and click a built-in table.

5 Word immediately inserts the table, and you can start replacing any placeholder text with your own text.

End

TIP

Editing Quick Tables You can customize a Quick Table and add your own text and other data. Just select any preset text and replace it with your own. You can also change the formatting, as needed. ■

APPLYING A TABLE STYLE

You can apply a preset table style to quickly add formatting to a table, such as cell borders and shading, or colors.

Garden Flowers

Perennial	Annual	Biennial
Speedwell	Petunia	Sweet William
Daylily	Geranium	Pansies
Coreopsis	Impatiens	Foxglove
Salvia	Zinnia	Primrose
Phlox	Sweet Pea	Hollyhocks
Sedum	Snapdragon	
Russian Sage		

Start

1 Click the upper-left corner of the table to select the entire table.

2 Click the Ribbon's **Design** tab.

3 Click the **More** button for Table Styles.

4 Click a style from the Quick Tables Gallery.

5 Word immediately applies the new style to the table.

End

TIP

Customize It and Save It   You can customize any preset table style to suit your own design needs; just make the necessary changes to the formatting. You can also save the new table formatting as a new table style to reuse again later. Select the customized table, and display the Quick Tables Gallery; click **New Table Style**. The Create New Style from Formatting dialog box opens; give the style a name and click **OK**. ∎

TIP

Formatting Tables   You can format table text just as you can any other text in Word. You can change fonts and sizes, apply color to text, add background shading to the cells, change the gridline colors, and more. ∎

You can add rows and columns in your table as you work. Naturally, your table expands to include new rows or columns.

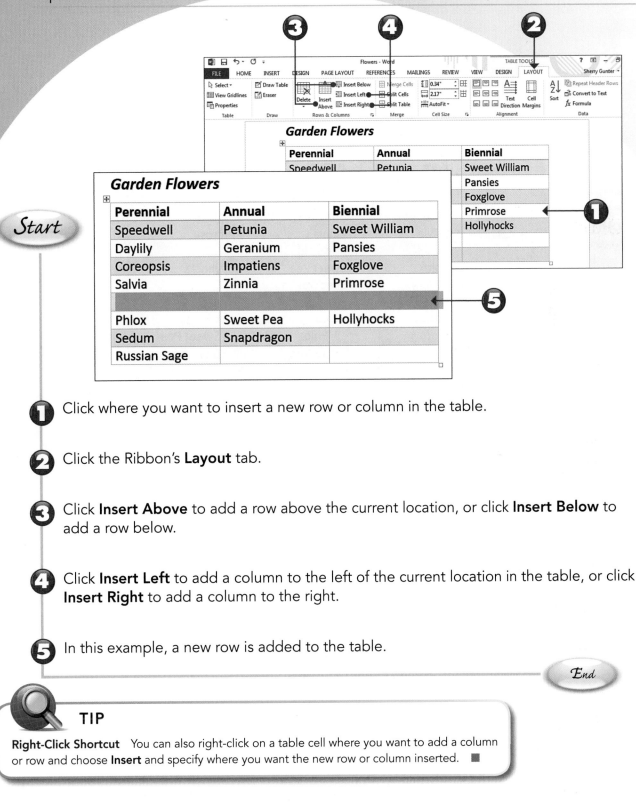

1. Click where you want to insert a new row or column in the table.

2. Click the Ribbon's **Layout** tab.

3. Click **Insert Above** to add a row above the current location, or click **Insert Below** to add a row below.

4. Click **Insert Left** to add a column to the left of the current location in the table, or click **Insert Right** to add a column to the right.

5. In this example, a new row is added to the table.

TIP

Right-Click Shortcut   You can also right-click on a table cell where you want to add a column or row and choose **Insert** and specify where you want the new row or column inserted. ■

DELETING ROWS AND COLUMNS

You can delete rows and columns you no longer need. When you delete columns and rows, the rest of the table structure shifts to fill in the space. Any data within the rows or columns is also deleted.

Start

1 Select the column or row you want to delete, or click in a corresponding cell.

2 Click the Ribbon's **Layout** tab.

3 Click **Delete**.

4 Click **Delete Columns** or **Delete Rows**.

5 Word removes the column or row; in this example a row is deleted.

End

TIP

Oops! If you accidentally delete the wrong row or column, click the **Undo** button on the Quick Access toolbar to quickly fix the mistake, or press **Ctrl+Z** on your keyboard. ■

TIP

Removing Cells You can also choose to delete cells in a table rather than entire rows or columns; click the **Delete** button on the Ribbon's **Layout** tab and then click **Delete Cells**. Deleting cells removes the cell and its content, and Word prompts you to choose how you want to fill in the gap, either by moving surrounding cells up or left. ■

DELETING A TABLE

You can easily delete a table you no longer need in a document. Just remember that deleting a table removes all the content as well.

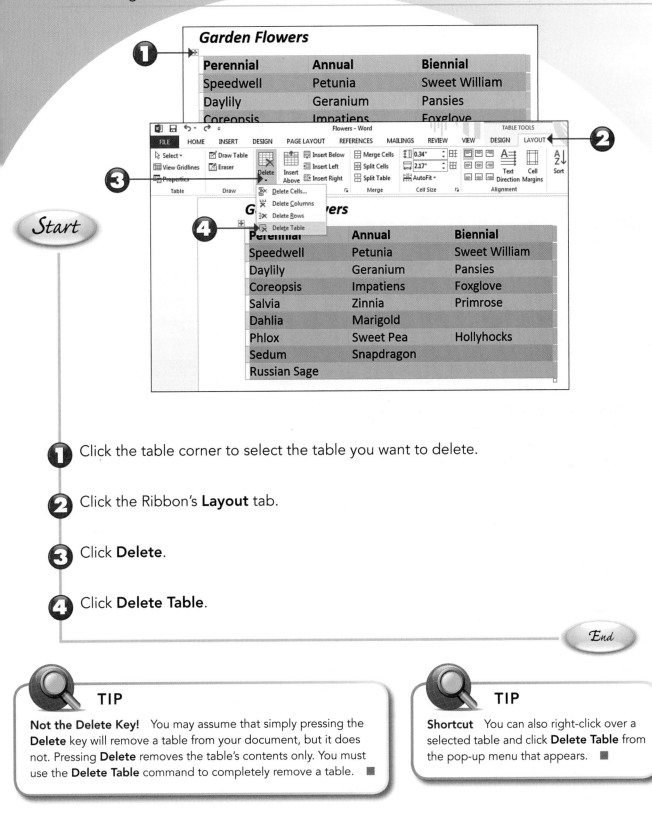

Start

1. Click the table corner to select the table you want to delete.

2. Click the Ribbon's **Layout** tab.

3. Click **Delete**.

4. Click **Delete Table**.

End

TIP

Not the Delete Key! You may assume that simply pressing the **Delete** key will remove a table from your document, but it does not. Pressing **Delete** removes the table's contents only. You must use the **Delete Table** command to completely remove a table. ■

TIP

Shortcut You can also right-click over a selected table and click **Delete Table** from the pop-up menu that appears. ■

MERGING TABLE CELLS

You can merge two or more cells in a table to create one larger cell. You might use this technique to create a title cell that spans across several columns, for example, or a large cell to contain a special note. You can merge cells across rows or down a column.

Perennial	Annual	Biennial
Speedwell	Petunia	Sweet William
Daylily	Geranium	Pansies

TABLE TOOLS

FILE | HOME | INSERT | DESIGN | PAGE LAYOUT | REFERENCES | MAILINGS | REVIEW | VIEW | DESIGN | LAYOUT

Select • | Draw Table | Insert Below | Merge Cells | 0.34" | Text Direction | Cell Margins | Sort
View Gridlines | Eraser | Delete | Insert Above | Insert Left | Split Cells | 4.33"
Properties | | | Insert Right | Split Table | AutoFit •

Table | Draw | Rows & Columns | Merge | Cell Size | Alignment

Perennial	Annual	Biennial
Speedwell	Petunia	Sweet William
Daylily	Geranium	Pansies
Coreopsis	Impatiens	Foxglove
Salvia	Zinnia	Primrose
Dahlia	Marigold	
Phlox	Sweet Pea	Hollyhocks
Sedum	Snapdragon	
Russian Sage		

Start

1. Select the cells you want to merge.

2. Click the Ribbon's **Layout** tab.

3. Click **Merge Cells**.

4. Word merges the cells.

End

TIP

Resize It You can easily resize your table, rows, and columns by dragging a border. For example, to resize a row, drag the top or bottom of the row's border. To resize a column, drag the left or right column border. ■

TIP

Splitting Tables You can also split a table into two tables using the **Split Table** command located directly below the **Split Cells** command on the Layout tab. ■

Just as you can merge cells to create one large cell, you can also split a large table cell into two or more cells. When you split a cell, Word prompts you to choose how to split the cell, either into row or column format. Any text contained within the cells is merged into one cell, unless you specify differently.

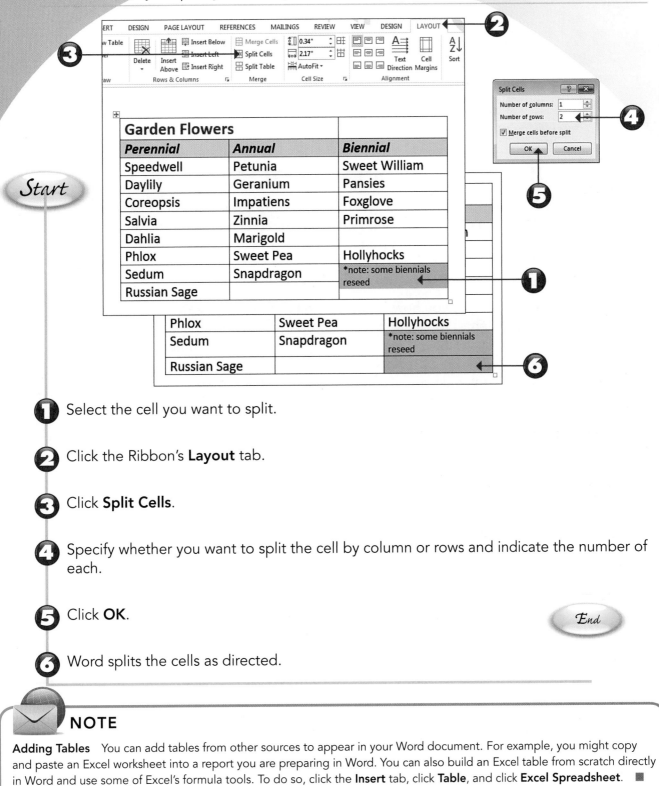

1. Select the cell you want to split.

2. Click the Ribbon's **Layout** tab.

3. Click **Split Cells**.

4. Specify whether you want to split the cell by column or rows and indicate the number of each.

5. Click **OK**.

6. Word splits the cells as directed.

End

NOTE

Adding Tables   You can add tables from other sources to appear in your Word document. For example, you might copy and paste an Excel worksheet into a report you are preparing in Word. You can also build an Excel table from scratch directly in Word and use some of Excel's formula tools. To do so, click the **Insert** tab, click **Table**, and click **Excel Spreadsheet**. ∎

Chapter 8

ENHANCING WORD DOCUMENTS

Basic formatting, such as changing a font or text color, can certainly spruce up a document's text. However, Word offers so much more to make your document appear polished and professional. You can add a variety of enhancements, such as page numbers, text boxes, headers and footers, and other page elements to give your document added pizzazz.

This chapter shows you how to use several of these key features to build better documents. You learn how to add pages, cover pages, and page numbers. When you work with longer documents, page numbers, headers and footers, and page breaks can help you organize your pages. You also learn how to enhance your document with special formatting features, such as text boxes, symbols, and drop caps.

ADDING HEADERS AND FOOTERS IN WORD

You can add headers and footers to your documents to add repeating page text, such as page numbers, author name, or document title

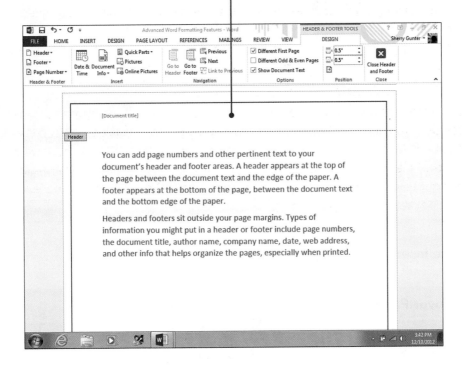

INSERTING A COVER PAGE

You can add a cover page to your document to display a title, author information, or other text of your choosing. Cover pages are simply templates with preset designs and placeholder text. Simply replace the template text with your own.

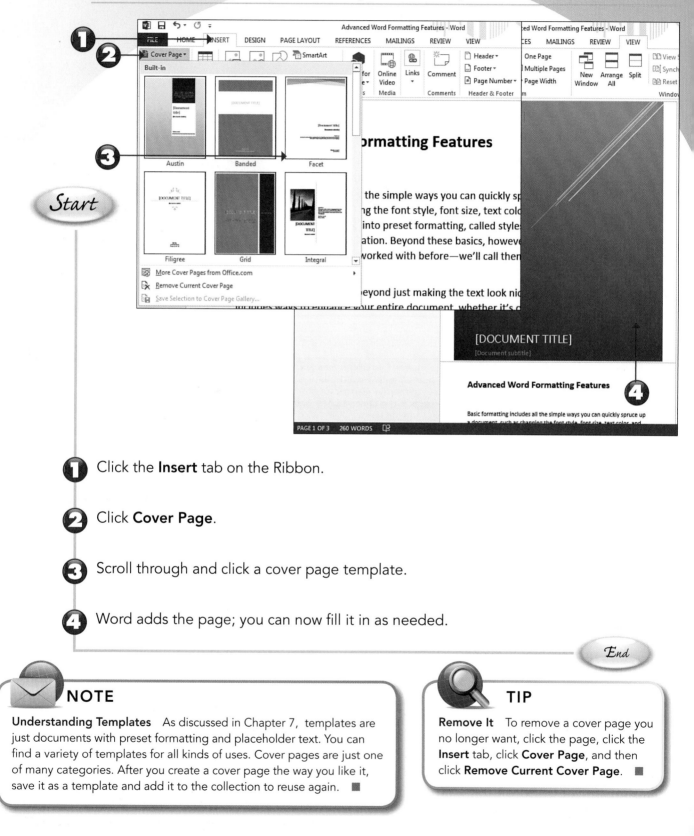

Start

1 Click the **Insert** tab on the Ribbon.

2 Click **Cover Page**.

3 Scroll through and click a cover page template.

4 Word adds the page; you can now fill it in as needed.

End

NOTE

Understanding Templates As discussed in Chapter 7, templates are just documents with preset formatting and placeholder text. You can find a variety of templates for all kinds of uses. Cover pages are just one of many categories. After you create a cover page the way you like it, save it as a template and add it to the collection to reuse again. ■

TIP

Remove It To remove a cover page you no longer want, click the page, click the **Insert** tab, click **Cover Page**, and then click **Remove Current Cover Page**. ■

INSERTING A BLANK PAGE

Although Word creates a new page for you as you type when you reach the end of the current page, you might also need to insert a blank page from time to time. For example, you might need a new page in the middle of two existing pages to insert a chart or graphic. It's easy to insert blank pages where you need them.

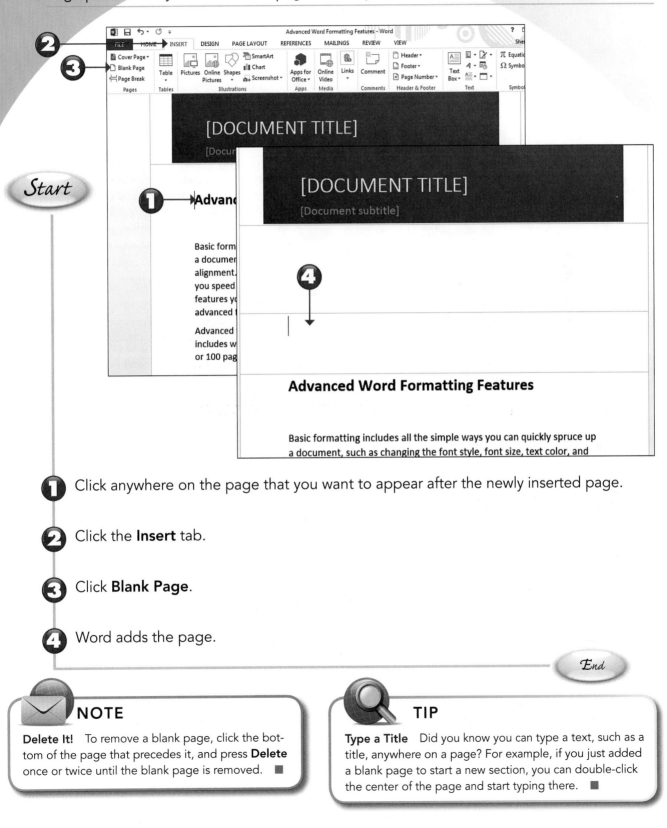

Start

1. Click anywhere on the page that you want to appear after the newly inserted page.

2. Click the **Insert** tab.

3. Click **Blank Page**.

4. Word adds the page.

End

TIP

Type a Title   Did you know you can type a text, such as a title, anywhere on a page? For example, if you just added a blank page to start a new section, you can double-click the center of the page and start typing there. ■

INSERTING A PAGE BREAK

You can insert a page break any time you need to manually start a new page. For example, you might want a longer paragraph at the end of a page to remain as a single block of text rather than broken onto two pages. You can also insert a page break to start a new chapter or topic.

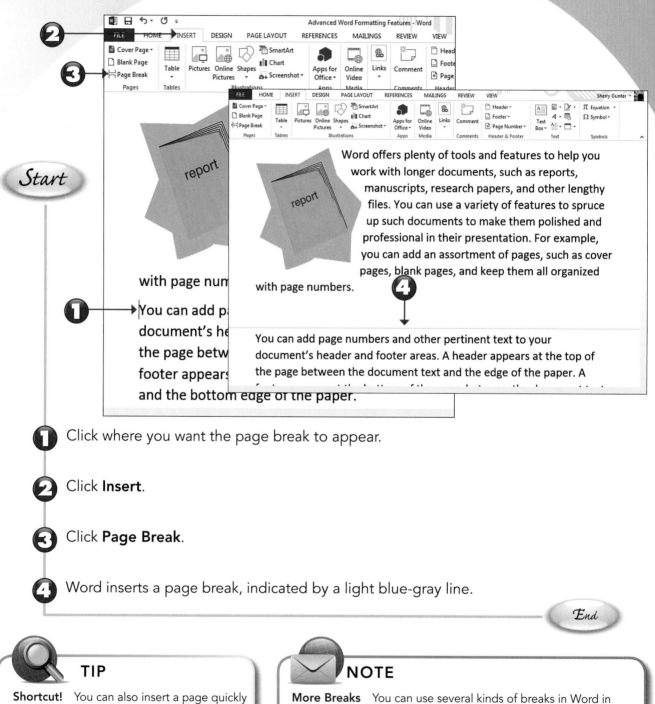

Word offers plenty of tools and features to help you work with longer documents, such as reports, manuscripts, research papers, and other lengthy files. You can use a variety of features to spruce up such documents to make them polished and professional in their presentation. For example, you can add an assortment of pages, such as cover pages, blank pages, and keep them all organized with page numbers.

You can add page numbers and other pertinent text to your document's header and footer areas. A header appears at the top of the page between the document text and the edge of the paper. A footer appears at the bottom of the page between the document text and the bottom edge of the paper.

1 Click where you want the page break to appear.

2 Click **Insert**.

3 Click **Page Break**.

4 Word inserts a page break, indicated by a light blue-gray line.

End

TIP

Shortcut! You can also insert a page quickly using the keyboard shortcut **Ctrl+Enter**. This command immediately starts a new page where the cursor currently sits. ■

NOTE

More Breaks You can use several kinds of breaks in Word in addition to page breaks. You can insert column breaks to control how text flows from one column to the next or section breaks to help manage long documents. To find more break options, click the **Page Layout** tab, and click the **Breaks** drop-down menu. ■

INSERTING PAGE NUMBERS

You can insert page numbers to appear in the header and footer areas of your documents. Page numbers are particularly helpful with longer documents, especially when you print them out and need to organize the pages.

Start

1 Click **Insert**.

2 Click **Page Number**.

3 Click a page location for the numbers.

4 Click a style.

5 Word applies the numbers to your document pages and opens the **Header & Footer Tools** on the Ribbon.

6 Click **Close Header and Footer** to exit.

End

NOTE

Format Them! To change font, size, or color for page numbers, select the page number in the header or footer area, and apply any formatting from the Home tab, such as making the numbers bold or red. To change the number style, click the **Page Number** drop-down menu on the **Header & Footer Tools Design** tab, and then click **Format Page Number**. This opens a dialog box where you can specify other styles, such as Roman numerals. ∎

ADDING HEADERS AND FOOTERS

You can use headers and footers in your documents to add special information to every page, such as a title and date at the top of each page, or a company name and address at the bottom. Header and footer information appears outside the regular text margins at the top (headers) or bottom (footers) of the document.

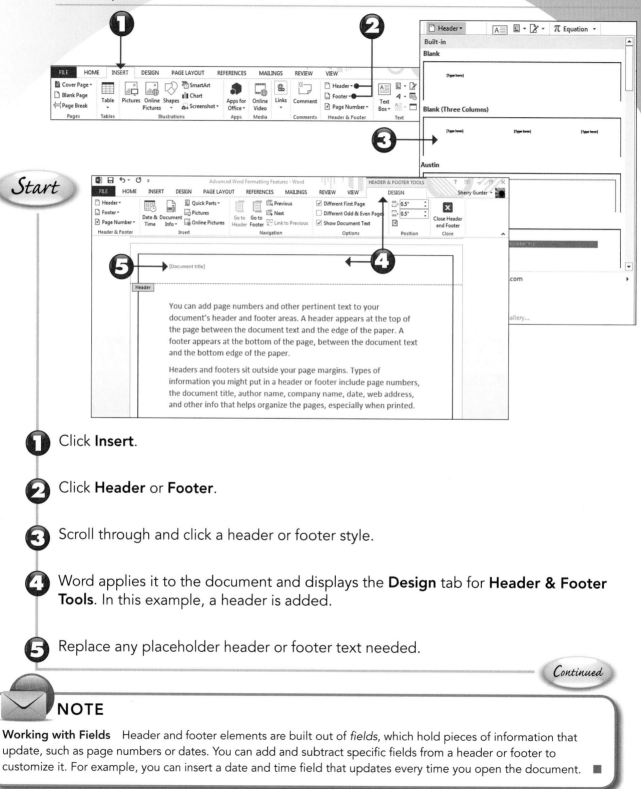

Start

1 Click **Insert**.

2 Click **Header** or **Footer**.

3 Scroll through and click a header or footer style.

4 Word applies it to the document and displays the **Design** tab for **Header & Footer Tools**. In this example, a header is added.

5 Replace any placeholder header or footer text needed.

Continued

NOTE

Working with Fields Header and footer elements are built out of *fields*, which hold pieces of information that update, such as page numbers or dates. You can add and subtract specific fields from a header or footer to customize it. For example, you can insert a date and time field that updates every time you open the document. ■

6 To insert a specific field, such as the document title or author name, click **Document Info** on the **Design** tab, and select a field.

7 Word inserts the specified field; in this example an author name field is added to the header.

8 To navigate between headers and footers, click the **Go to Header** or **Go to Footer** button.

9 To exit the header and footer area of a document, click the **Close Header and Footer** button.

End

TIP

Header and Footer Shortcuts When you work with headers and footers, a dotted line separates the header or footer area from the rest of the document page. If you double-click outside the header or footer area, or press **Esc**, Word automatically closes the Header/Footer view for you. To reopen the view again, double-click inside the header or footer area at the top or bottom of the page. ▪

EDITING HEADERS AND FOOTERS

You can edit your headers and footers to make changes to the text or fields. You can add new fields, remove others, and adjust the formatting to suit your preferences. You can also delete headers and footers you no longer want.

Start

All About Microsoft Word

Sherry Gunter

You can add page numbers and other pertinent text to your document's header and footer areas. A header appears at the top of the page between the document text and the edge of the paper. A footer appears at the bottom of the page, between the document text and the bottom edge of the paper.

Headers and f
information y
the document
and other inf

Advanced Word Formatting Features - Word

HEADER & FOOTER TOOLS

FILE   HOME   INSERT   DESIGN   PAGE LAYOUT   REFERENCES   MAILINGS   REVIEW   VIEW   DESIGN

Header ▾   Footer ▾   Page Number ▾ | Date & Document Time   Info ▾ | Quick Parts ▾   Pictures   Online Pictures | Go to Header   Go to Footer   Link to Previous | ☑ Different First Page   ☐ Different Odd & Even Pages   ☑ Show Document Text | 0.5"   0.5" | Close Header and Footer

Header & Footer   Insert   Navigation   Options   Position   Close

All About Microsoft Word
12/10/2012

Sherry Gunter

Header

① Double-click in the header or footer area you want to edit.

② Select and make any changes to the header or footer elements as needed, such as formatting, typing in different text, or adding more fields.

③ Use the **Options** tools to change how headers, footers, and document text appear while working in Header and Footer mode.

④ Use the **Position** tools to change the position and alignment of header and footer elements.

Continued

TIP

Navigating Tools   You can use the tools under the **Navigation** heading on the **Design** tab to navigate back and forth between header and footer areas in your document. For example, click the **Go to Footer** button to quickly view and make changes to the footer area. ■

5 To remove a header or footer, click the **Header** or **Footer** button on the **Design** tab.

6 Click **Remove Header** or **Remove Footer**.

7 Word removes the header or footer.

8 To exit the header and footer area, click the **Close Header and Footer** button.

End

TIP

Header and Footer Shortcuts When you work with headers and footers, a dotted line separates the header or footer area from the rest of the document page. If you double-click outside the header or footer area, or press **Esc**, Word automatically closes the Header/Footer view for you. To reopen the view again, double-click inside the header or footer area at the top or bottom of the page. ■

INSERTING A TEXT BOX

You can use a text box to add text to a picture, such as a caption or title, or to hold a picture, quote, or other element you want to appear separate from the main document text. Text boxes act as containers that you can move around on the document page.

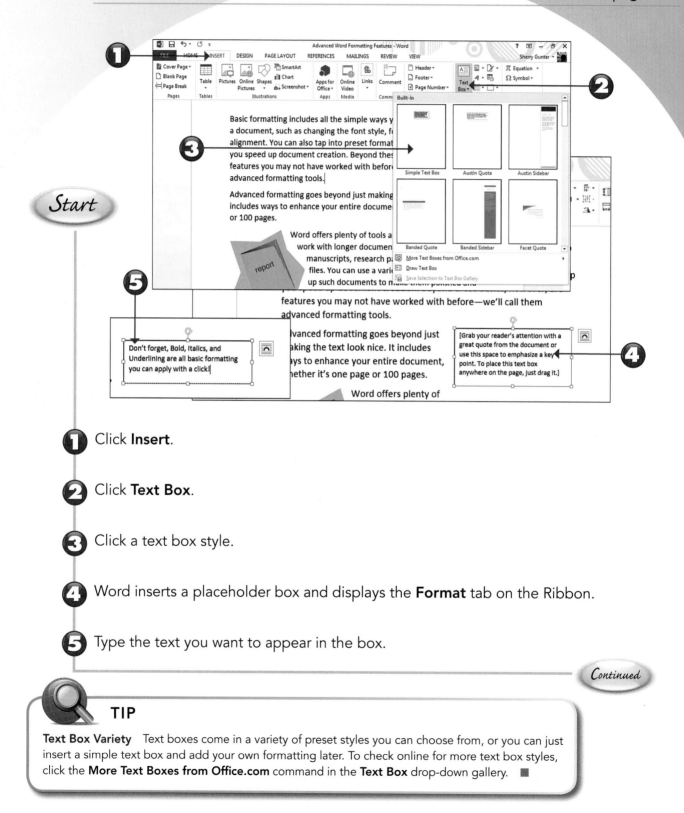

Start

1 Click **Insert**.

2 Click **Text Box**.

3 Click a text box style.

4 Word inserts a placeholder box and displays the **Format** tab on the Ribbon.

5 Type the text you want to appear in the box.

Continued

TIP

Text Box Variety   Text boxes come in a variety of preset styles you can choose from, or you can just insert a simple text box and add your own formatting later. To check online for more text box styles, click the **More Text Boxes from Office.com** command in the **Text Box** drop-down gallery. ∎

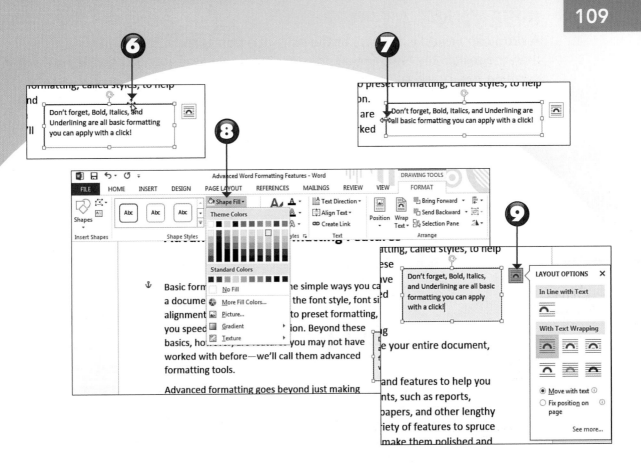

6 To move a text box, position the mouse pointer over an edge of the box, and then drag it to a new location onscreen.

7 To resize the box, click and drag a selection handle.

8 To add shading to a text box background, click the **Shape Fill** button, and choose a shading color.

9 To control additional layout options, click the **Layout Options** button, and choose a text wrap selection.

End

TIP

Easy Formatting You can format text within a text box using the same controls you use to format the rest of your document text. In addition, you can use the Drawing Tools **Format** tab to make changes to the text box shape, color, background, and alignment. ■

INSERTING A DROP CAP

A drop cap typically appears at the start of a paragraph, usually much larger in size than the rest of the text. Drop caps are commonly used in book publishing to mark the opening paragraph of a new chapter. You can use drop caps to add visual emphasis to your text.

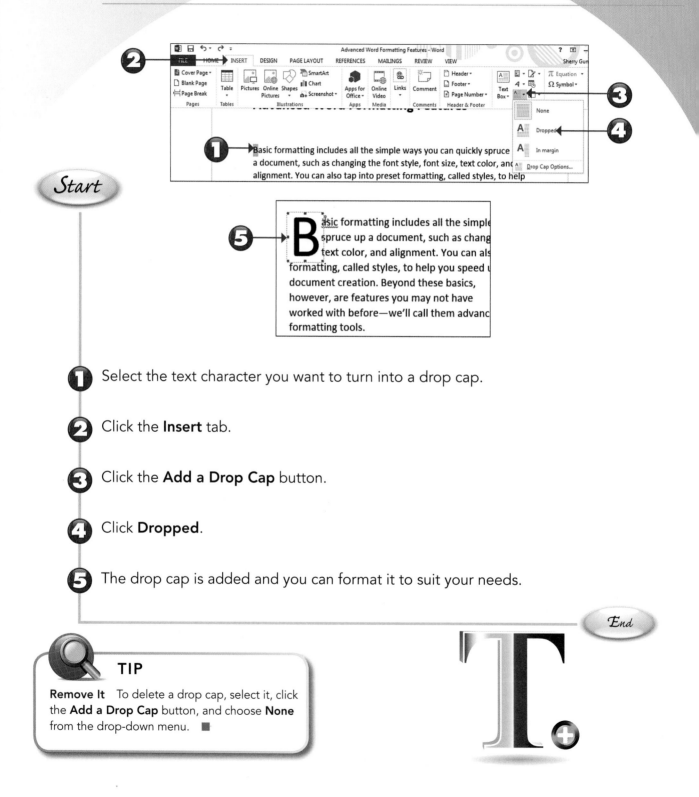

Start

1. Select the text character you want to turn into a drop cap.

2. Click the **Insert** tab.

3. Click the **Add a Drop Cap** button.

4. Click **Dropped**.

5. The drop cap is added and you can format it to suit your needs.

End

TIP

Remove It To delete a drop cap, select it, click the **Add a Drop Cap** button, and choose **None** from the drop-down menu. ■

INSERTING A DATE

You can insert a date or time field into a document that automatically updates every time you open the file. You can also keep the date static (that is, unchanging) if you like.

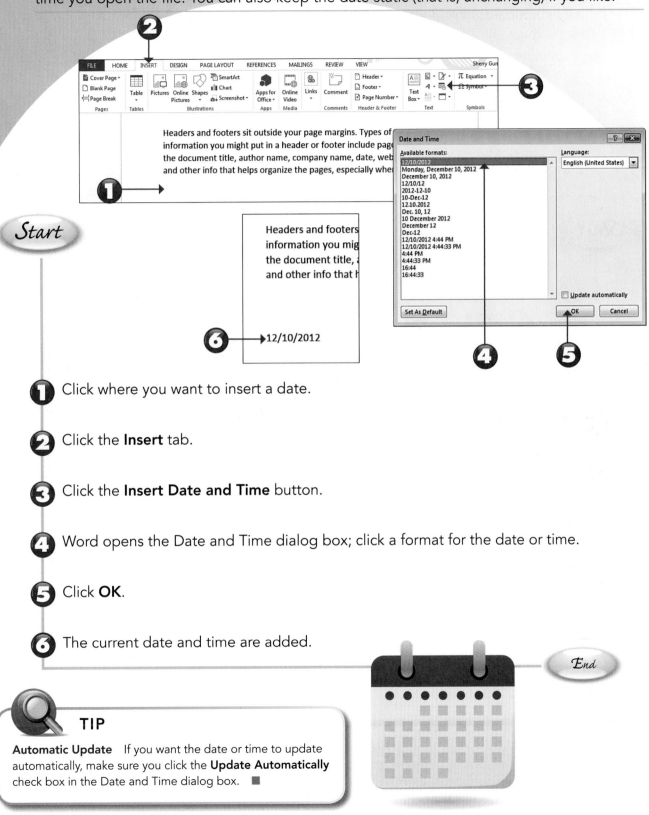

Start

Headers and footers sit outside your page margins. Types of information you might put in a header or footer include page the document title, author name, company name, date, web and other info that helps organize the pages, especially whe

Headers and footers
information you mig
the document title, a
and other info that h

12/10/2012

1 Click where you want to insert a date.

2 Click the **Insert** tab.

3 Click the **Insert Date and Time** button.

4 Word opens the Date and Time dialog box; click a format for the date or time.

5 Click **OK**.

6 The current date and time are added.

End

TIP

Automatic Update If you want the date or time to update automatically, make sure you click the **Update Automatically** check box in the Date and Time dialog box. ∎

INSERTING A SYMBOL

You might need to insert special symbols or characters from time to time, such as a copyright symbol or a registered trademark. Special symbols also include mathematical signs, special quotes, foreign language symbols, and more.

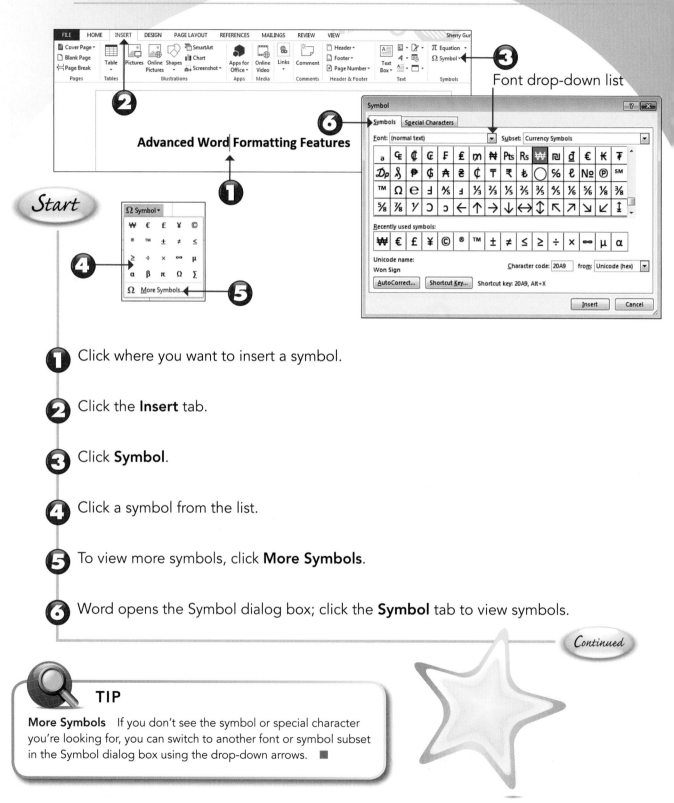

Font drop-down list

Advanced Word Formatting Features

Start

1. Click where you want to insert a symbol.

2. Click the **Insert** tab.

3. Click **Symbol**.

4. Click a symbol from the list.

5. To view more symbols, click **More Symbols**.

6. Word opens the Symbol dialog box; click the **Symbol** tab to view symbols.

Continued

TIP

More Symbols If you don't see the symbol or special character you're looking for, you can switch to another font or symbol subset in the Symbol dialog box using the drop-down arrows. ■

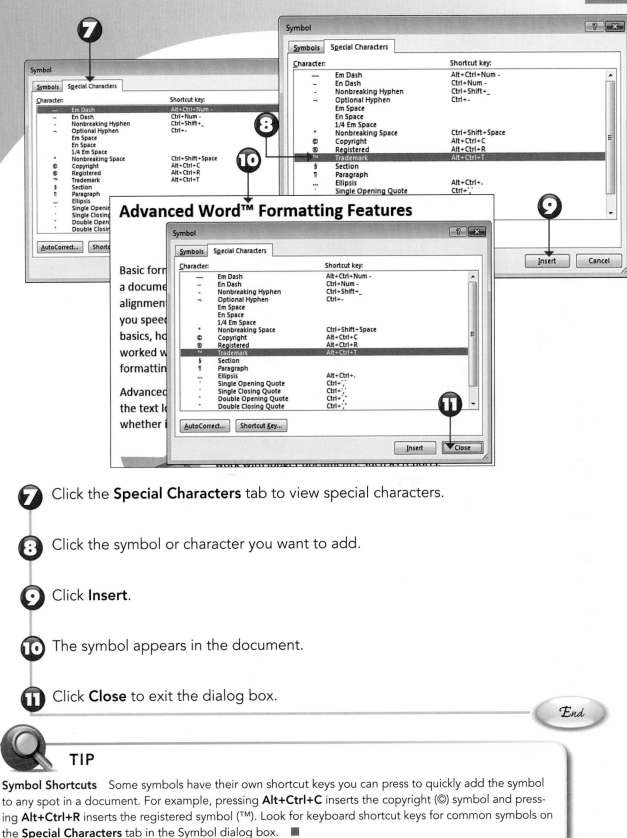

Advanced Word™ Formatting Features

Basic form
a docume
alignmen
you speed
basics, ho
worked w
formattin

Advanced
the text l
whether i

⓻ Click the **Special Characters** tab to view special characters.

⓼ Click the symbol or character you want to add.

⓽ Click **Insert**.

⓾ The symbol appears in the document.

⓫ Click **Close** to exit the dialog box.

End

TIP

Symbol Shortcuts   Some symbols have their own shortcut keys you can press to quickly add the symbol to any spot in a document. For example, pressing **Alt+Ctrl+C** inserts the copyright (©) symbol and pressing **Alt+Ctrl+R** inserts the registered symbol (™). Look for keyboard shortcut keys for common symbols on the **Special Characters** tab in the Symbol dialog box. ∎

INSERTING A HYPERLINK

You can insert a hyperlink into a document that, when clicked, jumps you to another location in the document, another document stored elsewhere on your computer or in the cloud, or a web page on the Internet.

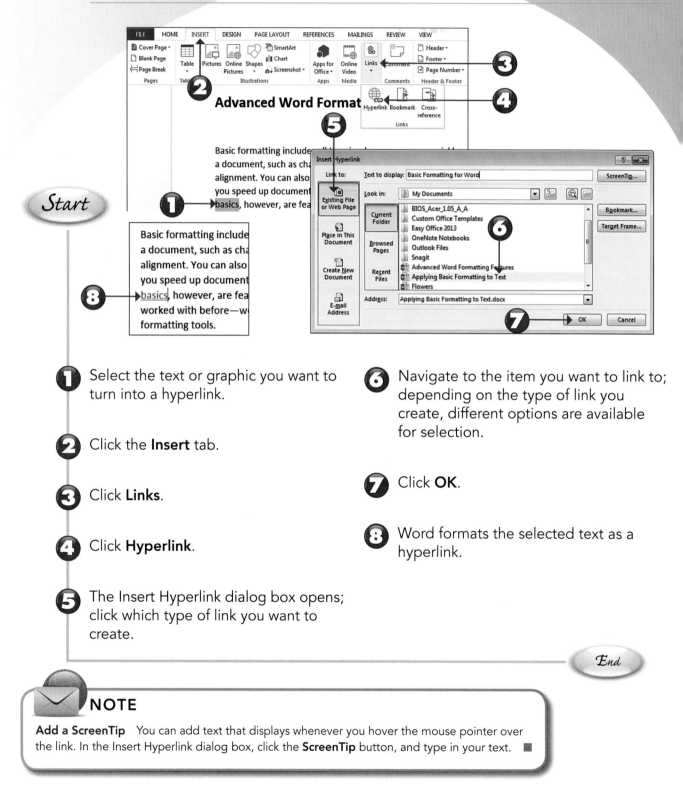

Start

1. Select the text or graphic you want to turn into a hyperlink.

2. Click the **Insert** tab.

3. Click **Links**.

4. Click **Hyperlink**.

5. The Insert Hyperlink dialog box opens; click which type of link you want to create.

6. Navigate to the item you want to link to; depending on the type of link you create, different options are available for selection.

7. Click **OK**.

8. Word formats the selected text as a hyperlink.

End

NOTE

Add a ScreenTip   You can add text that displays whenever you hover the mouse pointer over the link. In the Insert Hyperlink dialog box, click the **ScreenTip** button, and type in your text. ■

INSERTING A BOOKMARK

You can add bookmarks to lengthy documents that jump you to another location within the document. The bookmark naming policy is strict, however. You cannot use spaces, and every bookmark name must start with a letter.

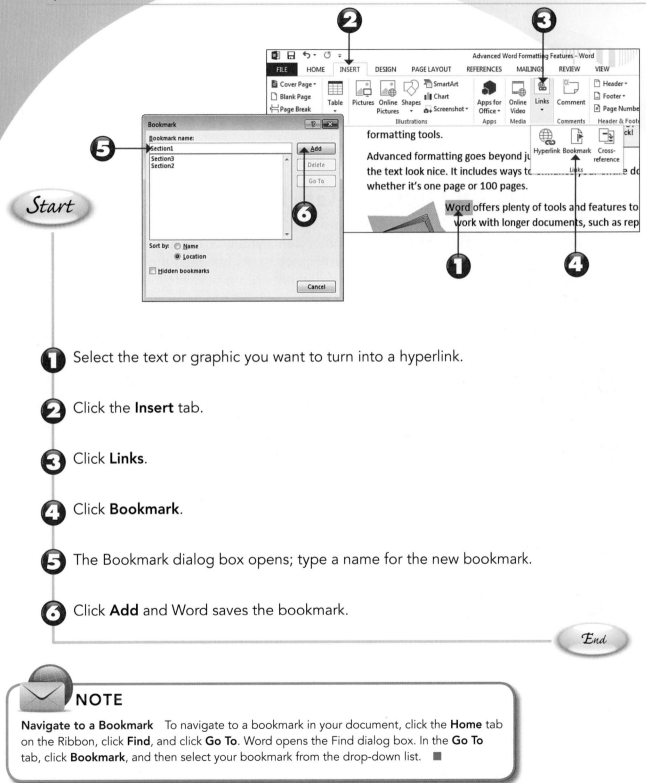

Start

1. Select the text or graphic you want to turn into a hyperlink.

2. Click the **Insert** tab.

3. Click **Links**.

4. Click **Bookmark**.

5. The Bookmark dialog box opens; type a name for the new bookmark.

6. Click **Add** and Word saves the bookmark.

End

NOTE

Navigate to a Bookmark   To navigate to a bookmark in your document, click the **Home** tab on the Ribbon, click **Find**, and click **Go To**. Word opens the Find dialog box. In the **Go To** tab, click **Bookmark**, and then select your bookmark from the drop-down list. ■

Chapter 9

CONTROLLING PAGE LAYOUT

Page layout refers to how you place and position elements on a page, including text and graphics, and any other items you insert in a document. Margins, for example, control how much space exists between the text and the outer edge of the page, whereas alignment controls how text lines up with a margin. Learning how to use Word's page layout features can help you create polished, professional looking documents. You can find most of Word's page layout tools on the Ribbon's Page Layout tab, including access to the Page Setup features to help you ready a document for printing.

In this chapter, you find out how to change the default margins to suit your document. You also see how to change the page orientation from portrait, which is the default setting, to landscape. This chapter shows you how to change the page size and add special borders, create columns on a page, and apply a theme.

CONTROLLING PAGE LAYOUT IN WORD

The Page Layout tab offers a variety of tools for controlling the layout of elements on a document page

Find preset themes you can apply on the Design tab

Page layout refers to how you place and position elements on a page, including text and pictures, and any other items you insert in a document. Margins, for example, control how much space exists between the text and outer edges of the page, while alignment controls how text lines up with a margin.

Learning how to utilize Words page layout features can help you create polished,

CHANGING PAGE MARGINS

Page margins control how text is positioned on a page as it relates to the edges of the page. By default, Word sets margins to 1" on all sides of the page: top, bottom, left, and right. You can change any or all margins as needed, or choose from several presets.

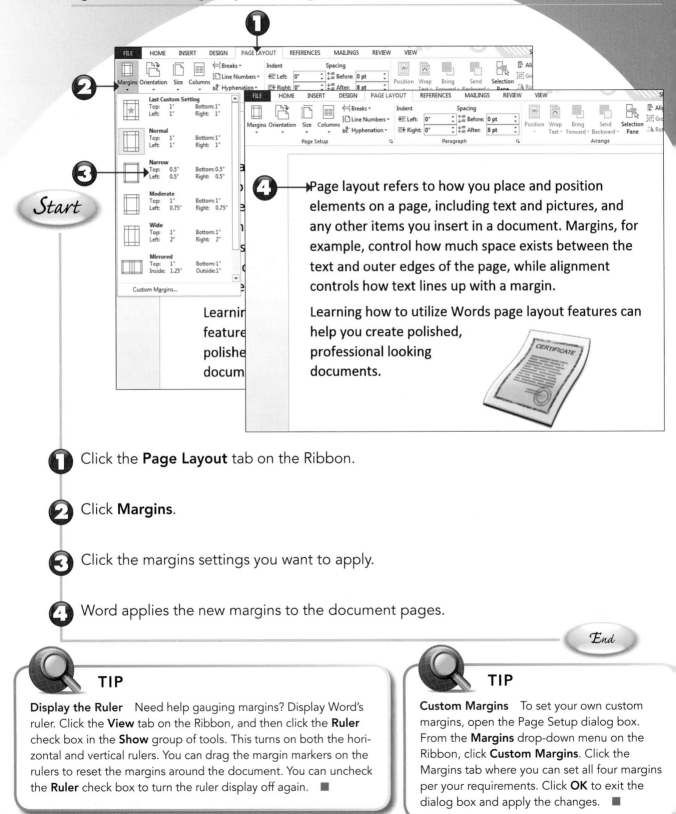

Page layout refers to how you place and position elements on a page, including text and pictures, and any other items you insert in a document. Margins, for example, control how much space exists between the text and outer edges of the page, while alignment controls how text lines up with a margin.

Learning how to utilize Words page layout features can help you create polished, professional looking documents.

Start

End

1 Click the **Page Layout** tab on the Ribbon.

2 Click **Margins**.

3 Click the margins settings you want to apply.

4 Word applies the new margins to the document pages.

TIP

Display the Ruler   Need help gauging margins? Display Word's ruler. Click the **View** tab on the Ribbon, and then click the **Ruler** check box in the **Show** group of tools. This turns on both the horizontal and vertical rulers. You can drag the margin markers on the rulers to reset the margins around the document. You can uncheck the **Ruler** check box to turn the ruler display off again. ■

TIP

Custom Margins   To set your own custom margins, open the Page Setup dialog box. From the **Margins** drop-down menu on the Ribbon, click **Custom Margins**. Click the Margins tab where you can set all four margins per your requirements. Click **OK** to exit the dialog box and apply the changes. ■

MODIFYING PAGE ORIENTATION

By default, Word applies a portrait page orientation, which means the page is taller than it is wide (8.5" x 11"). If your document needs to be wider than it is tall (11" x 8.5"), you can switch it to landscape orientation.

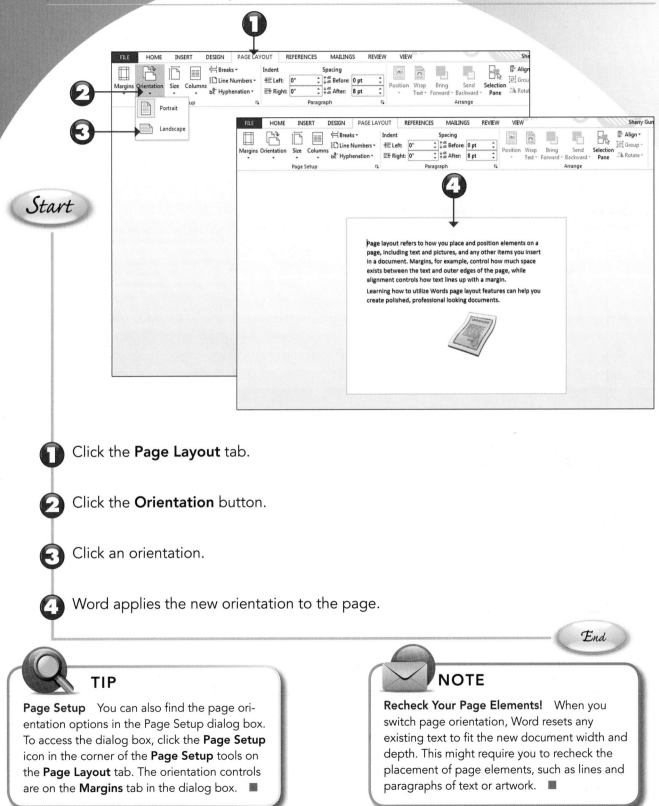

Start

1. Click the **Page Layout** tab.

2. Click the **Orientation** button.

3. Click an orientation.

4. Word applies the new orientation to the page.

End

TIP

Page Setup You can also find the page orientation options in the Page Setup dialog box. To access the dialog box, click the **Page Setup** icon in the corner of the **Page Setup** tools on the **Page Layout** tab. The orientation controls are on the **Margins** tab in the dialog box. ■

NOTE

Recheck Your Page Elements! When you switch page orientation, Word resets any existing text to fit the new document width and depth. This might require you to recheck the placement of page elements, such as lines and paragraphs of text or artwork. ■

CHANGING PAGE SIZE

Depending on your printer's capabilities, you can create and print all kinds of document sizes in Word. For example, you can type up an address and return address in Word to print on an envelope, or you can print legal size pages, and so on.

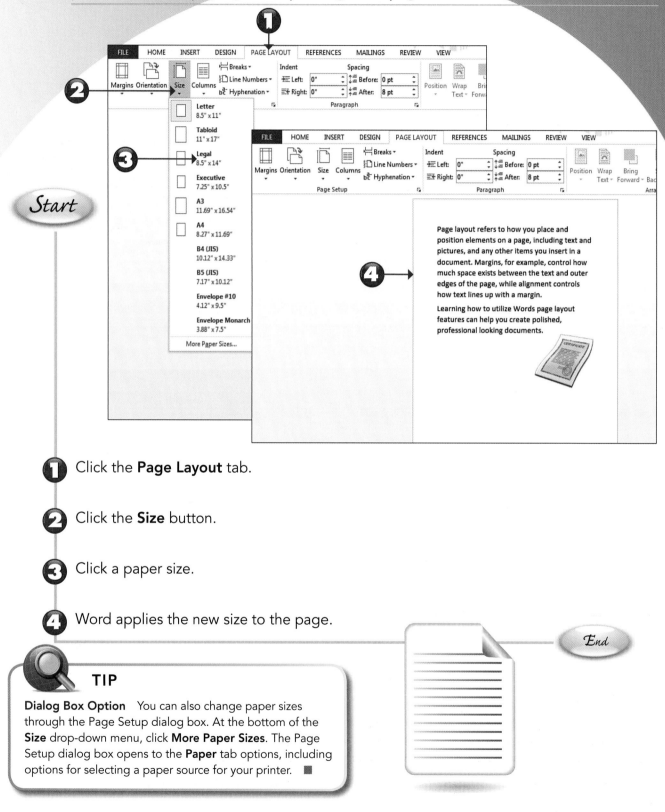

Start

1 Click the **Page Layout** tab.

2 Click the **Size** button.

3 Click a paper size.

4 Word applies the new size to the page.

End

TIP

Dialog Box Option   You can also change paper sizes through the Page Setup dialog box. At the bottom of the **Size** drop-down menu, click **More Paper Sizes**. The Page Setup dialog box opens to the **Paper** tab options, including options for selecting a paper source for your printer. ■

CREATING COLUMNS

You can turn a page of text into columns, much like those found in a newspaper or magazine. With the column feature, text flows from column to column on a page.

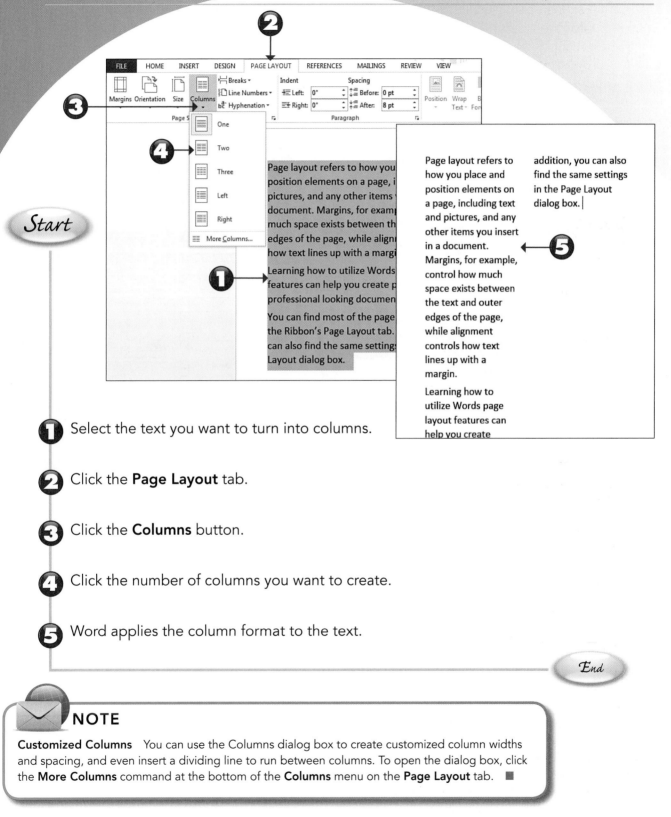

Select the text you want to turn into columns.

Click the **Page Layout** tab.

Click the **Columns** button.

Click the number of columns you want to create.

Word applies the column format to the text.

NOTE

Customized Columns   You can use the Columns dialog box to create customized column widths and spacing, and even insert a dividing line to run between columns. To open the dialog box, click the **More Columns** command at the bottom of the **Columns** menu on the **Page Layout** tab. ■

APPLYING PAGE BORDERS

You can add a border to a document using the Borders and Shading tools. You can specify a border type, such as a box or shadow effect, and choose from a variety of line styles, such as solid, dots, or dashes. In addition, you can specify a color and thickness for the border.

Start

1 Click the **Design** tab.

2 Click the **Page Borders** button.

3 Choose a border type.

4 Click a style.

Continued

TIP

Custom Borders You can also create a custom page border that has only one or two sides. Using the edging buttons in the **Preview** area of the Borders and Shading dialog box, you can turn borders on or off for the top, bottom, right, and left edges of the document. ■

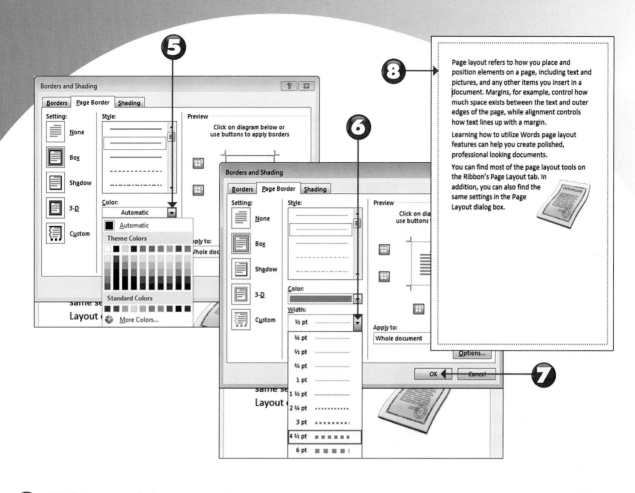

5 Click here and choose a color.

6 Click the **Width** drop-down arrow to choose a line thickness.

7 Click **OK**.

8 Word applies the border to your page.

End

TIP

More Options If you click the **Options** button in the Borders and Shading dialog box, you can open the Border and Shading Options dialog box and specify margin settings for your page border. By default, Word sets the page border at 1/2 points all around, but you can customize the setting to suit your own document. ∎

ADDING INDENTS

You can use indents to move text horizontally from the page margin to set it apart from surrounding text. The Increase Indent and Decrease Indent commands create left indents in increments. You can set more precise indents using the Page Layout tab, including tools for indenting from the right side of a page.

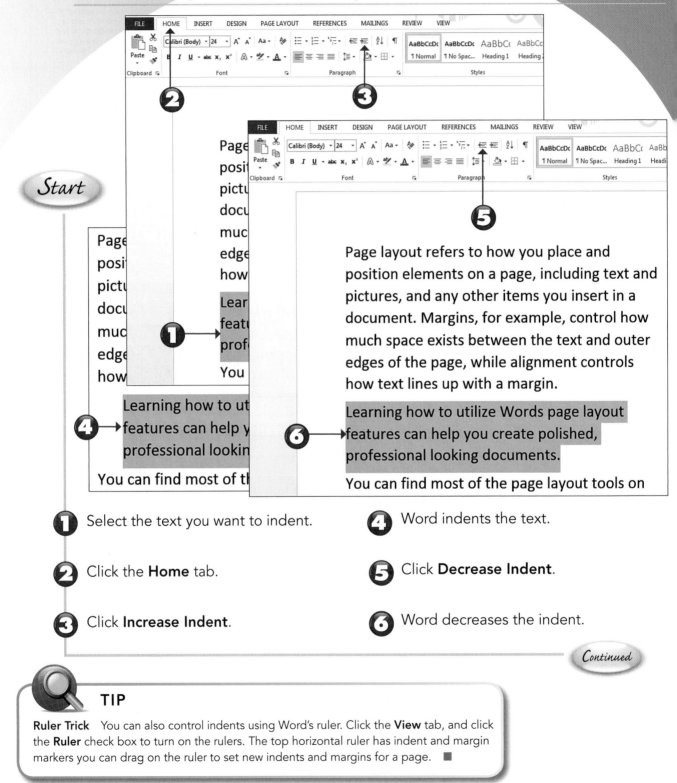

Page layout refers to how you place and position elements on a page, including text and pictures, and any other items you insert in a document. Margins, for example, control how much space exists between the text and outer edges of the page, while alignment controls how text lines up with a margin.

Learning how to utilize Words page layout features can help you create polished, professional looking documents.

You can find most of the page layout tools on

1 Select the text you want to indent.

2 Click the **Home** tab.

3 Click **Increase Indent**.

4 Word indents the text.

5 Click **Decrease Indent**.

6 Word decreases the indent.

Continued

TIP

Ruler Trick You can also control indents using Word's ruler. Click the **View** tab, and click the **Ruler** check box to turn on the rulers. The top horizontal ruler has indent and margin markers you can drag on the ruler to set new indents and margins for a page. ■

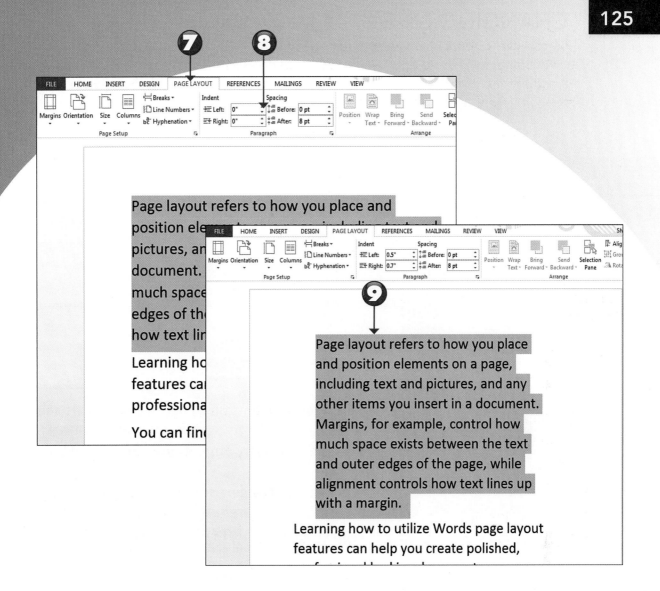

7 Click the **Page Layout** tab.

8 Click the spinner arrows for the **Left** or **Right** indents to specify an indentation amount.

9 Word applies the indent to the selected text.

End

NOTE

Types of Indents You can set several types of indents in Word, including left and right indents. You can also set a First Line indent, which indents just the first line of text in a paragraph, or a Hanging Indent, which indents everything in the paragraph except the first line. You can find draggable markers for these indents on the horizontal ruler; click the **View** tab and click **Ruler** to display the ruler. You can also find special indents through the Paragraph dialog box; click the **Paragraph Settings** icon in the **Paragraph** group of tools on the **Home** tab. ∎

CHANGING LINE SPACING

Line spacing refers to the amount of space between lines of text and paragraphs. You can choose from several preset line spacing amounts. By default, Multiple line spacing is assigned unless you specify something else.

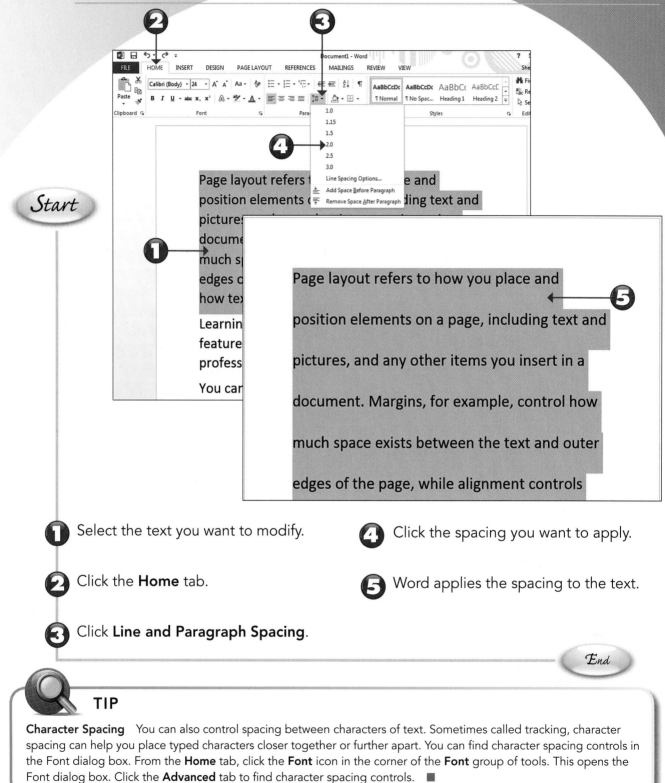

Select the text you want to modify.

Click the **Home** tab.

Click **Line and Paragraph Spacing**.

Click the spacing you want to apply.

Word applies the spacing to the text.

TIP

Character Spacing   You can also control spacing between characters of text. Sometimes called tracking, character spacing can help you place typed characters closer together or further apart. You can find character spacing controls in the Font dialog box. From the **Home** tab, click the **Font** icon in the corner of the **Font** group of tools. This opens the Font dialog box. Click the **Advanced** tab to find character spacing controls. ■

Word adds extra space below every paragraph by default. You can control the spacing to suit your own document needs. You can specify how much space to include before and after paragraphs.

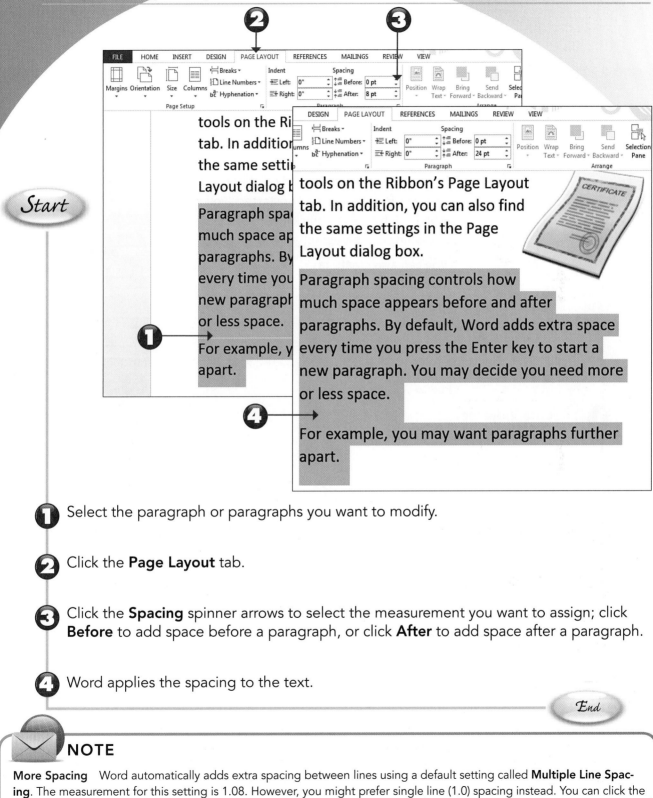

Start

tools on the Ribbon's Page Layout tab. In addition, you can also find the same settings in the Page Layout dialog box.

Paragraph spacing controls how much space appears before and after paragraphs. By default, Word adds extra space every time you press the Enter key to start a new paragraph. You may decide you need more or less space.

For example, you may want paragraphs further apart.

1. Select the paragraph or paragraphs you want to modify.

2. Click the **Page Layout** tab.

3. Click the **Spacing** spinner arrows to select the measurement you want to assign; click **Before** to add space before a paragraph, or click **After** to add space after a paragraph.

4. Word applies the spacing to the text.

End

NOTE

More Spacing Word automatically adds extra spacing between lines using a default setting called **Multiple Line Spacing**. The measurement for this setting is 1.08. However, you might prefer single line (1.0) spacing instead. You can click the **Home** tab and click **Line and Paragraph Spacing** to change the line spacing. ■

SETTING TABS

You can use tab stops to line up text in a document or create columns for organized lists. Word's tabs indent text by one-half an inch. You can use a default tab stop simply by pressing the Tab key. To define your own tab stops, you can use Word's ruler.

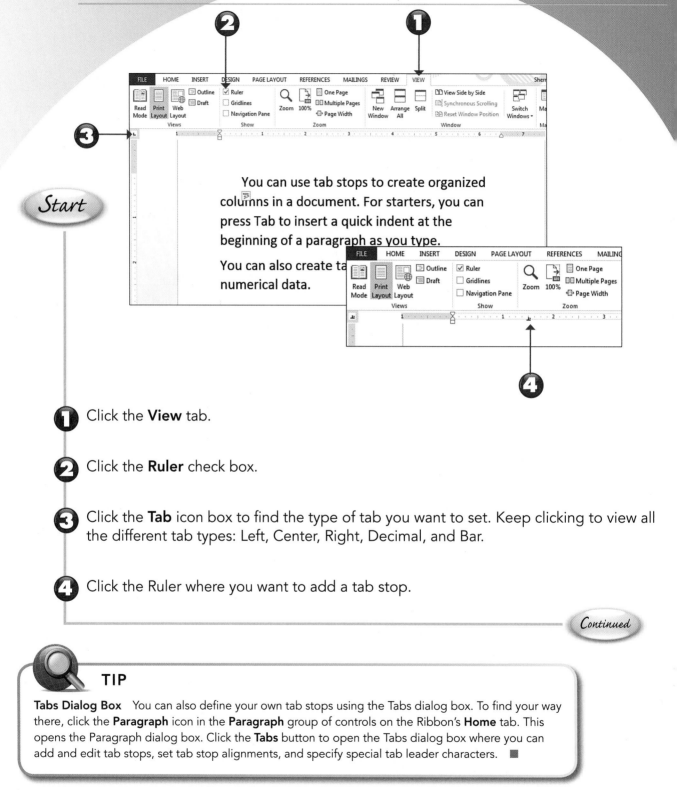

Start

1 Click the **View** tab.

2 Click the **Ruler** check box.

3 Click the **Tab** icon box to find the type of tab you want to set. Keep clicking to view all the different tab types: Left, Center, Right, Decimal, and Bar.

4 Click the Ruler where you want to add a tab stop.

Continued

TIP

Tabs Dialog Box You can also define your own tab stops using the Tabs dialog box. To find your way there, click the **Paragraph** icon in the **Paragraph** group of controls on the Ribbon's **Home** tab. This opens the Paragraph dialog box. Click the **Tabs** button to open the Tabs dialog box where you can add and edit tab stops, set tab stop alignments, and specify special tab leader characters. ■

You can use tab stops to create organized columns in a document. For starters, you can press Tab to insert a quick indent at the beginning of a paragraph as you type.

You can also create tabbed columns to present numerical data.

5 ➤ 123.5

6 ➤ 65.0

8.75

7

You can use tab stops to create organized columns in a document. For starters, you can press Tab to insert a quick indent at the beginning of a paragraph as you type.

You can also create tabbed columns to present numerical data.

123.5

65.0

8.75

You can use ta columns in a docu press Tab **8** inser beginning of a par

You can also creat numerical data.

123.5

65.0

8.75

5 Press **Tab** and type your text.

6 Continue adding as many tab stops as you need and entering your tabbed text. In this example, a Decimal tab is applied, causing all the decimal points to line up in a column.

7 To move a tab, drag it to a new location on the ruler.

8 To remove a tab stop, drag it off the ruler.

End

NOTE

Leader Characters   Leader characters are simply characters that appear between tab stops. Dots, for example, are a common character used, or a dash or solid line. Leader characters extend from one tabbed column to the next, filling in the extra space between columns. You can set leader characters through the Tabs dialog box; click the **Paragraph** icon in the corner of the **Paragraph** tools on the **Home** tab and then click the **Tabs** button. ■

APPLYING A THEME

Another way to add formatting to an entire document is to apply a theme. Themes include a set of coordinating colors, fonts, and effects you can apply to make sure your documents present a professional appearance. You can choose from a variety of preset themes or browse for more themes online.

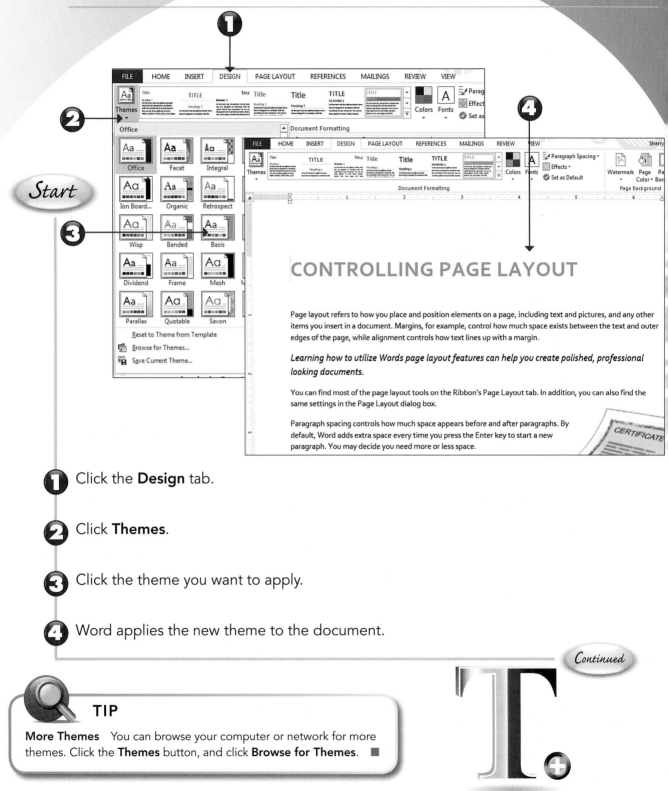

Start

CONTROLLING PAGE LAYOUT

Page layout refers to how you place and position elements on a page, including text and pictures, and any other items you insert in a document. Margins, for example, control how much space exists between the text and outer edges of the page, while alignment controls how text lines up with a margin.

Learning how to utilize Words page layout features can help you create polished, professional looking documents.

You can find most of the page layout tools on the Ribbon's Page Layout tab. In addition, you can also find the same settings in the Page Layout dialog box.

Paragraph spacing controls how much space appears before and after paragraphs. By default, Word adds extra space every time you press the Enter key to start a new paragraph. You may decide you need more or less space.

1 Click the **Design** tab.

2 Click **Themes**.

3 Click the theme you want to apply.

4 Word applies the new theme to the document.

Continued

TIP

More Themes You can browse your computer or network for more themes. Click the **Themes** button, and click **Browse for Themes**. ■

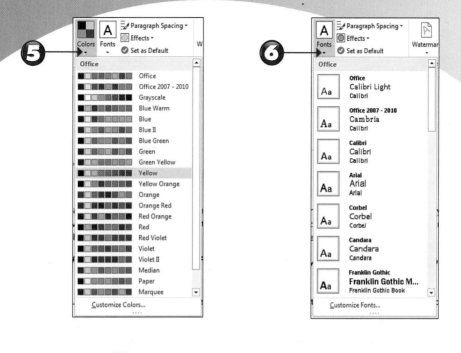

 Click the **Colors** drop-down arrow to change the color scheme associated with the theme.

6 Click the **Fonts** drop-down arrow to change the fonts associated with the theme.

7 To change the document formatting, make a selection from the palette, or click the **More** button to view all the choices and choose a style.

 End

NOTE

What's in a Theme? When you assign a theme, Word looks for and replaces the formats of each of the styles to the document elements. A theme includes fonts for any headings and body text assigned, including color, type style, and spacing. Themes also include 3-D effects, shadows, and lighting effects. ■

TIP

Default Theme Any blank documents you start in Word already have a default theme assigned—the Office theme. To return to this default, select **Office** from the Themes palette that appears when you click the **Themes** button. ■

Chapter 10

REVIEWING AND VIEWING WORD DOCUMENTS

Word offers a lot of tools to help you review your documents, including spelling and grammar checking, AutoCorrect to instantly fix common mistakes while you type, and find and replace tools to help you look through documents for words or phrases you need to change or check. In addition to these basic proofreading tools, you can also use tracking tools to help you keep review changes made by multiple users to the same document. For example, if you share a report with several co-workers, you can turn on the Track Changes feature and easily see who makes what changes and compare them all.

Word also offers numerous ways to view your documents using View modes. You can switch View modes to see how your document looks when printed or in a Web browser, or you can use the Read mode to read through your document just like a book. You can also zoom in or out of your document to get a better look at text or page elements and layout.

REVIEW TOOLS IN WORD

The Review tab houses all kinds of tools and features for editing a document with other reviewers

Use the Reviewing Pane to check revisions to a shared document

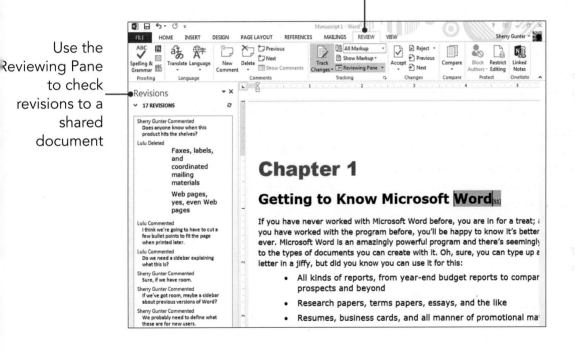

TRACKING CHANGES WITH DOCUMENT REVIEWERS

If you share your documents with other Word users in an editorial environment, you can turn on Word's Track Changes feature and keep track of who makes what changes to the text.

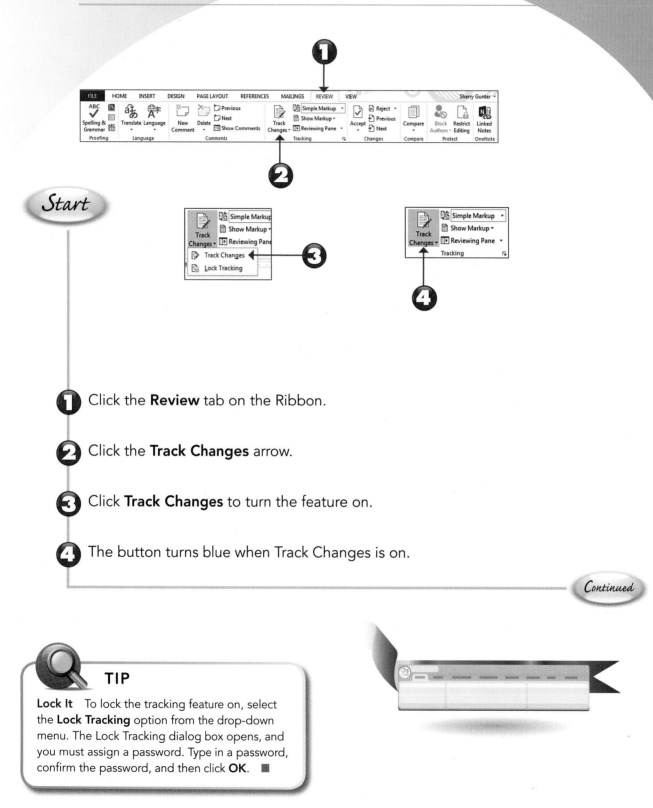

Start

1 Click the **Review** tab on the Ribbon.

2 Click the **Track Changes** arrow.

3 Click **Track Changes** to turn the feature on.

4 The button turns blue when Track Changes is on.

Continued

TIP

Lock It To lock the tracking feature on, select the **Lock Tracking** option from the drop-down menu. The Lock Tracking dialog box opens, and you must assign a password. Type in a password, confirm the password, and then click **OK**. ■

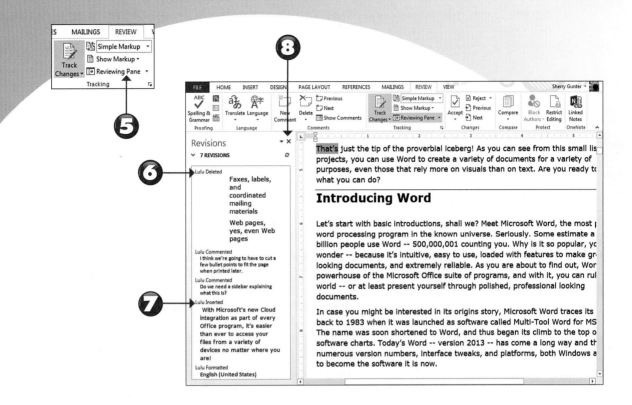

 5 Click **Reviewing Pane**.

6 Any revisions made to the document appear in this pane, along with the name of the person who made the changes.

7 Click an item in the list to quickly move to its location in the document.

8 To close the pane, click here.

 TIP

Review Changes   When everyone finishes editing a document, you can review the changes. See the task "Accepting or Rejecting Changes" later in this chapter to learn how. ■

TIP

Change the Pane   You can click the **Reviewing Pane** arrow on the **Review** tab and choose whether you want to display the pane on the left side or bottom of the document. ■

You can use comments to add notations to your document that are not meant to be printed. Comments are handy when you want to leave a note for someone else reading the document. Comments appear in a balloon off to the side of the document.

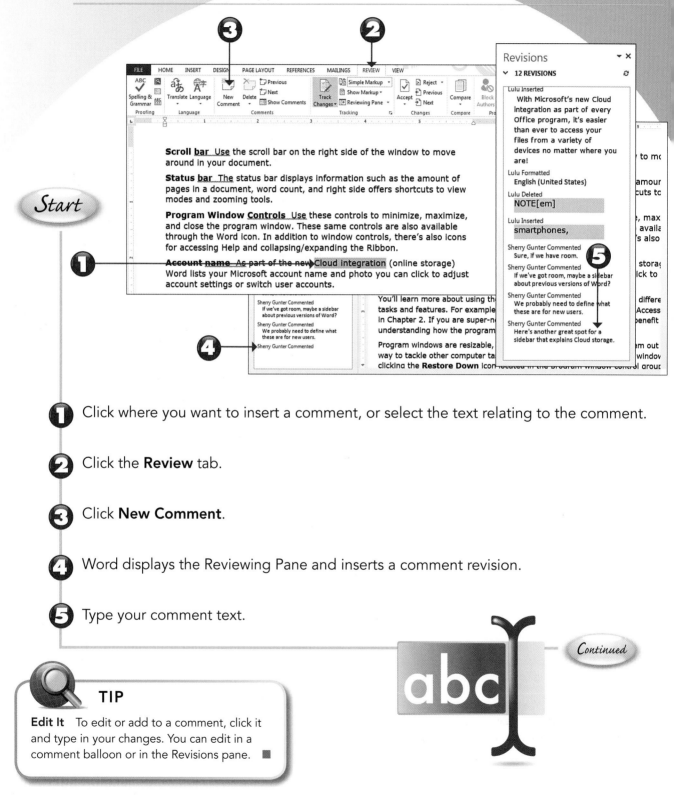

1. Click where you want to insert a comment, or select the text relating to the comment.

2. Click the **Review** tab.

3. Click **New Comment**.

4. Word displays the Reviewing Pane and inserts a comment revision.

5. Type your comment text.

Continued

TIP

Edit It   To edit or add to a comment, click it and type in your changes. You can edit in a comment balloon or in the Revisions pane. ■

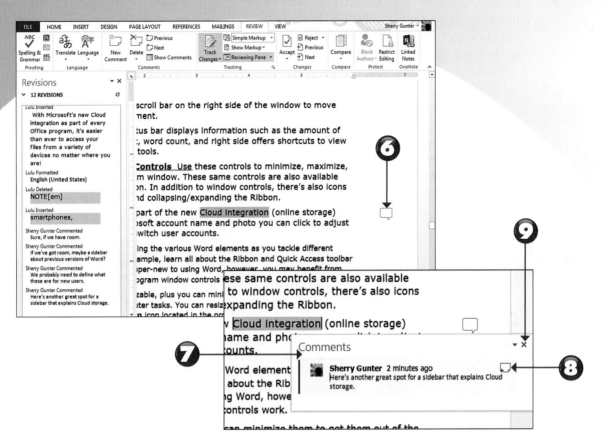

 Word also displays comments as balloons in the right margin; to view a comment, click its balloon icon.

The comment balloon opens.

Click to add a reply to a comment.

Click to close a comment.

End

TIP

Remove It To delete a comment, click it and click the **Delete Comment** button that appears in the **Review** tab. ∎

VIEWING DOCUMENT MARKUP

If you are reviewing a document and keeping track of changes you and other users make, you can change the way in which you view those changes—called *markup*. You can choose to view all the changes, just the simple changes, no markup at all, or the original document.

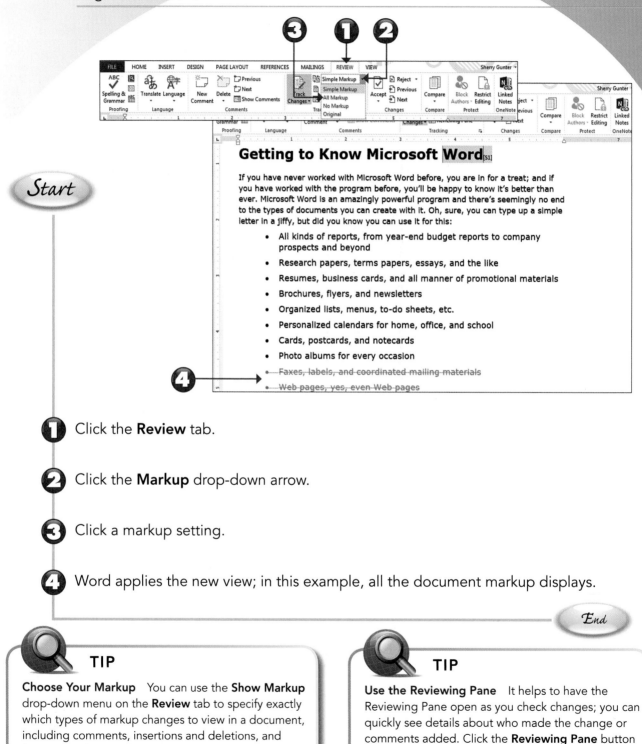

1 Click the **Review** tab.

2 Click the **Markup** drop-down arrow.

3 Click a markup setting.

4 Word applies the new view; in this example, all the document markup displays.

TIP

Choose Your Markup You can use the **Show Markup** drop-down menu on the **Review** tab to specify exactly which types of markup changes to view in a document, including comments, insertions and deletions, and formatting changes. ■

TIP

Use the Reviewing Pane It helps to have the Reviewing Pane open as you check changes; you can quickly see details about who made the change or comments added. Click the **Reviewing Pane** button on the **Review** tab to display the pane. ■

After using Word's Track Changes feature to record everyone's changes to a document, you can go through and decide which edits to keep or disregard.

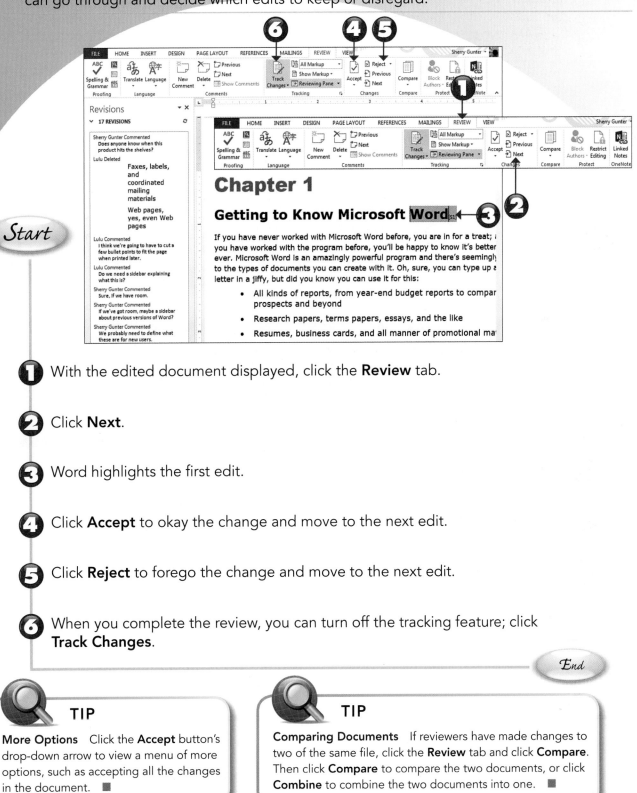

Start

1. With the edited document displayed, click the **Review** tab.

2. Click **Next**.

3. Word highlights the first edit.

4. Click **Accept** to okay the change and move to the next edit.

5. Click **Reject** to forego the change and move to the next edit.

6. When you complete the review, you can turn off the tracking feature; click **Track Changes**.

End

TIP

More Options Click the **Accept** button's drop-down arrow to view a menu of more options, such as accepting all the changes in the document. ■

TIP

Comparing Documents If reviewers have made changes to two of the same file, click the **Review** tab and click **Compare**. Then click **Compare** to compare the two documents, or click **Combine** to combine the two documents into one. ■

EXPLORING DOCUMENT VIEWS

Word offers several different view modes you can use to view your document. The default view, Print Layout, shows you how your document will look when printed. You can switch to Web Layout view to see how your document looks in a Web browser, or Read Mode to view your document much like a book, with side-by-side pages.

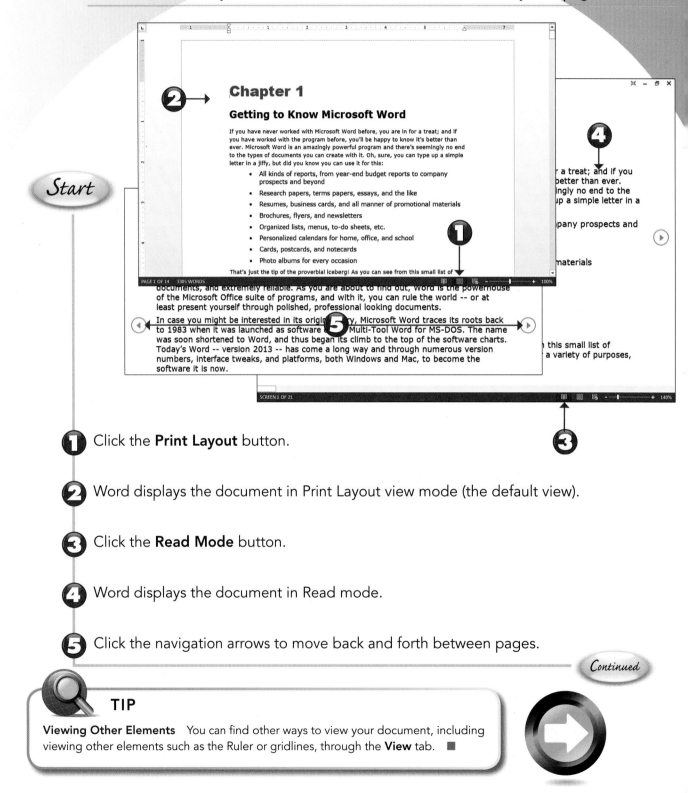

Click the **Print Layout** button.

Word displays the document in Print Layout view mode (the default view).

Click the **Read Mode** button.

Word displays the document in Read mode.

Click the navigation arrows to move back and forth between pages.

Continued

TIP

Viewing Other Elements You can find other ways to view your document, including viewing other elements such as the Ruler or gridlines, through the **View** tab. ■

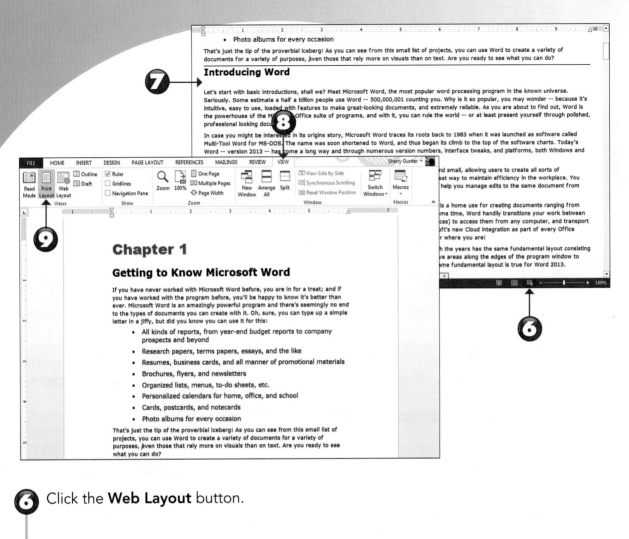

6 Click the **Web Layout** button.

7 Word displays the document in Web Layout view mode.

8 You can also change view modes through the Ribbon's **View** tab; click the **View** tab.

9 Click a view mode.

End

TIP

More Views You can also view your document in Draft mode, which hides any graphics elements, so you can focus on just the text. If your document is composed of headings and document levels, you can use Outline mode to see your document in an outline format. Both options are available as buttons on the **View** tab. See Word's Help feature to learn more about using Draft and Outline modes. ■

ZOOMING IN AND OUT OF DOCUMENTS

You can use the Zoom controls to zoom in and out of a document. Zooming in increases the magnification level, allowing you to enlarge the document for a closer look. Zooming out decreases the magnification level, allowing you to see more of the page.

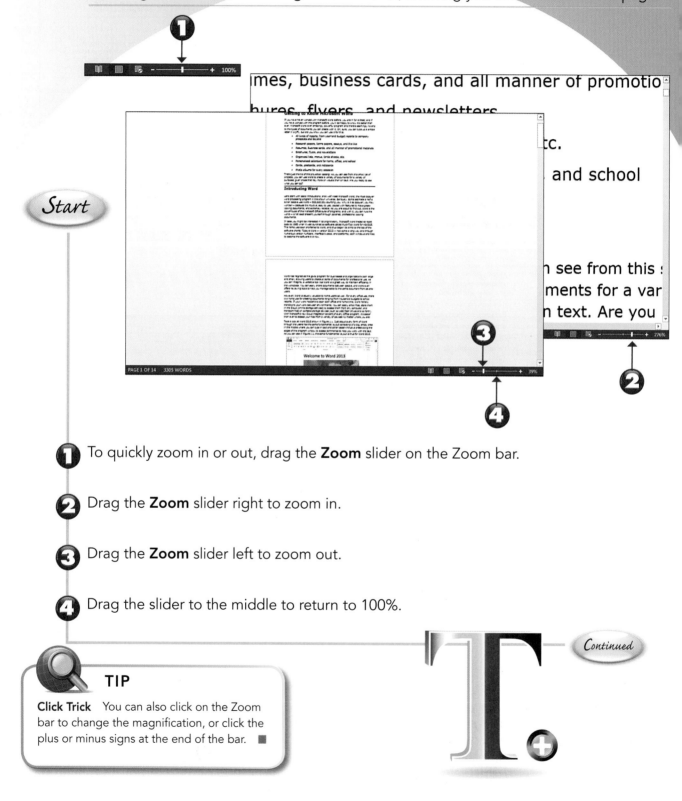

1 To quickly zoom in or out, drag the **Zoom** slider on the Zoom bar.

2 Drag the **Zoom** slider right to zoom in.

3 Drag the **Zoom** slider left to zoom out.

4 Drag the slider to the middle to return to 100%.

Continued

TIP

Click Trick   You can also click on the Zoom bar to change the magnification, or click the plus or minus signs at the end of the bar. ■

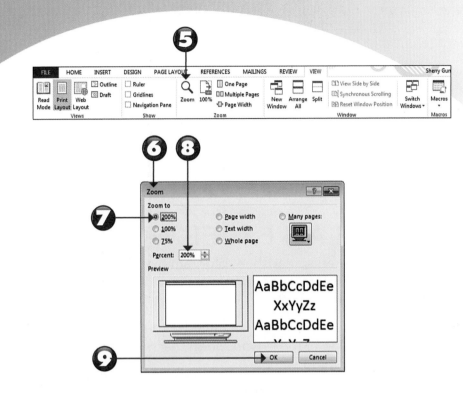

To set a specific zoom percentage, click the **Zoom** button on the **View** tab.

Word opens the Zoom dialog box.

Choose a zoom setting.

You can also type in a percentage number here.

Click **OK** and Word applies the zoom.

End

TIP

More Zoom Tools The View tab includes buttons for zooming quickly to 100% or choosing to display multiple pages, full page width, or a single page. ■

Chapter 11

CREATING AN EXCEL WORKBOOK

Excel is the full-featured spreadsheet program that's part of Microsoft Office 2013. You can use Excel to perform calculations, create charts, and analyze data.

An Excel file is called a *workbook*, identified with the extension .xls. Each workbook contains one or more *worksheets*, each identified with a unique tab at the bottom of the screen.

A worksheet consists of a series of columns and rows; up to 256 columns and 16,384 rows, if you need them. At the intersection of a column and row is a cell, where you enter data and perform calculations.

GETTING STARTED WITH EXCEL

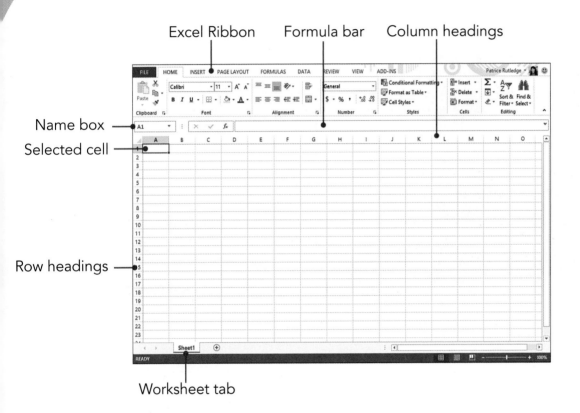

Excel Ribbon   Formula bar   Column headings

Name box

Selected cell

Row headings

Worksheet tab

CREATING A WORKBOOK FROM A TEMPLATE

Creating an Excel workbook from a template helps you save time because you can use a ready-made spreadsheet customized to your needs.

Search for more options online

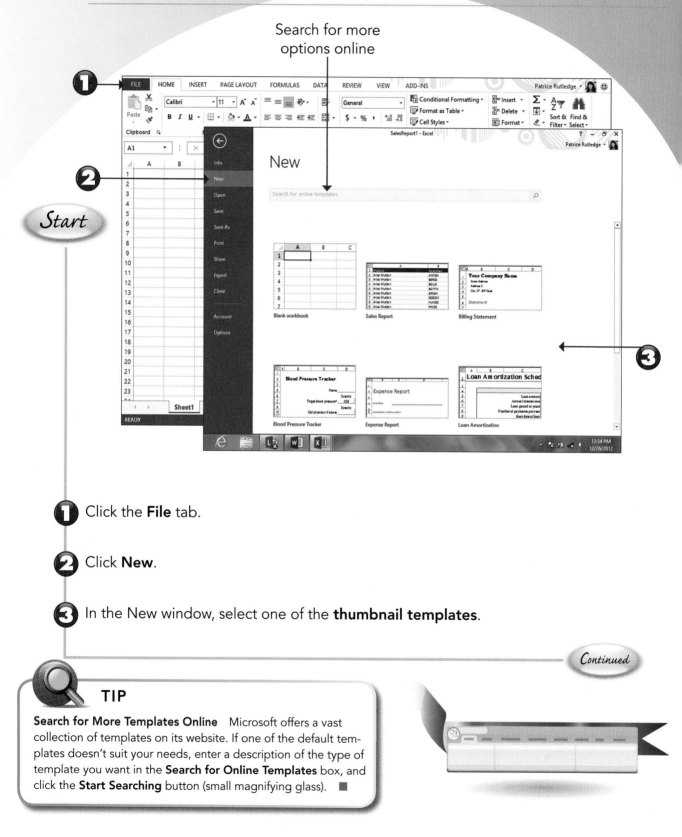

Start

1 Click the **File** tab.

2 Click **New**.

3 In the New window, select one of the **thumbnail templates**.

Continued

TIP

Search for More Templates Online Microsoft offers a vast collection of templates on its website. If one of the default templates doesn't suit your needs, enter a description of the type of template you want in the **Search for Online Templates** box, and click the **Start Searching** button (small magnifying glass). ■

| B2 | ▼ | : | × | ✓ | fx | Personal Monthly Budget |

Personal Monthly Budget

			Income 1	$2,500		PROJECTED BALANCE (Projected income minus expenses)
PROJECTED MONTHLY INCOME			Extra income	$500		
			Total monthly income	$3,000		ACTUAL BALANCE (Actual income minus expenses)
			Income 1	$2,500		
ACTUAL MONTHLY INCOME			Extra income	$500		DIFFERENCE (Actual minus projected)
			Total monthly income	$3,000		

HOUSING	Projected Cost	Actual Cost	Difference		ENTERTAINMENT	Projected Cost	Actual Cost	Diff
Mortgage or rent	$1,500	$1,400	$100		Video/DVD		$0	$50
Phone	$60	$100	-$40		CDs			
Electricity	$50	$60	-$10		Movies			
Gas	$200	$180	$20		Concerts			
Water and sewer			$0		Sporting events			
Cable			$0		Live theater			
Waste removal			$0		Other			
Maintenance or repairs			$0		Other			
Supplies			$0		Other			
Other			$0		Total		$0	$50

Personal Monthly Budget ⊕

 **4** Excel opens a new workbook based on the template you select.

End

TIP

Save Your Workbook Remember to save your new workbook by clicking the **Save** button on the Quick Access toolbar. ■

NOTE

Template Examples Some sample Excel templates include billing statements, expense reports, sales reports, personal budgets, time cards, and more. It's very likely that a template exists for the exact type of workbook you want to create. ■

CREATING A BLANK WORKBOOK

If you just need a basic spreadsheet, you can create a blank workbook.

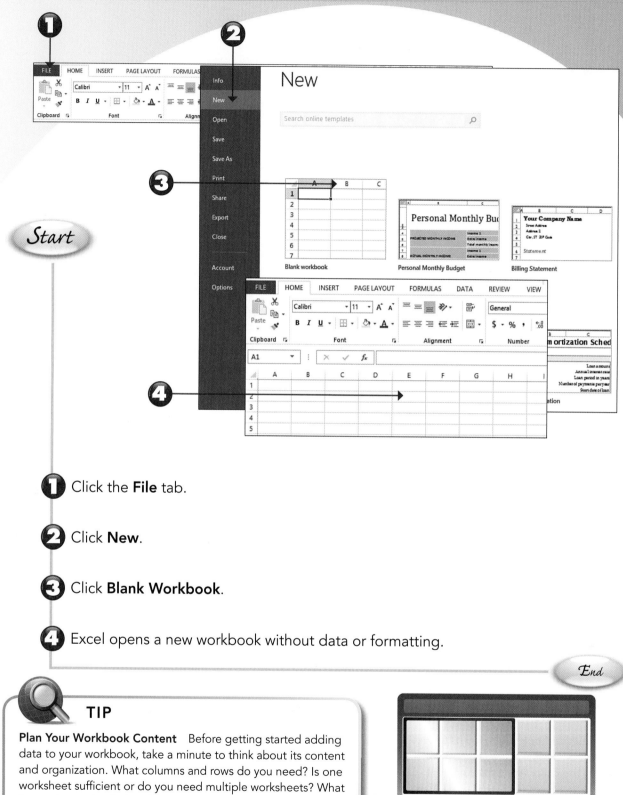

Start

1 Click the **File** tab.

2 Click **New**.

3 Click **Blank Workbook**.

4 Excel opens a new workbook without data or formatting.

End

TIP

Plan Your Workbook Content   Before getting started adding data to your workbook, take a minute to think about its content and organization. What columns and rows do you need? Is one worksheet sufficient or do you need multiple worksheets? What formatting and coloring do you want to apply? ■

You can use your mouse or keyboard to quickly navigate in an Excel worksheet.

Cell address

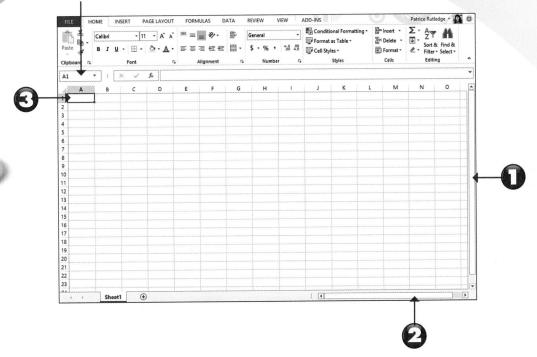

1 Select and drag the **vertical scroll bar** with your mouse until the row you are looking for is visible.

2 Select and drag the **horizontal scroll bar** until the column you are looking for is visible.

3 Click a **cell** to select it.

End

NOTE

Cell Address   The name box in the upper-left corner of the screen displays the *cell address* of the selected cell. A cell address is composed of the column letter and row number, such as cell A1 or cell D8. ■

TIP

Other Ways to Navigate a Worksheet   You can also navigate your worksheet using the arrow keys on your keyboard to move one cell at a time up, down, left, or right. Using the Page Up and Page Down keys is another navigation option. ■

ENTERING DATA

You can enter a variety of data on an Excel worksheet such as numbers, text, dates, or times.

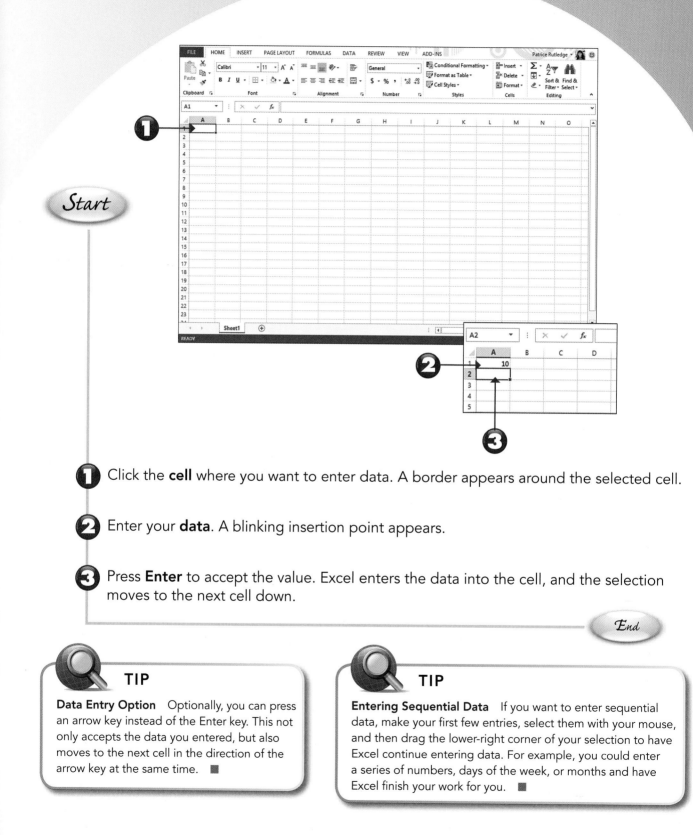

Start

1 Click the **cell** where you want to enter data. A border appears around the selected cell.

2 Enter your **data**. A blinking insertion point appears.

3 Press **Enter** to accept the value. Excel enters the data into the cell, and the selection moves to the next cell down.

End

TIP

Data Entry Option Optionally, you can press an arrow key instead of the Enter key. This not only accepts the data you entered, but also moves to the next cell in the direction of the arrow key at the same time. ∎

TIP

Entering Sequential Data If you want to enter sequential data, make your first few entries, select them with your mouse, and then drag the lower-right corner of your selection to have Excel continue entering data. For example, you could enter a series of numbers, days of the week, or months and have Excel finish your work for you. ∎

Occasionally, you might need to insert a row into the middle of data that you have already entered. Inserting a row moves existing data down one row.

Start

1 Click the **Home** tab.

2 Click the **row heading number** where you want to insert the new row. Excel selects the entire row.

3 Click the **Insert** button.

4 Excel moves the existing row down and inserts a new blank row.

End

TIP

Enter Multiple Rows To enter more than one row, select the number of rows you want to enter with your mouse, and click the **Insert** button. For example, if you select rows 7 through 9, Excel moves the existing rows down and inserts three blank rows, numbered 7 through 9. ■

INSERTING A NEW COLUMN

You can also insert a new column on a worksheet with existing data. Inserting a column moves the existing data to the right of the new column.

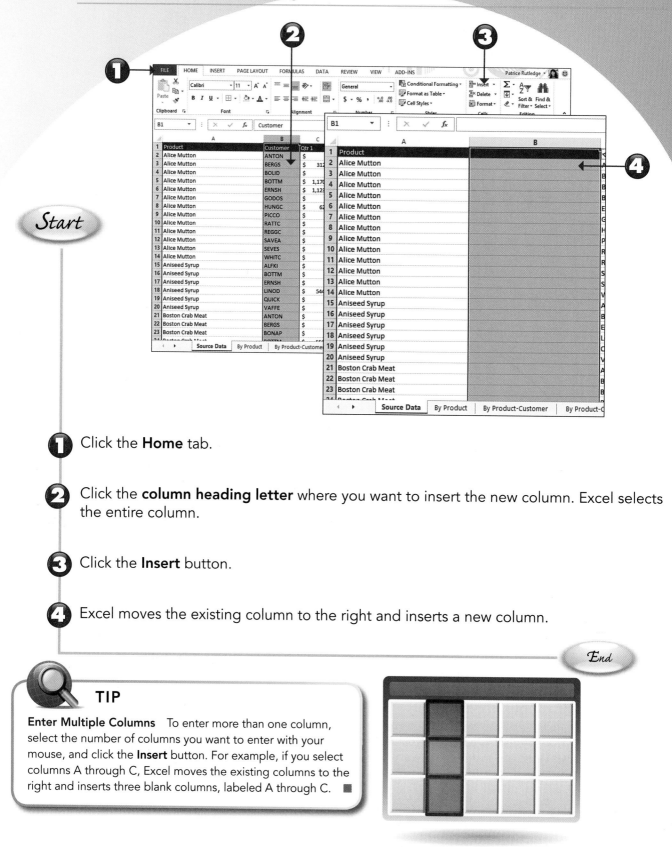

Start

1 Click the **Home** tab.

2 Click the **column heading letter** where you want to insert the new column. Excel selects the entire column.

3 Click the **Insert** button.

4 Excel moves the existing column to the right and inserts a new column.

End

TIP

Enter Multiple Columns To enter more than one column, select the number of columns you want to enter with your mouse, and click the **Insert** button. For example, if you select columns A through C, Excel moves the existing columns to the right and inserts three blank columns, labeled A through C. ■

DELETING ROWS AND COLUMNS

You can delete Excel rows and columns easily and quickly. Remember that deleting a row or column removes all content from the selected row or column, not just the content of a single cell.

Start

1 Click the **Home** tab.

2 Click the **column heading letter** or **row heading number** of the column or row you want to delete.

3 Click the **Delete** button. Excel deletes the selected content.

End

TIP

Delete Multiple Columns or Rows To delete more than one column or row, select the content you want to delete with your mouse, and click the **Delete** button. For example, if you select the row heading numbers for rows 7 through 9, Excel deletes those rows. ■

INSERTING A NEW WORKSHEET

By default, a new Excel workbook contains a single worksheet named Sheet1. If you like, you can add more worksheets to your workbook. For example, you might want a worksheet for every month of the year, for specific products or projects, and so forth.

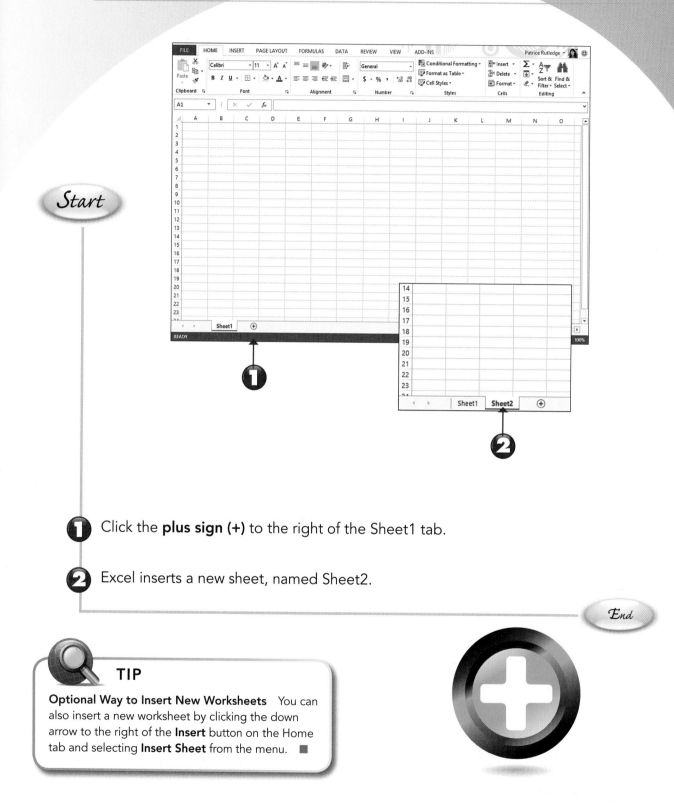

Start

1 Click the **plus sign (+)** to the right of the Sheet1 tab.

2 Excel inserts a new sheet, named Sheet2.

End

TIP

Optional Way to Insert New Worksheets You can also insert a new worksheet by clicking the down arrow to the right of the **Insert** button on the Home tab and selecting **Insert Sheet** from the menu. ■

Excel names your worksheets consecutively as Sheet1, Sheet2, Sheet3, and so forth. You can easily customize these tab names to something more meaningful, however.

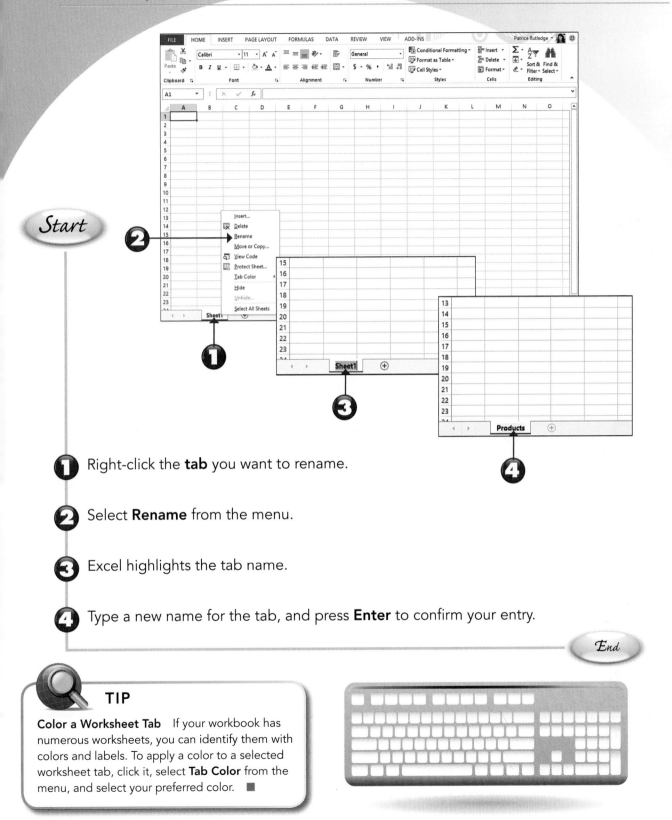

1. Right-click the **tab** you want to rename.

2. Select **Rename** from the menu.

3. Excel highlights the tab name.

4. Type a new name for the tab, and press **Enter** to confirm your entry.

TIP

Color a Worksheet Tab   If your workbook has numerous worksheets, you can identify them with colors and labels. To apply a color to a selected worksheet tab, click it, select **Tab Color** from the menu, and select your preferred color. ■

DELETING A WORKSHEET

If you no longer need a worksheet, or create one by mistake, you can delete it.

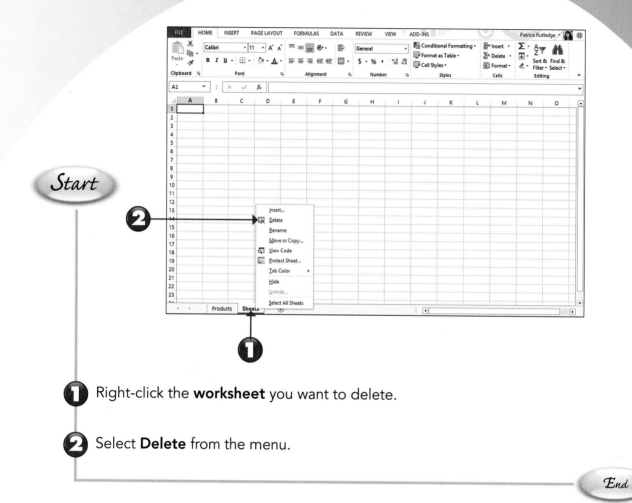

Start

1. Right-click the **worksheet** you want to delete.

2. Select **Delete** from the menu.

End

TIP

Delete Multiple Worksheets If you want to delete more than one worksheet, press the Ctrl key, and select the worksheets you no longer want. Then, right-click and select **Delete** from the menu. ■

CAUTION

Excel Workbooks Require at Least One Worksheet Because Excel requires at least one worksheet, you can't delete all the worksheets in your workbook. If you no longer need any of the worksheets in a workbook, you should delete the entire workbook instead. ■

HIDING A WORKSHEET

If you aren't ready to delete a worksheet, but don't want it to display in your workbook, you can hide it.

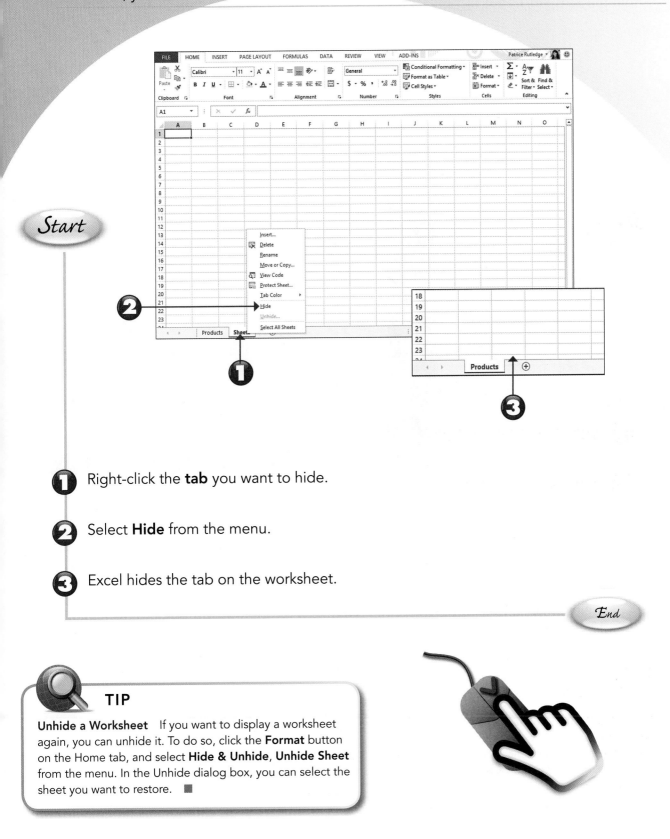

1. Right-click the **tab** you want to hide.

2. Select **Hide** from the menu.

3. Excel hides the tab on the worksheet.

Start

End

TIP

Unhide a Worksheet If you want to display a worksheet again, you can unhide it. To do so, click the **Format** button on the Home tab, and select **Hide & Unhide**, **Unhide Sheet** from the menu. In the Unhide dialog box, you can select the sheet you want to restore. ■

PROTECTING A WORKBOOK WITH A PASSWORD

If your workbook contains confidential information that you want to share only with a select audience, you can protect it with a password. This way, only people who have the password can open the workbook and view its contents.

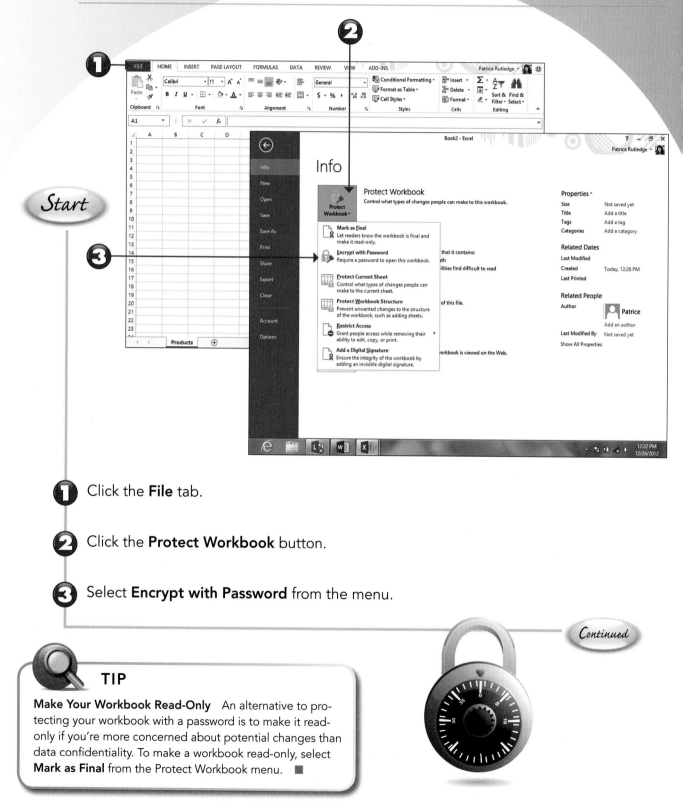

Start

1 Click the **File** tab.

2 Click the **Protect Workbook** button.

3 Select **Encrypt with Password** from the menu.

Continued

TIP

Make Your Workbook Read-Only An alternative to protecting your workbook with a password is to make it read-only if you're more concerned about potential changes than data confidentiality. To make a workbook read-only, select **Mark as Final** from the Protect Workbook menu. ■

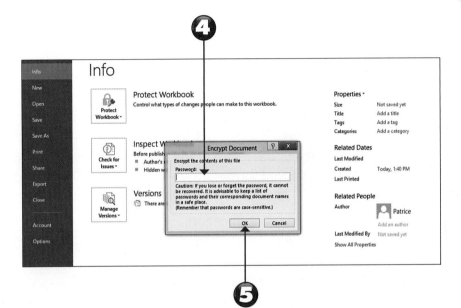

4 In the Encrypt Document dialog box, enter a case-sensitive **password** for your workbook.

5 Click **OK**.

End

TIP

Protect Worksheet Data Another alternative to protecting an entire workbook is to protect specific worksheet data. Doing this enables people to open your workbook but not perform functions you specify, such as format, insert, or delete rows and columns. To protect a worksheet, right-click it and select **Protect Sheet** from the menu. ■

Chapter 12

FORMATTING WORKSHEET DATA

Excel makes formatting data easy with many simple, yet powerful, tools. In addition to applying traditional formatting common to all Office applications, you can also wrap cell text and merge columns to create headings in Excel.

As expected for a spreadsheet application, Excel offers many options for formatting numbers, including formatting as currency, percentages, fractions, dates, times, and more.

If your worksheet contains a lot of data, Excel makes it easy for you to find a specific cell or even replace cell content automatically. Freezing row numbers and column letters also makes it easier to find what you're looking for.

Formatting your worksheet data using colored cell styles or as a table are other options that enhance your table's design and functionality.

FORMATTING BASICS

Wrap text Format as a table Find data

Merge and
center data

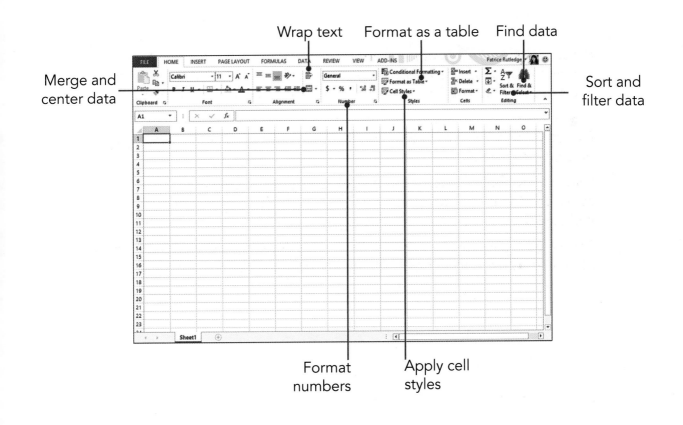

Sort and
filter data

Format
numbers

Apply cell
styles

WRAPPING TEXT

Wrapping text in cells is useful when the text is too long to fit in one cell and you don't want it to overlap to the next cell.

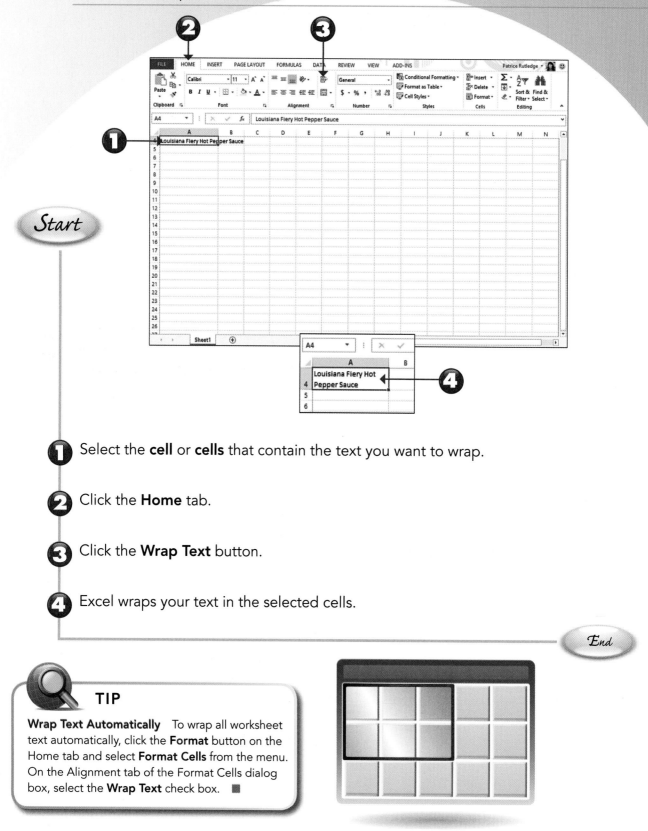

Start

1. Select the **cell** or **cells** that contain the text you want to wrap.

2. Click the **Home** tab.

3. Click the **Wrap Text** button.

4. Excel wraps your text in the selected cells.

End

TIP

Wrap Text Automatically   To wrap all worksheet text automatically, click the **Format** button on the Home tab and select **Format Cells** from the menu. On the Alignment tab of the Format Cells dialog box, select the **Wrap Text** check box. ■

The Merge & Center button makes it easy to create attractive headings that display across multiple columns. For example, if your worksheet contains data in columns A through H, you could merge and center a heading across these columns.

Start

1. Select the **cells** to be included in the heading.

2. Click the **Home** tab.

3. Click the **Merge & Center** button.

4. Excel merges and centers the selected cells.

End

NOTE

Identifying Merged Cells Notice the gridlines have disappeared, and the cells appear to be joined together. ■

FORMATTING NUMBERS

By default, values display as general numbers. You can also display values as currency, percentages, fractions, dates, or in many other formats.

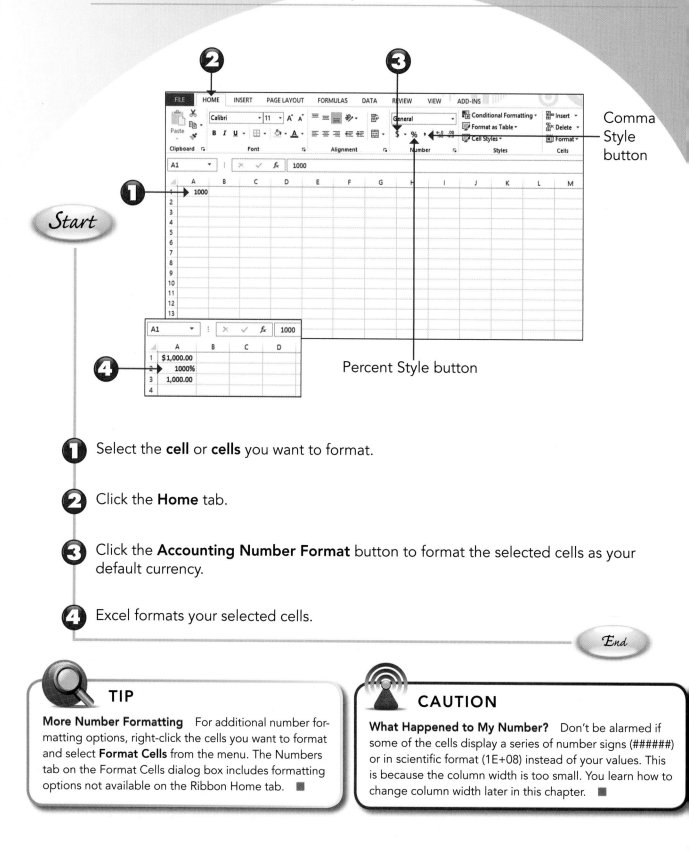

Comma Style button

Percent Style button

Start

1 Select the **cell** or **cells** you want to format.

2 Click the **Home** tab.

3 Click the **Accounting Number Format** button to format the selected cells as your default currency.

4 Excel formats your selected cells.

End

TIP

More Number Formatting For additional number formatting options, right-click the cells you want to format and select **Format Cells** from the menu. The Numbers tab on the Format Cells dialog box includes formatting options not available on the Ribbon Home tab. ■

CAUTION

What Happened to My Number? Don't be alarmed if some of the cells display a series of number signs (######) or in scientific format (1E+08) instead of your values. This is because the column width is too small. You learn how to change column width later in this chapter. ■

Cell styles enable you to apply colored formatting instantly to your worksheets. These styles can make your data easier to read.

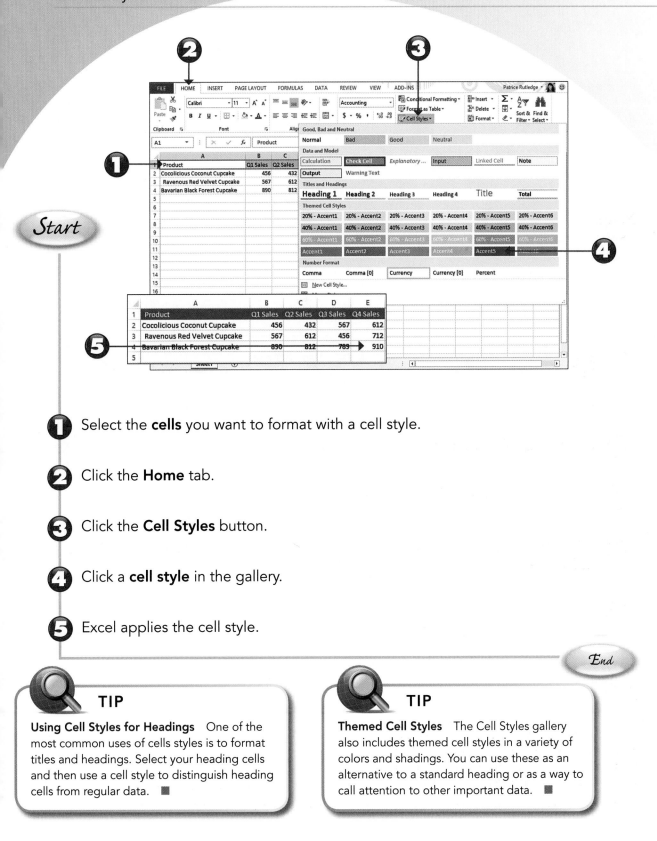

Start

1. Select the **cells** you want to format with a cell style.

2. Click the **Home** tab.

3. Click the **Cell Styles** button.

4. Click a **cell style** in the gallery.

5. Excel applies the cell style.

End

TIP

Using Cell Styles for Headings One of the most common uses of cells styles is to format titles and headings. Select your heading cells and then use a cell style to distinguish heading cells from regular data. ■

TIP

Themed Cell Styles The Cell Styles gallery also includes themed cell styles in a variety of colors and shadings. You can use these as an alternative to a standard heading or as a way to call attention to other important data. ■

FORMATTING AS A TABLE

Formatting worksheet data as a table is another way to distinguish cell data with color. You can also filter and summarize table data using the tools on the Table Tools-Design tab.

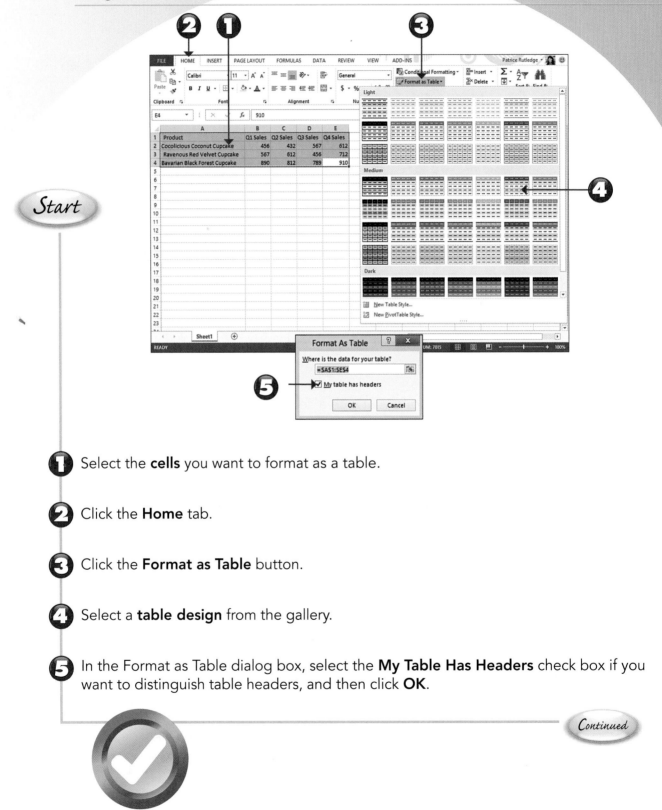

Start

1 Select the **cells** you want to format as a table.

2 Click the **Home** tab.

3 Click the **Format as Table** button.

4 Select a **table design** from the gallery.

5 In the Format as Table dialog box, select the **My Table Has Headers** check box if you want to distinguish table headers, and then click **OK**.

Continued

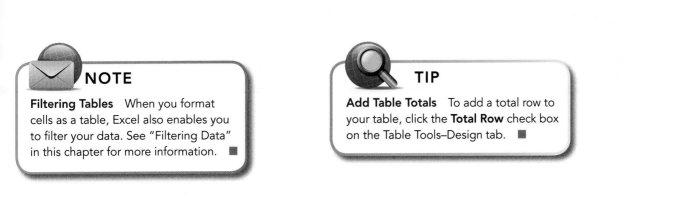

6 Excel applies the table design you selected.

7 The **Table Tools–Design tab** displays, offering additional table formatting options.

End

NOTE

Filtering Tables   When you format cells as a table, Excel also enables you to filter your data. See "Filtering Data" in this chapter for more information. ■

TIP

Add Table Totals   To add a total row to your table, click the **Total Row** check box on the Table Tools–Design tab. ■

ADJUSTING COLUMN WIDTH

The default width of an Excel column is 8.43 characters, but you can adjust each individual column from 0 to 255 characters wide.

Start

1 Position the **mouse pointer** to the right of the column you want to adjust. The mouse pointer becomes a crosshair.

2 Press and hold the mouse button, and **drag the column line** to the right to increase the column width or to the left to decrease it.

3 Release the **mouse button**. The column width will be changed.

End

TIP

Adjust Columns Automatically To automatically adjust column width to exactly fit the contents of the cell, double-click the mouse after the pointer becomes a crosshair. ■

The default height of an Excel row is 15 points, but you can adjust each individual row from 0 to 409 points.

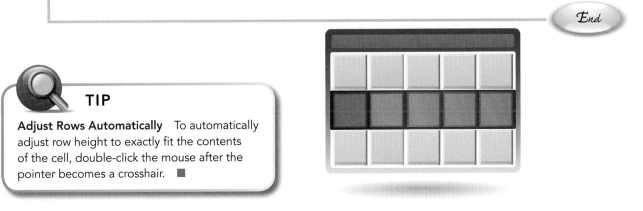

Start

1 Position the **mouse pointer** below the row you want to adjust. The mouse pointer becomes a crosshair.

2 Press and hold the mouse button and **drag the row line** down to increase the row height or up to decrease it.

3 Release the **mouse button**. The row height will be changed.

End

TIP

Adjust Rows Automatically To automatically adjust row height to exactly fit the contents of the cell, double-click the mouse after the pointer becomes a crosshair. ■

FINDING DATA

If your worksheet contains a lot of data, it can be hard to find the right cell at times. Fortunately, Excel makes it easy to search your worksheet data.

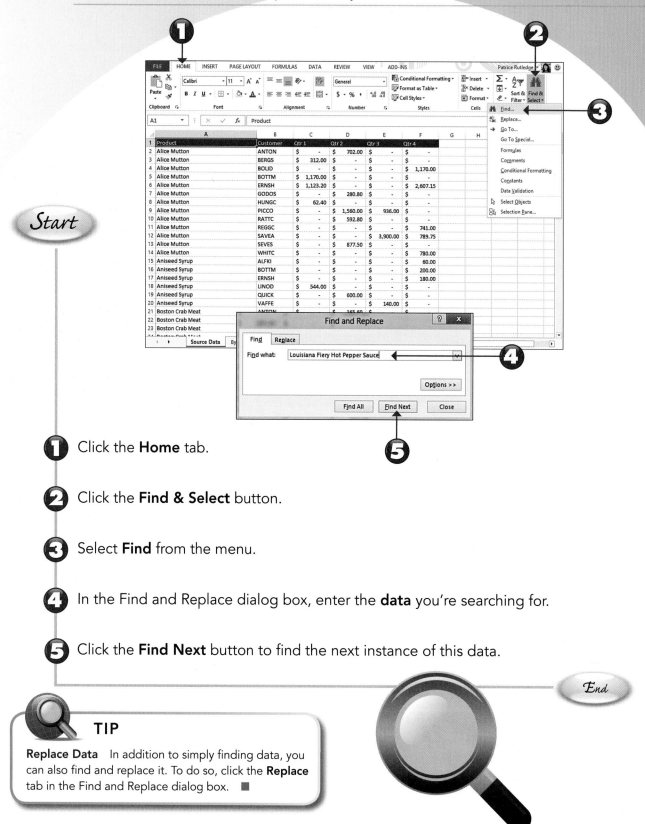

Start

1 Click the **Home** tab.

2 Click the **Find & Select** button.

3 Select **Find** from the menu.

4 In the Find and Replace dialog box, enter the **data** you're searching for.

5 Click the **Find Next** button to find the next instance of this data.

End

TIP

Replace Data In addition to simply finding data, you can also find and replace it. To do so, click the **Replace** tab in the Find and Replace dialog box. ■

You can freeze columns, rows, or both so that column letters and row numbers remain in view as you scroll instead of scrolling off the screen with the rest of the worksheet. This is particularly helpful with larger worksheets.

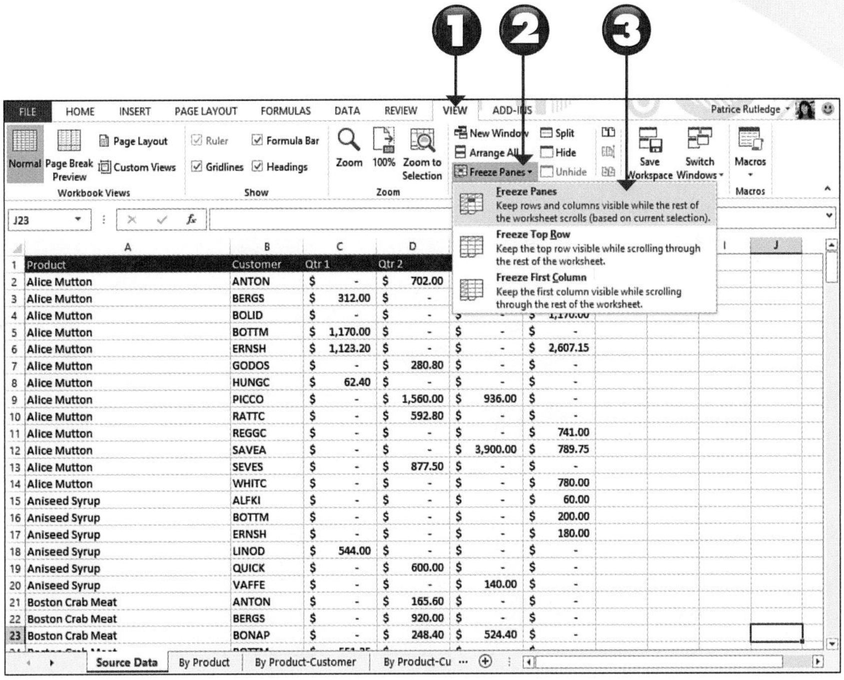

Start

1 Click the **View** tab.

2 Click the **Freeze Panes** button.

3 Select **Freeze Panes** from the menu to free both columns and rows.

End

TIP

Unfreeze Panes To unfreeze panes, click the **Freeze** button, and select **Unfreeze Panes** from the menu. ■

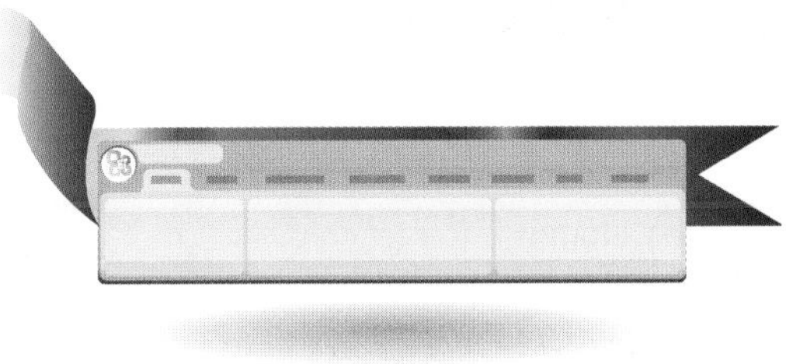

SORTING DATA

If your worksheet data isn't in the right order, you can sort it.

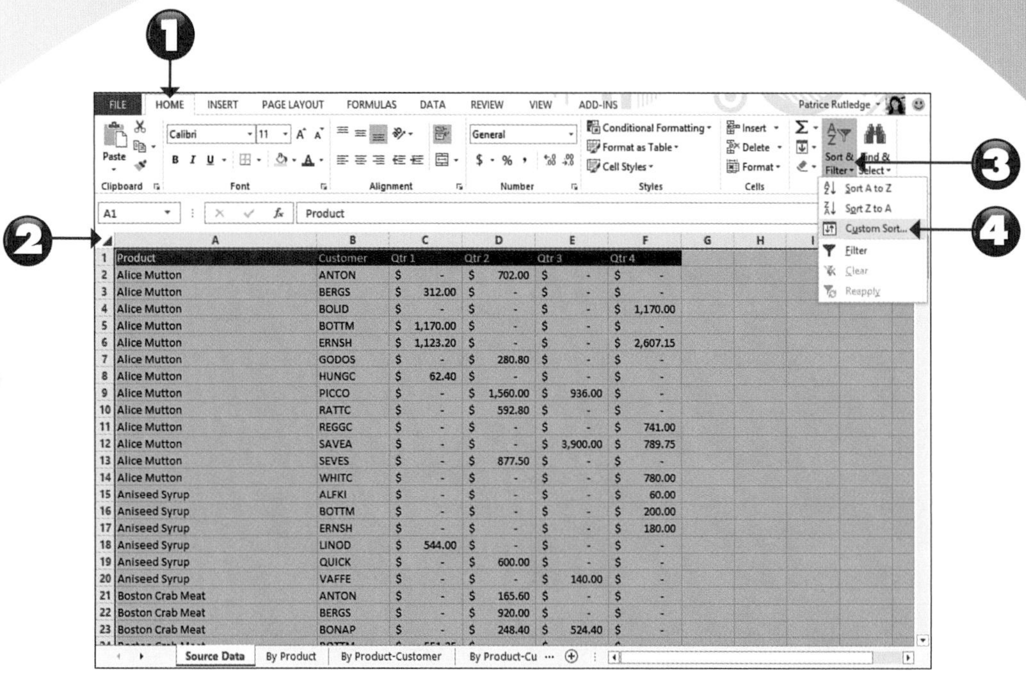

Start

1 Click the **Home** tab.

2 Click the **Select All** button to select all your worksheet data.

3 Click the **Sort & Filter** button.

4 Select **Custom Sort** from the menu.

Continued

TIP

Sorting on Multiple Columns   To sort on more than one column, click the **Add Level** button in the Sort dialog box, and add an additional column. ■

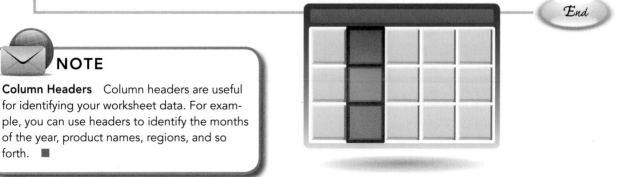

5 Select the **My Data Has Headers** check box if your worksheet includes column headers.

6 Specify the **column** you want to sort by.

7 Specify your preferred **sort order**, such as A to Z or Z to A.

8 Click **OK**.

End

NOTE

Column Headers Column headers are useful for identifying your worksheet data. For example, you can use headers to identify the months of the year, product names, regions, and so forth. ■

FILTERING DATA

Filtering data is another way to control what displays on your Excel worksheet. By applying a filter, you can hide data temporarily, making it easy to focus on the data you need to see.

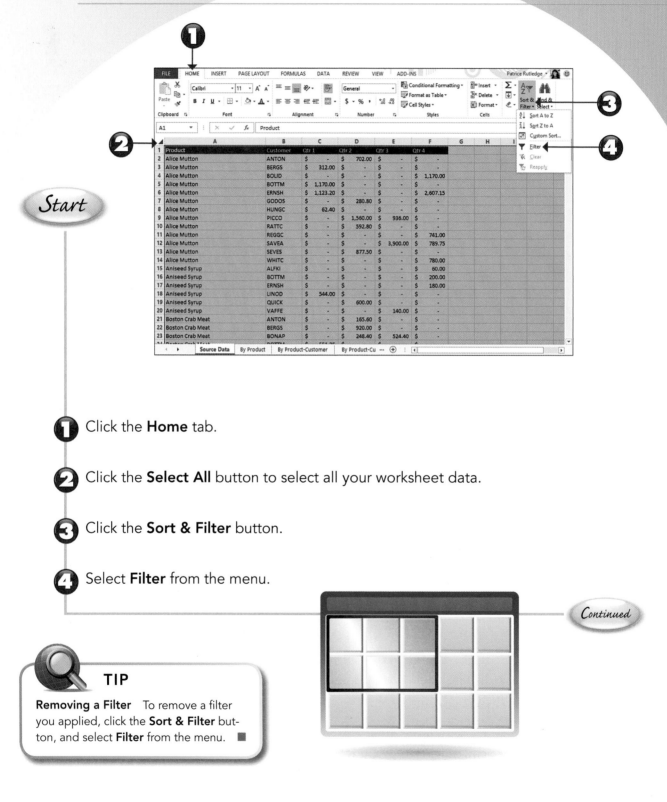

Start

1 Click the **Home** tab.

2 Click the **Select All** button to select all your worksheet data.

3 Click the **Sort & Filter** button.

4 Select **Filter** from the menu.

Continued

TIP

Removing a Filter   To remove a filter you applied, click the **Sort & Filter** button, and select **Filter** from the menu. ■

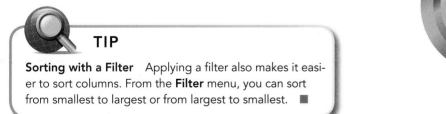

5 Excel displays a down arrow to the right of each column. Click the **arrow** to right of the column you want to filter.

6 Remove the **check box** next to any data you don't want to display.

End

TIP

Sorting with a Filter Applying a filter also makes it easier to sort columns. From the **Filter** menu, you can sort from smallest to largest or from largest to smallest. ■

Chapter 13

WORKING WITH CELL FORMULAS AND FUNCTIONS

Formulas in an Excel worksheet perform calculations, such as adding, subtracting, averaging, or multiplying numbers. They're also dynamic—for example, if you reference a cell address in a formula, the formula changes if the data in the cell changes.

At times, formulas can be complex and time-consuming to build. To simplify creating formulas, Excel also has a solid collection of different functions to assist you with your calculations. For example, you could use the AVERAGE function to average a series of numbers.

CELL FORMULA BASICS

Formulas tab for advanced features

Formula bar

AutoSum button

Cell with calculated formula

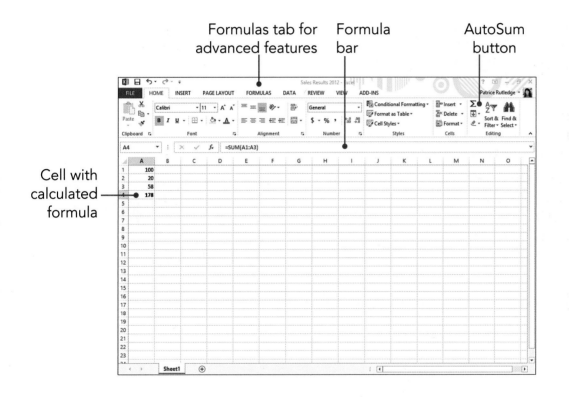

CREATING A SIMPLE FORMULA

You can use a simple formula to add, subtract, multiply, or divide two numbers. An example of a simple formula is =A1+A2, which adds the contents of cells A1 and A2.

The formula also displays in the Formula bar

Formula are not case-sensitive—A5 is the same as a5

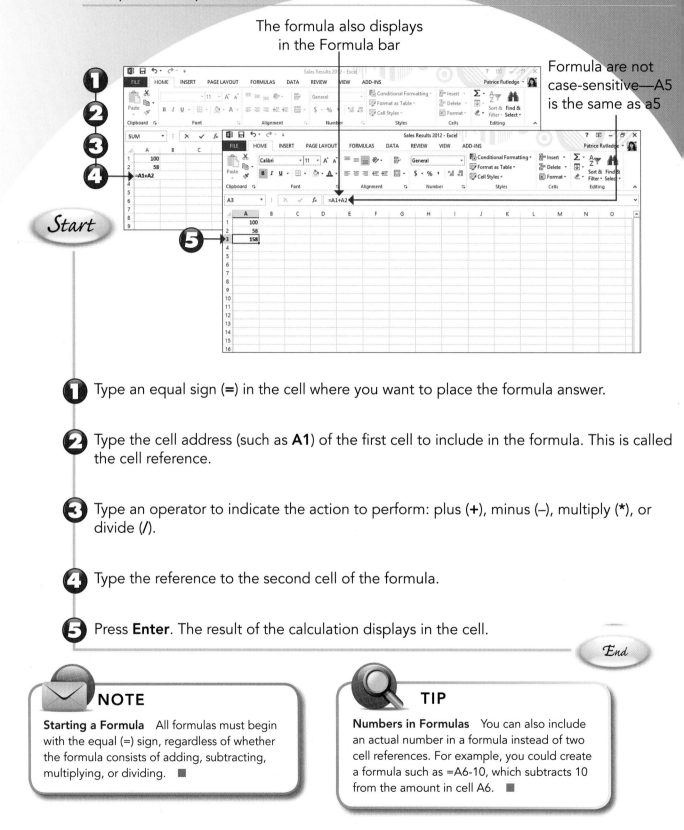

Start

1 Type an equal sign (**=**) in the cell where you want to place the formula answer.

2 Type the cell address (such as **A1**) of the first cell to include in the formula. This is called the cell reference.

3 Type an operator to indicate the action to perform: plus (**+**), minus (**–**), multiply (*****), or divide (**/**).

4 Type the reference to the second cell of the formula.

5 Press **Enter**. The result of the calculation displays in the cell.

End

NOTE

Starting a Formula All formulas must begin with the equal (=) sign, regardless of whether the formula consists of adding, subtracting, multiplying, or dividing. ■

TIP

Numbers in Formulas You can also include an actual number in a formula instead of two cell references. For example, you could create a formula such as =A6-10, which subtracts 10 from the amount in cell A6. ■

COPYING FORMULAS USING FILL

Similar to filling a pattern of days or months, Excel can also fill cells with the pattern of a formula. For example, you might want to copy a formula if you have multiple rows or columns that require the same calculation.

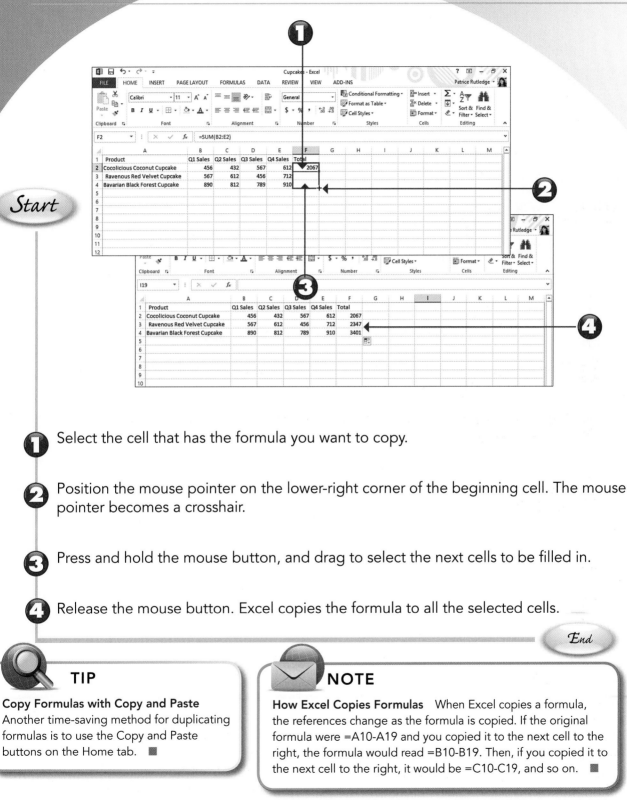

Start

1. Select the cell that has the formula you want to copy.

2. Position the mouse pointer on the lower-right corner of the beginning cell. The mouse pointer becomes a crosshair.

3. Press and hold the mouse button, and drag to select the next cells to be filled in.

4. Release the mouse button. Excel copies the formula to all the selected cells.

End

TIP

Copy Formulas with Copy and Paste
Another time-saving method for duplicating formulas is to use the Copy and Paste buttons on the Home tab. ◼

NOTE

How Excel Copies Formulas When Excel copies a formula, the references change as the formula is copied. If the original formula were =A10-A19 and you copied it to the next cell to the right, the formula would read =B10-B19. Then, if you copied it to the next cell to the right, it would be =C10-C19, and so on. ◼

CREATING A COMPOUND FORMULA

If you need more than one operator for a calculation, you can use a compound formula. Examples of a compound formula include =B7+B8+B12 or =B11-B19-A23.

Start

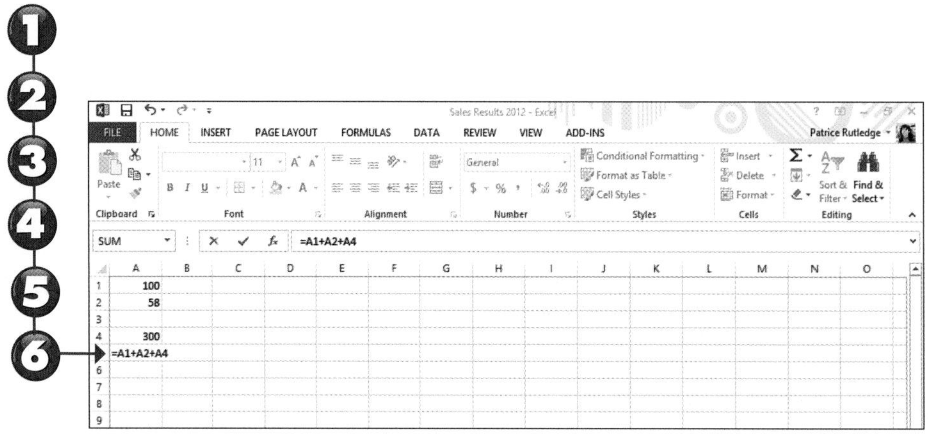

① Type an equal sign (=) in the cell where you want to place the formula answer.

② Type the reference to the first cell of the formula.

③ Type the operator.

④ Type the reference to the second cell of the formula.

⑤ Type the next operator.

⑥ Type the reference to the third cell of the formula.

Continued

TIP

Update Formulas Automatically Try changing one of the values you originally typed in the worksheet and watch the answer to the formula change. ■

7 Repeat steps 5 and 6 until the formula is complete, adding parentheses wherever necessary.

8 Press **Enter** to accept the formula. The result of the calculation displays in the cell.

End

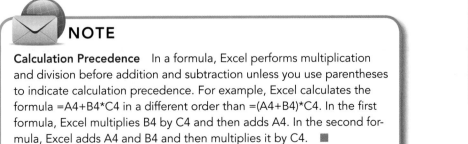

NOTE

Calculation Precedence   In a formula, Excel performs multiplication and division before addition and subtraction unless you use parentheses to indicate calculation precedence. For example, Excel calculates the formula =A4+B4*C4 in a different order than =(A4+B4)*C4. In the first formula, Excel multiplies B4 by C4 and then adds A4. In the second formula, Excel adds A4 and B4 and then multiplies it by C4. ■

CREATING AN ABSOLUTE REFERENCE IN A FORMULA

Sometimes when you copy a formula, you don't want one of the cell references to change. That's when you need to create an absolute reference. You use the dollar sign ($) to indicate an absolute reference.

Start

1 Type the equal (**=**) sign in the cell where you want to place the formula answer.

2 Type the reference to the first cell of the formula. If this reference is to be an absolute reference, add dollar signs (**$**) in front of both the column reference and the row reference.

3 Type the operator.

4 Type the reference to the second cell of the formula. If this reference is to be an absolute reference, add dollar signs (**$**) in front of both the column reference and the row reference.

Continued

NOTE

Understanding Absolute References It's called an *absolute reference* because when you copy it, it absolutely stays that cell reference and never changes. An example of a formula with an absolute reference might be =B21*B23. The reference to cell B23 will not change when copied. ■

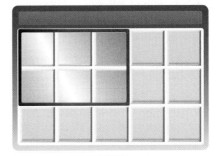

5 Press **Enter**. The result of the calculation displays in the cell.

6 Copy the formula to the adjacent cells using either the Fill or Copy and Paste method.

End

NOTE

Compound Formulas Although this example uses a simple formula, compound formulas can also have absolute references. ◼

USING THE SUM FUNCTION

The SUM function totals a range of values. The syntax for this function is =SUM (*range of values to total*). An example might be =SUM(B7:D7).

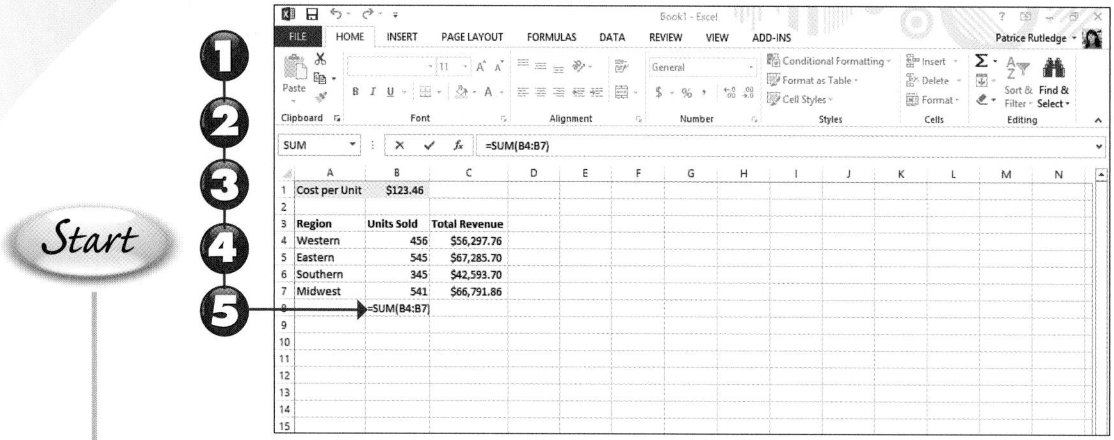

Start

1 Type the equal (**=**) sign in the cell where you want to place the sum of values.

2 Type the function name **SUM**.

3 Type the open parentheses symbol.

4 Type the range to be totaled, such as **B7:D7**.

5 Type the close parentheses symbol.

Continued

185

	A	B	C	D	E	F	G	H	I	J	K	L	M	N
1	Cost per Unit	$123.46												
2														
3	Region	Units Sold	Total Revenue											
4	Western	456	$56,297.76											
5	Eastern	545	$67,285.70											
6	Southern	345	$42,593.70											
7	Midwest	541	$66,791.86											
8		1887												
9														
10														
11														

B8 =SUM(B4:B7)

6 Press **Enter**. The result of the calculation displays in the cell.

End

NOTE

Nonsequential Sums There are two ways to reference a range of values. If the cells to be included are sequential, they are separated by a colon (:). If the range is nonsequential, the cells are separated by a comma (,). For example, the range (B8:D8) would include cells B8, C8, and D8; the range (B8:D8, F4) would include cells B8, C8, D8, and F4. ■

USING THE AUTOSUM BUTTON

Excel's AutoSum button simplifies creating a basic addition formula. You can calculate a string of numbers in either a row or a column using this easy feature.

Start

	A	B	C	D	E	F
1	Cost per Unit	$123.46				
2						
3	**Region**	**Units Sold**	**Total Revenue**			
4	Western	456	$56,297.76			
5	Eastern	545	$67,285.70			
6	Southern	345	$42,593.70			
7	Midwest	541	$66,791.86			
8		➤ 1887				
9						
10						

B8   =SUM(B4:B7)

1 Select the cell below or to the right of the values to be totaled.

2 On the Home tab, click the **AutoSum** button.

3 Press **Enter**. The result of the calculation displays in the selected cell.

End

CAUTION

AutoSum Looks for Sequential Numbers   AutoSum adds only sequential numbers. If you have empty cells in a column or row, AutoSum adds only the cells following the empty cell. For example, if cells A1 through A10 have numbers, cell A11 is blank, and cells A12 through A14 have numbers; using AutoSum in cell A15 adds only cells A12 through A14. ■

NOTE

Sum Directions   Excel sums the values directly above the selected cell first. If no values are above it, Excel looks for values in the cells to the left. ■

USING THE AVERAGE FUNCTION

The AVERAGE function finds an average value of a range of cells. The syntax for this function is =AVERAGE(*range of values to average*). An example might be =AVERAGE(B7:D7).

Start

1 Type the equal (**=**) sign in the cell where you want to place the average.

2 Type the function name **AVERAGE**.

3 Type the open parentheses symbol.

4 Type or highlight the range to be averaged.

5 Type the close parentheses symbol.

6 Press **Enter**. Excel averages the values in the selected range.

End

NOTE

Consider Other Functions   Similar functions include the =MAX, =MIN, and =COUNT functions. The =MAX function finds the largest value in a range of cells. The =MIN function finds the smallest value in a range of cells. The =COUNT function counts the nonblank cells in a range of cells. Examples might include =MAX(C7:C15) or =COUNT(C7:C15). ∎

Chapter 14

WORKING WITH CHARTS, PIVOTTABLES, AND SPARKLINES

Although Excel is an excellent tool for tracking and calculating data, there are times when you might want to summarize this data or display it in a more visual way. Fortunately, Excel offers several easy options to accomplish this.

Creating a *chart* is an effective way to illustrate the data in your worksheet. It can make relationships between numbers easier to see because it turns numbers into shapes, and the shapes can then be compared to one another. If your worksheet contains data you want to summarize, consider creating a *PivotTable* report. A final option is to create a mini chart called a *sparkline* in a cell adjacent to your data.

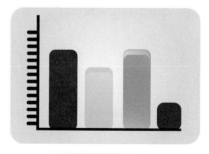

CHART AND PIVOTTABLE TOOLS

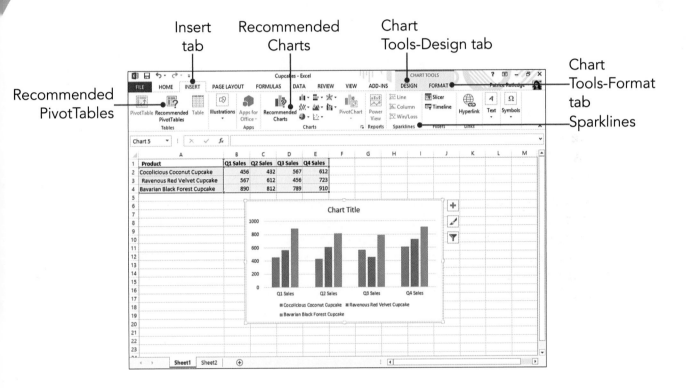

INSERTING A CHART

The Recommended Charts tool simplifies creating an Excel chart by suggesting the best chart types for your selected data. This is particularly useful if you are new to charts and aren't familiar with the Excel chart types available.

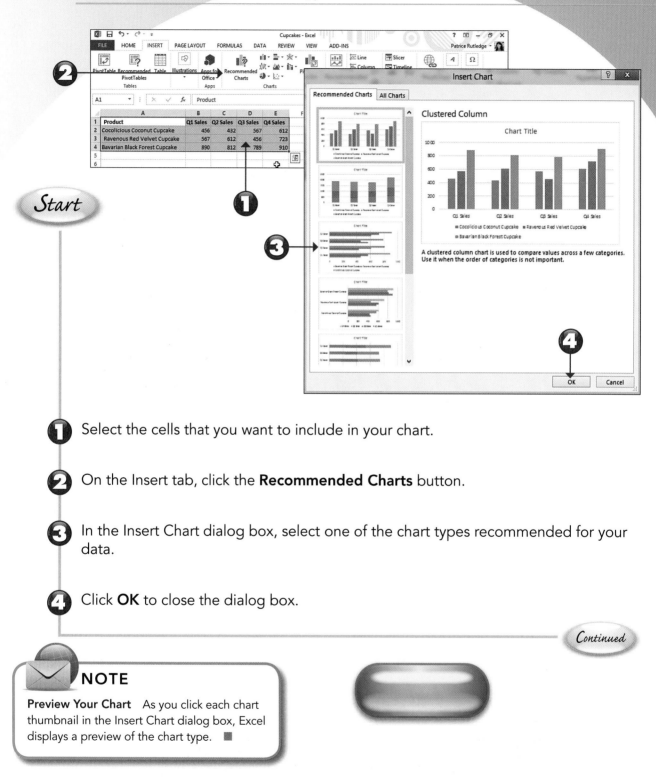

Start

1. Select the cells that you want to include in your chart.

2. On the Insert tab, click the **Recommended Charts** button.

3. In the Insert Chart dialog box, select one of the chart types recommended for your data.

4. Click **OK** to close the dialog box.

Continued

NOTE

Preview Your Chart   As you click each chart thumbnail in the Insert Chart dialog box, Excel displays a preview of the chart type. ■

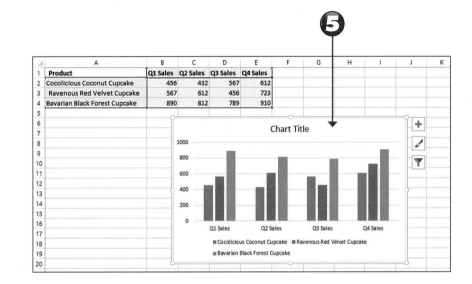

5 Excel displays the chart on your worksheet.

End

APPLYING A CHART STYLE
One easy way to modify the appearance of a chart is to apply a new chart style.

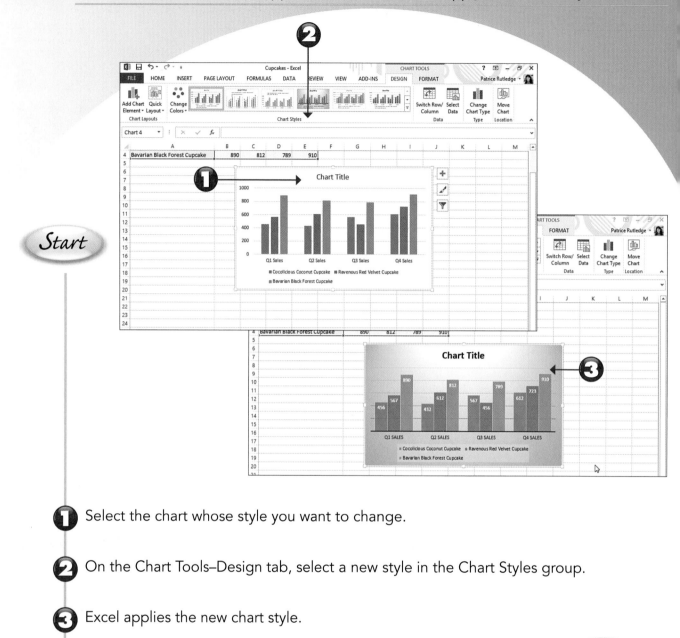

 Start

End

1. Select the chart whose style you want to change.

2. On the Chart Tools–Design tab, select a new style in the Chart Styles group.

3. Excel applies the new chart style.

NOTE

Chart Styles   The chart styles available for a chart are associated with that workbook's theme and its colors. You can apply a new theme by clicking the **Themes** button on the Page Layout tab. ■

TIP

Preview Chart Styles   Pause the mouse over each option in the Chart Styles group to preview its effect on your chart. ■

MODIFYING A CHART

Although Excel automates chart creation, you most likely still want to make a few changes. In this section, you learn several ways to modify an existing chart using the Chart Tools–Design tab.

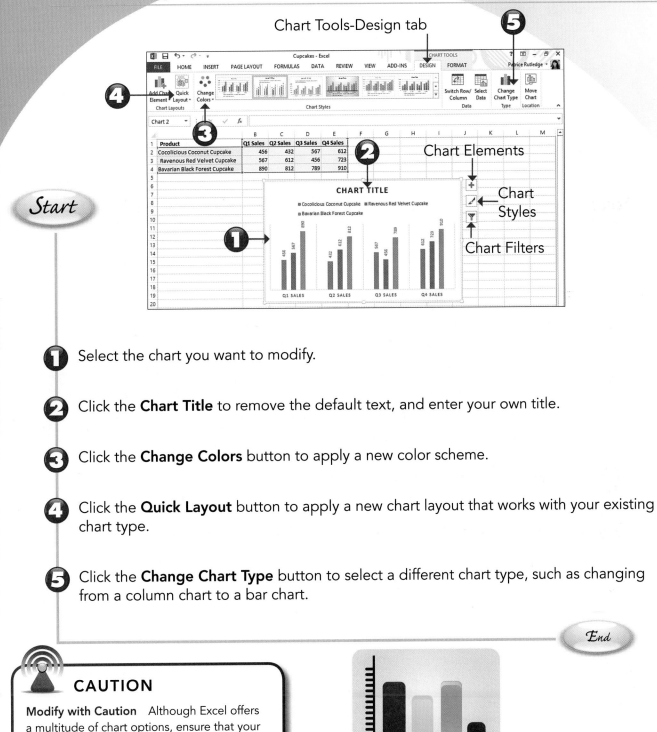

Chart Tools-Design tab

Chart Elements

Chart Styles

Chart Filters

Start

1 Select the chart you want to modify.

2 Click the **Chart Title** to remove the default text, and enter your own title.

3 Click the **Change Colors** button to apply a new color scheme.

4 Click the **Quick Layout** button to apply a new chart layout that works with your existing chart type.

5 Click the **Change Chart Type** button to select a different chart type, such as changing from a column chart to a bar chart.

End

CAUTION

Modify with Caution   Although Excel offers a multitude of chart options, ensure that your chart is still readable after making changes. ■

CREATING A PIVOTTABLE

If your worksheet contains extensive data, you can summarize it using a PivotTable report. For example, say you have a worksheet that lists every sale by product and customer over the past four quarters. You could use a PivotTable to summarize sales by product, customer, or quarter.

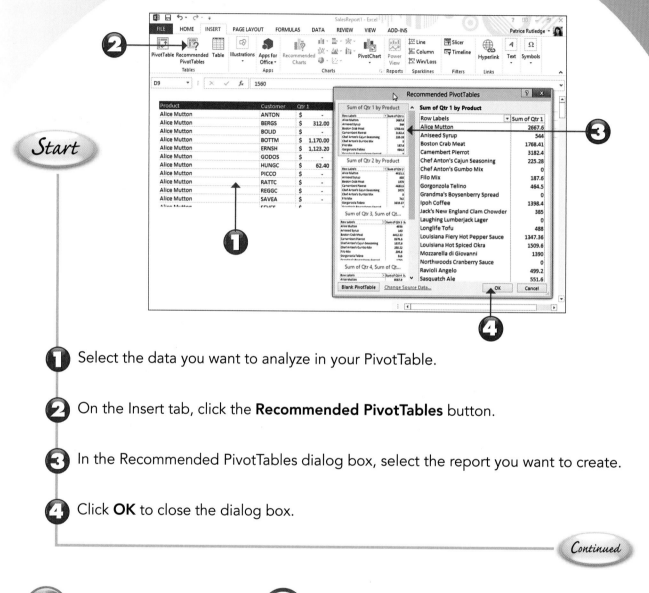

Start

1. Select the data you want to analyze in your PivotTable.

2. On the Insert tab, click the **Recommended PivotTables** button.

3. In the Recommended PivotTables dialog box, select the report you want to create.

4. Click **OK** to close the dialog box.

Continued

TIP

PivotTable Headings If you don't like the headings in your PivotTable report, you can edit them. ■

CAUTION

Not All Data Is Right for a PivotTable Excel displays a warning message if your selected data won't work well as a PivotTable. ■

Edit headings

PivotTable styles

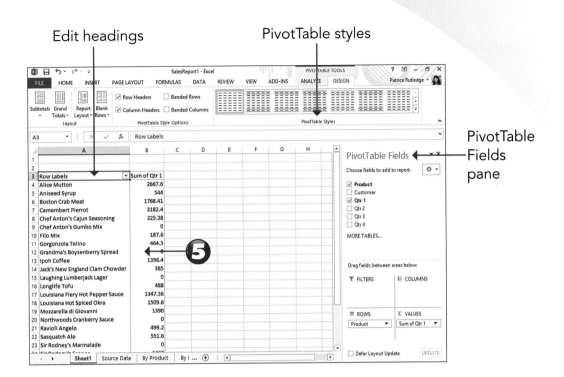

PivotTable Fields pane

 Excel displays the PivotTable report in a new worksheet in your workbook.

 End

PivotTable Fields Pane You can modify your PivotTable on the PivotTable Fields pane, which displays when you select a PivotTable. For example, you can add and remove the fields analyzed. ■

TIP

PivotTable Styles To apply a style to your PivotTable, select it, and choose one of the PivotTable styles on the PivotTable Tools–Design tab. ■

ADDING A SPARKLINE

Creating a sparkline—a mini chart that displays in a single cell—is another option for representing your worksheet data visually. In particular, a sparkline is a great tool for showing data trends.

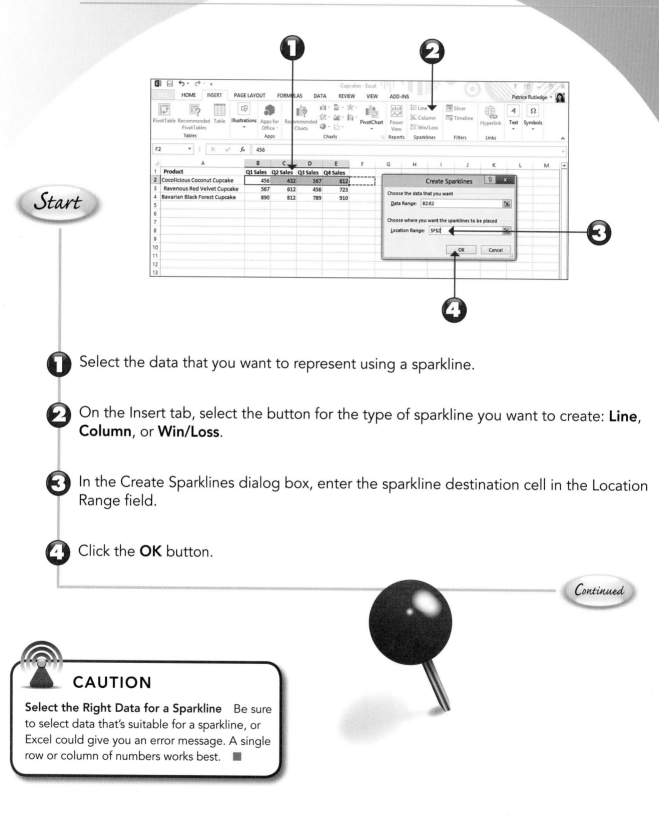

1. Select the data that you want to represent using a sparkline.

2. On the Insert tab, select the button for the type of sparkline you want to create: **Line**, **Column**, or **Win/Loss**.

3. In the Create Sparklines dialog box, enter the sparkline destination cell in the Location Range field.

4. Click the **OK** button.

Continued

CAUTION

Select the Right Data for a Sparkline Be sure to select data that's suitable for a sparkline, or Excel could give you an error message. A single row or column of numbers works best. ∎

Change sparkline type · · · · · Sparkline styles

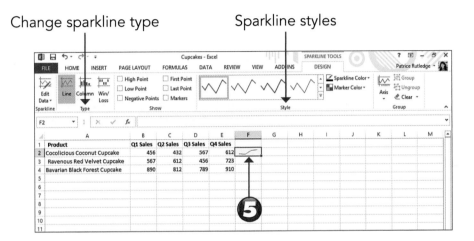

 Excel displays the sparkline in the selected cell.

End

NOTE

Sparkline Types Excel offers three different kinds of sparklines: line, column, and win/loss. If you've created an Excel chart, you should be familiar with line and column sparklines. A win/loss sparkline is useful if your data contains negative numbers and you want to graphically represent losses in relation to gains (wins). ■

TIP

Sparkline Tools–Design tab When you select a sparkline, the Sparkline Tools–Design tab displays. On this tab, you can apply sparkline styles, modify your sparkline content, or change its colors. ■

Chapter 15

CREATING AND MANAGING POWERPOINT PRESENTATIONS

With PowerPoint, you design a series of slides—enhanced with text, images, media, and animation—to create a presentation that you can deliver in person, on the Web, or on mobile devices. PowerPoint simplifies creating an effective, well-designed presentation with easy-to-use tools and color-coordinated themes.

Remember, however, that no matter how easy it is to create a basic series of slides, a great presentation requires strategic content, quality images, and a powerful delivery to truly motivate, inspire, and educate your audience.

GETTING STARTED WITH POWERPOINT

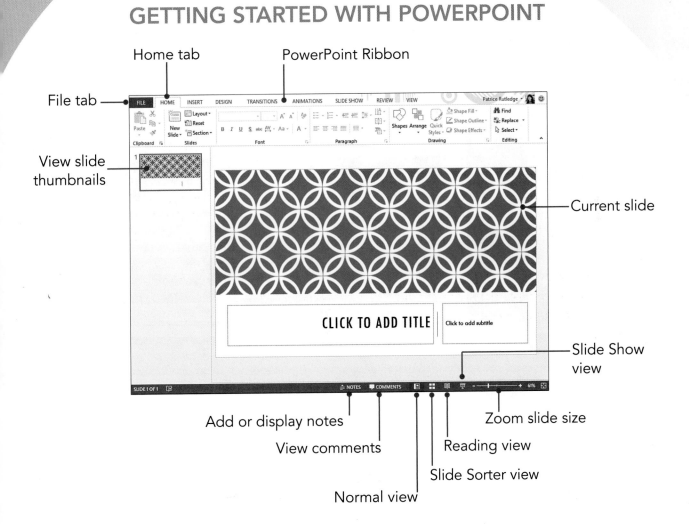

Home tab

PowerPoint Ribbon

File tab

View slide thumbnails

Current slide

Slide Show view

Add or display notes

View comments

Normal view

Slide Sorter view

Reading view

Zoom slide size

CREATING A NEW POWERPOINT PRESENTATION

PowerPoint's professionally-designed themes make it easy to create a quality presentation—even for the design-challenged.

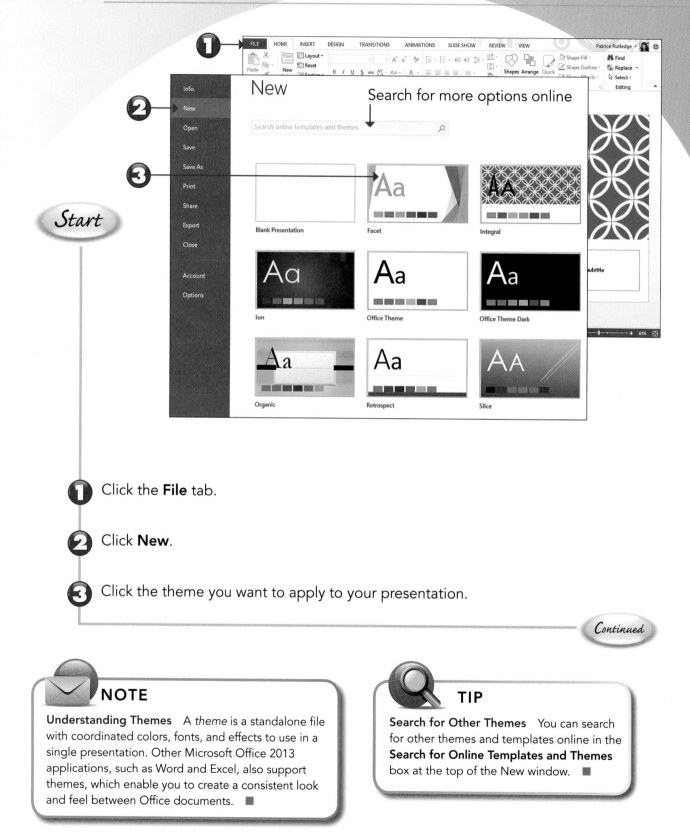

Search for more options online

Start

Continued

Click the **File** tab.

Click **New**.

Click the theme you want to apply to your presentation.

NOTE

Understanding Themes   A *theme* is a standalone file with coordinated colors, fonts, and effects to use in a single presentation. Other Microsoft Office 2013 applications, such as Word and Excel, also support themes, which enable you to create a consistent look and feel between Office documents. ■

TIP

Search for Other Themes   You can search for other themes and templates online in the **Search for Online Templates and Themes** box at the top of the New window. ■

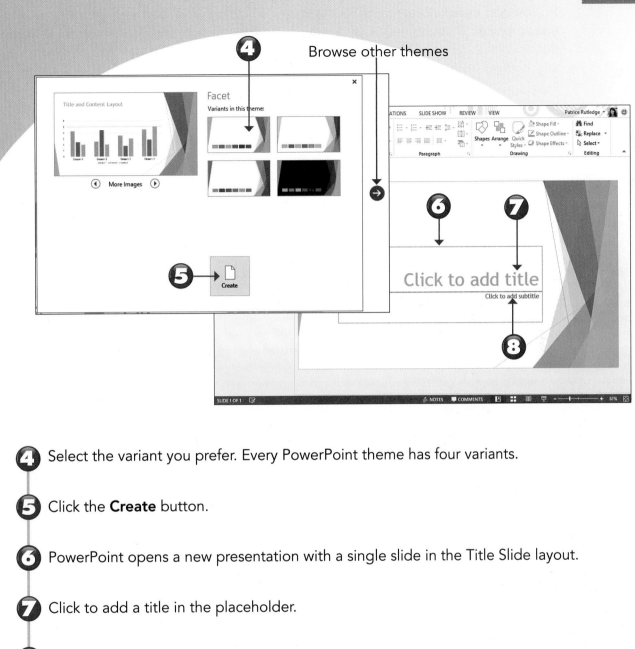

Browse other themes

4 Select the variant you prefer. Every PowerPoint theme has four variants.

5 Click the **Create** button.

6 PowerPoint opens a new presentation with a single slide in the Title Slide layout.

7 Click to add a title in the placeholder.

8 Click to add a subtitle in the placeholder.

End

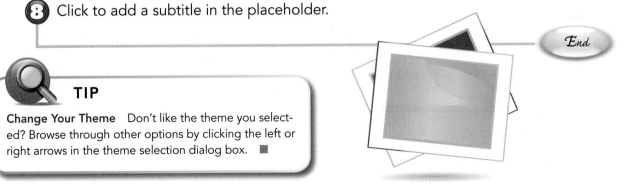

TIP

Change Your Theme   Don't like the theme you selected? Browse through other options by clicking the left or
right arrows in the theme selection dialog box. ■

EXPLORING NORMAL VIEW

PowerPoint includes several different *views*, which are arrangements of slides and tools on the screen that you use to work with and view your presentation. Normal view is PowerPoint's default view. This is where you do most of your presentation design, so it's a good idea to explore this view and get to know its key elements.

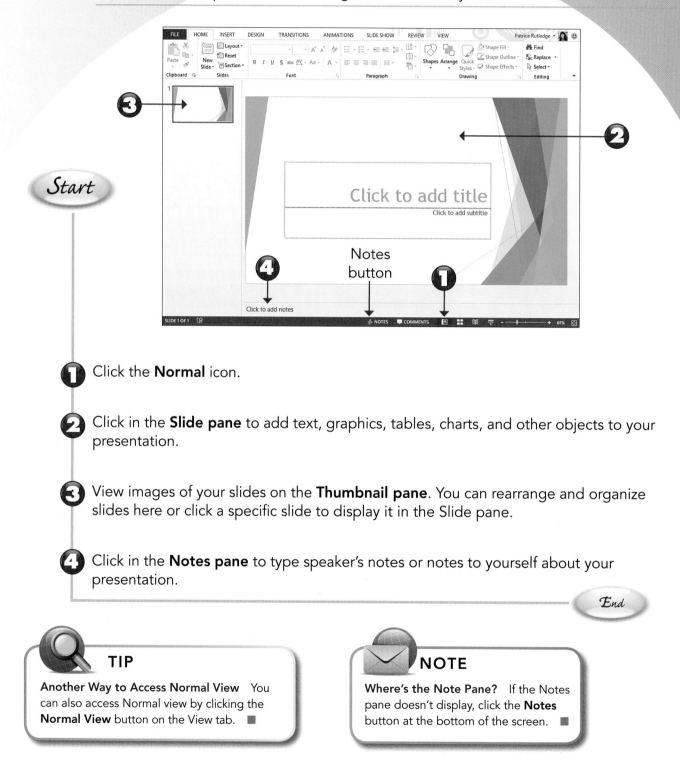

Start

1. Click the **Normal** icon.

2. Click in the **Slide pane** to add text, graphics, tables, charts, and other objects to your presentation.

3. View images of your slides on the **Thumbnail pane**. You can rearrange and organize slides here or click a specific slide to display it in the Slide pane.

4. Click in the **Notes pane** to type speaker's notes or notes to yourself about your presentation.

End

TIP

Another Way to Access Normal View You can also access Normal view by clicking the **Normal View** button on the View tab. ■

NOTE

Where's the Note Pane? If the Notes pane doesn't display, click the **Notes** button at the bottom of the screen. ■

You can add new slides to any open PowerPoint presentation. When you add a new slide, PowerPoint prompts you to select a predesigned slide layout.

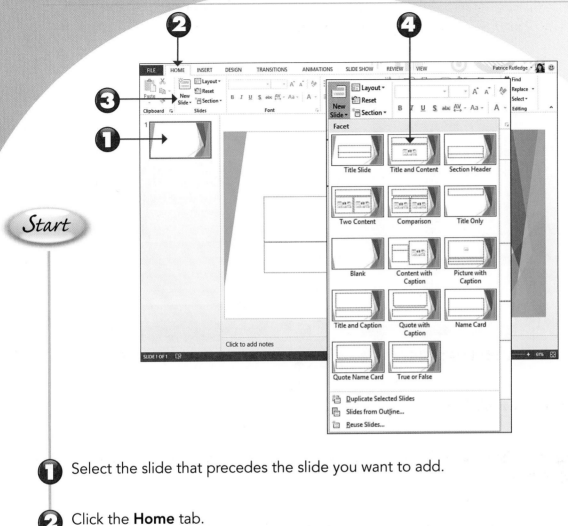

Start

1. Select the slide that precedes the slide you want to add.

2. Click the **Home** tab.

3. Click the lower portion of the **New Slide** button.

4. Select a slide layout from the gallery that displays.

Continued

NOTE

Understanding Slide Layouts A _slide layout_ helps you add specific types of content to your slides, such as text, tables, charts, and pictures. Slide layouts include placeholders that enable you to position content in the right location. ■

TIP

New Slide Shortcut Clicking the top portion of the **New Slide** button adds a slide in the layout of the active slide automatically without opening the gallery. Pressing **Ctrl+M** also performs this same task. ■

5 PowerPoint creates a new presentation with an initial slide in the layout you selected.

6 Add slide content in the placeholders.

7 If you selected a layout that includes the content palette, click the button on the palette that matches the type of content you want to insert. PowerPoint opens a dialog box that helps you insert that content type.

End

NOTE

Exploring the Content Palette The content palette enables you to add a table, chart, SmartArt graphic, picture, online picture, or video to your slide. Pause your mouse over each button on the content palette to view a description of the type of content that button inserts. ■

TIP

Switch to a New Layout Didn't choose the right layout? Click the **Layout** button on the Home tab to apply a new layout to an existing slide. ■

ADDING A SLIDE WITH A BULLET LIST

Although there is no slide layout specifically for bullet lists, you can create a list easily with the Title and Content layout.

Start

1. In the Thumbnail pane, select the slide that precedes the slide you want to add.

2. Click the **Home** tab.

3. Click the lower portion of the **New Slide** button.

4. Click the **Title and Content** slide layout.

5. Click the title placeholder and type your slide title.

6. Click the starter bullet and start typing your bullet list, pressing the Enter key to move to a new line.

End

TIP

Other Slide Layout Options You can also create a bullet list by choosing any of the other slide layouts that include the content palette, including the following: Title and Content, Two Content, Comparison, and Content with Caption. ■

ADDING SECTIONS TO YOUR PRESENTATION

Sections are particularly useful for large presentations where it's easy to get lost in a sea of slides. You can use sections to define presentation topics or distinguish between presenters, for example.

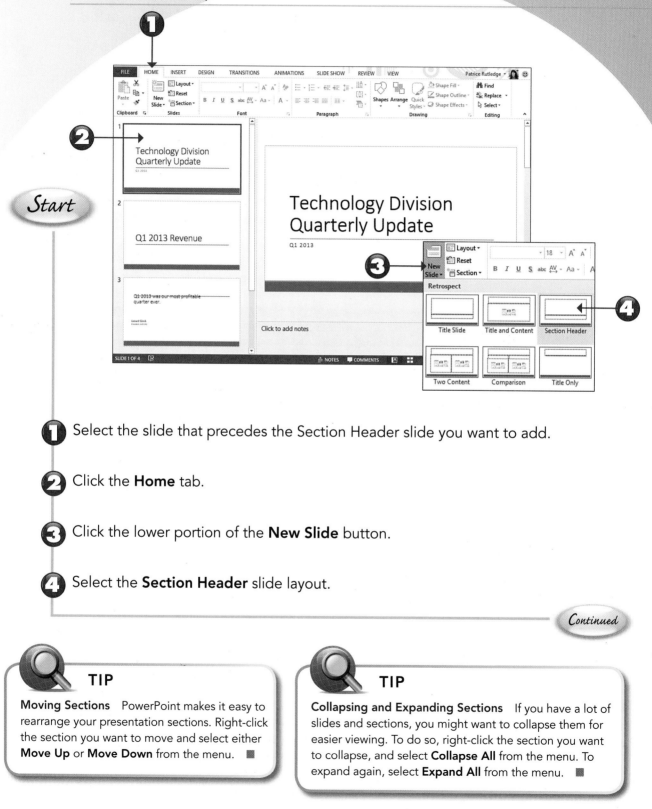

Start

1. Select the slide that precedes the Section Header slide you want to add.

2. Click the **Home** tab.

3. Click the lower portion of the **New Slide** button.

4. Select the **Section Header** slide layout.

Continued

TIP

Moving Sections PowerPoint makes it easy to rearrange your presentation sections. Right-click the section you want to move and select either **Move Up** or **Move Down** from the menu. ■

TIP

Collapsing and Expanding Sections If you have a lot of slides and sections, you might want to collapse them for easier viewing. To do so, right-click the section you want to collapse, and select **Collapse All** from the menu. To expand again, select **Expand All** from the menu. ■

5 On the new slide, type a section title in the placeholder.

6 Click the **Section** button, and select **Add Section** from the menu.

7 On the left side of the screen, right-click **Untitled Section**.

8 Select **Rename Section** from the menu.

9 Enter a **Section Name** in the Rename Section dialog box.

10 Click the **Rename** button.

End

TIP

Removing a Section On the left pane, right-click the section you want to remove, and select **Remove Section** from the menu. PowerPoint deletes the section marker but not the slides in that section. If you want to remove all the slides in a section and not just the section marker, select **Remove Section and Slides** from the menu. To remove *all* sections, select **Remove All Sections** from the menu.

abc

CREATING A PRESENTATION OUTLINE

A solid, well-organized outline helps you achieve the goals of your presentation. In Outline view, PowerPoint organizes outline content in levels. For example, a slide is the first level on your outline. If your slide contains a bullet list, those bullets are the second level. If you have indented bullets, they are the third level of your outline.

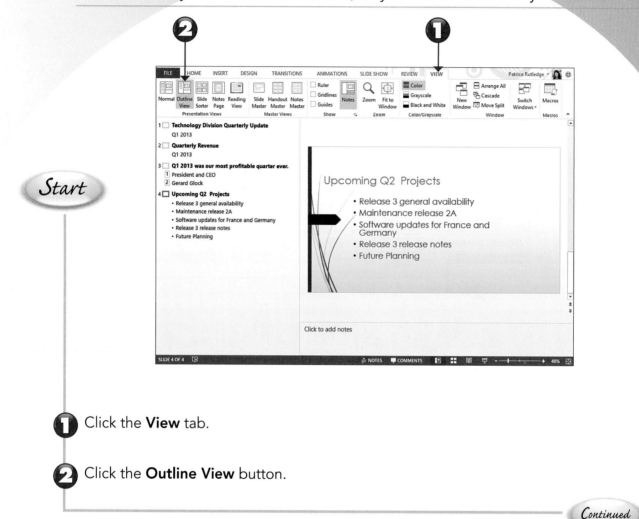

1 Click the **View** tab.

2 Click the **Outline View** button.

Continued

CAUTION

When Not to Use Outline View   Outline view works best for slides that contain a lot of text, such as bullet lists. Pictures, tables, charts, and other objects don't display in an outline. If your slides emphasize other types of content, such as graphics and charts, you'll find it to be more convenient to rearrange content directly on your slides. ■

TIP

Deleting Content   Select any outline content you want to delete, and press the **Delete** key on your keyboard. For example, you could delete a single bullet point or one or more slides. ■

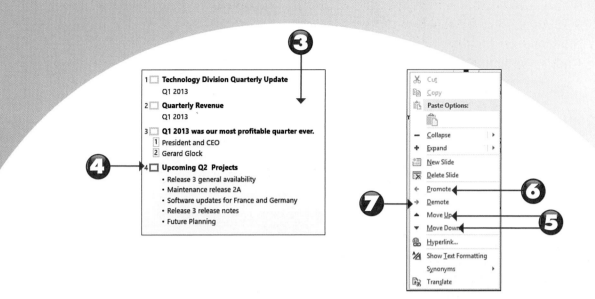

3 View an outline of your presentation. Each slide is numbered and followed by a slide icon and the title text.

4 Type new content, and press the **Enter** key on your keyboard to move to the next point.

5 Right-click a slide or slide content, and select **Move Up** or **Move Down** to move your selection.

6 Right-click slide content, and select **Promote** to change the selected text's outline level to the previous higher level.

7 Right-click slide content, and select **Demote** to change the selected text's outline level to the next lower level. Demoting a slide title moves the text of the selected slide to the previous slide.

End

TIP

Collapsing and Expanding Your Outline Collapsing hides all slide body text, which can make it easier to organize a long presentation. Right-click the Slide view, and then select **Collapse** and **Collapse All** from the menu. To expand again, select **Expand** and then **Expand All**. ■

TIP

Import an Outline If you create an outline in another application, such as Microsoft Word, you can import it into PowerPoint. Click the lower portion of the **New Slide** button, and select **Slides from Outline**. ■

Chapter 16

EDITING AND FORMATTING PRESENTATIONS

After you create a presentation, you'll most likely want to modify its appearance. Fortunately, it's easy to modify and organize slides, content, and presentations in PowerPoint using automated tools, the Slide Sorter, and slide masters.

When you finish with your presentation, you can print it for a final review or create handouts from your slides.

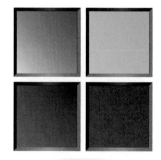

POWERPOINT DESIGN OPTIONS

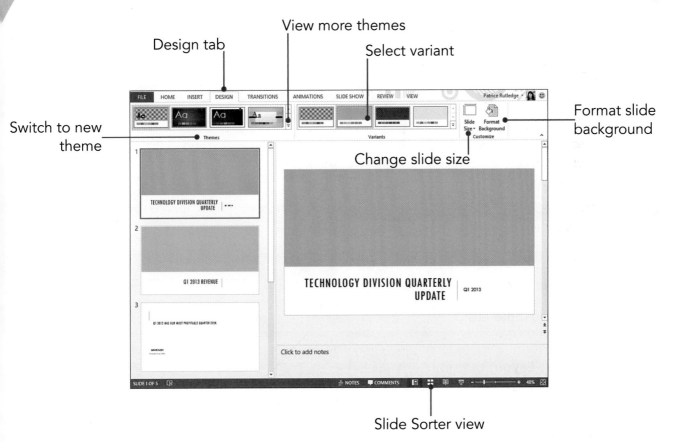

View more themes

Design tab

Select variant

Switch to new theme

Format slide background

Change slide size

Slide Sorter view

APPLYING A NEW SLIDE LAYOUT

If you don't like the slide layout you applied to a slide—or you selected the wrong layout—you can apply a new layout easily.

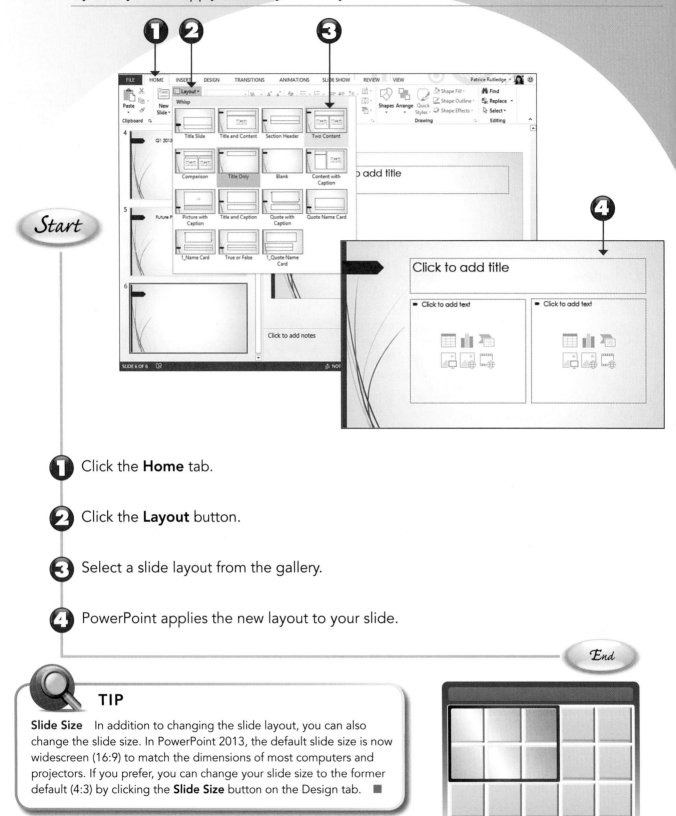

Start

1 Click the **Home** tab.

2 Click the **Layout** button.

3 Select a slide layout from the gallery.

4 PowerPoint applies the new layout to your slide.

End

TIP

Slide Size In addition to changing the slide layout, you can also change the slide size. In PowerPoint 2013, the default slide size is now widescreen (16:9) to match the dimensions of most computers and projectors. If you prefer, you can change your slide size to the former default (4:3) by clicking the **Slide Size** button on the Design tab. ■

APPLYING A NEW THEME

When you create a presentation, PowerPoint automatically applies a theme: a coordinated set of colors, fonts, and effects. However, you can easily change the existing theme in a matter of seconds.

Your current theme

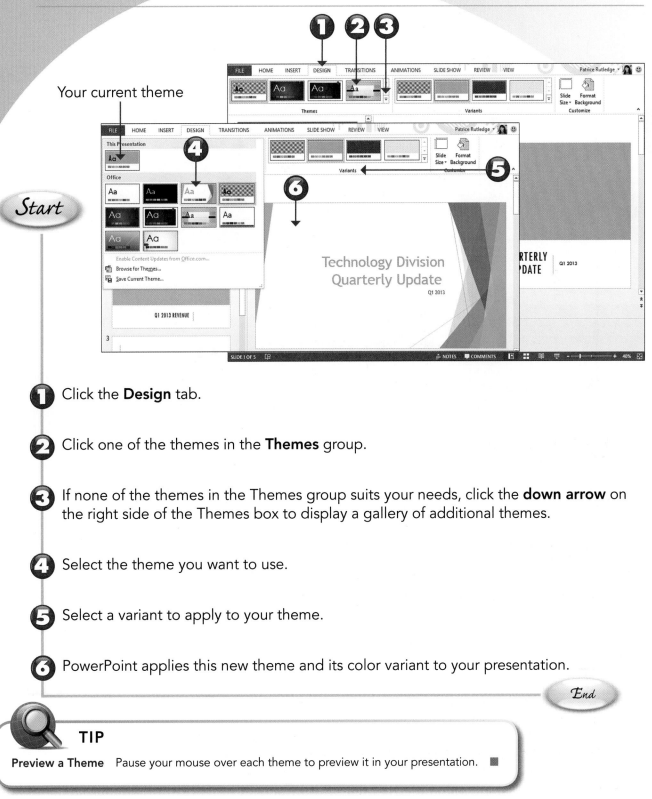

Start

1. Click the **Design** tab.

2. Click one of the themes in the **Themes** group.

3. If none of the themes in the Themes group suits your needs, click the **down arrow** on the right side of the Themes box to display a gallery of additional themes.

4. Select the theme you want to use.

5. Select a variant to apply to your theme.

6. PowerPoint applies this new theme and its color variant to your presentation.

End

TIP

Preview a Theme   Pause your mouse over each theme to preview it in your presentation.   ■

FORMATTING A SLIDE'S BACKGROUND

You can further customize your theme by applying, removing, and modifying its background. In addition to specific color backgrounds, you can also add special effects such as shading, patterns, textures, and pictures.

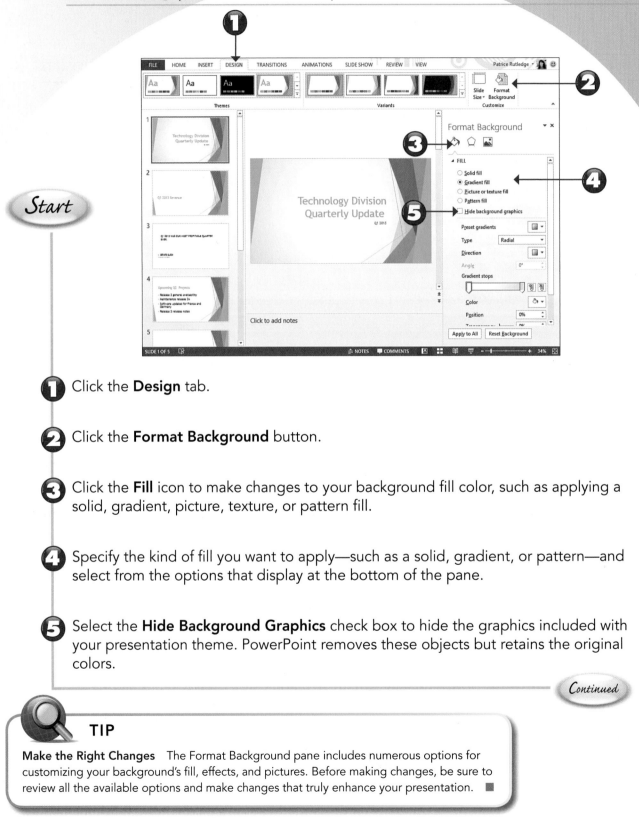

Start

① Click the **Design** tab.

② Click the **Format Background** button.

③ Click the **Fill** icon to make changes to your background fill color, such as applying a solid, gradient, picture, texture, or pattern fill.

④ Specify the kind of fill you want to apply—such as a solid, gradient, or pattern—and select from the options that display at the bottom of the pane.

⑤ Select the **Hide Background Graphics** check box to hide the graphics included with your presentation theme. PowerPoint removes these objects but retains the original colors.

Continued

TIP

Make the Right Changes The Format Background pane includes numerous options for customizing your background's fill, effects, and pictures. Before making changes, be sure to review all the available options and make changes that truly enhance your presentation. ■

Effects icon   Picture icon

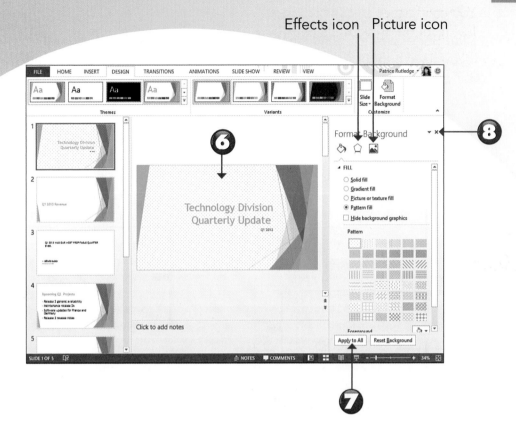

6 PowerPoint previews your changes in the Slide pane.

7 Click **Apply to All** if you want to apply this format to all slides in your presentation.

8 Click the **Close** button to close the Format Background pane and apply your changes.

End

TIP

Starting Over If you don't like the formatting options you applied, click the **Reset Background** button to start again. ■

NOTE

Formatting Effects and Pictures You can also click the **Effects** icon or **Picture** icon to make additional background changes. Be aware that these formatting options are available for some, but not all, backgrounds. ■

ORGANIZING YOUR PRESENTATION WITH SLIDE SORTER VIEW

Slide Sorter view displays smaller versions of your slides in several rows and columns. If you have a lot of reorganization to do, it's usually easier to accomplish this task in Slide Sorter view than in Normal view.

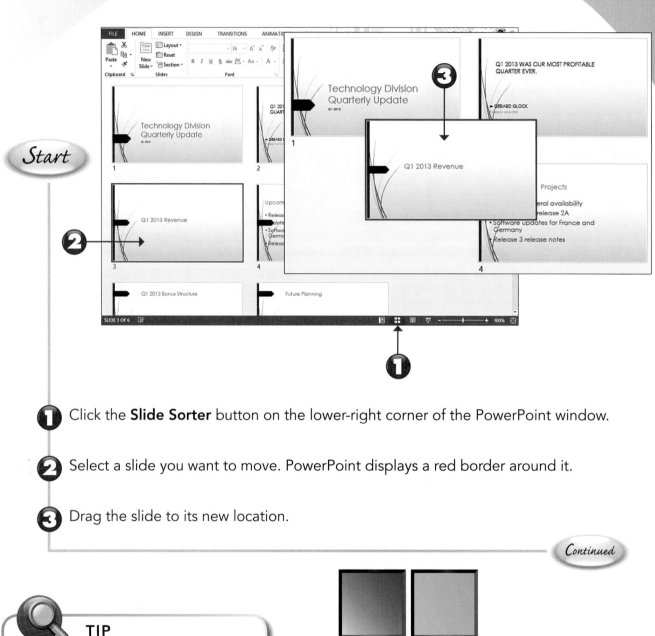

1. Click the **Slide Sorter** button on the lower-right corner of the PowerPoint window.

2. Select a slide you want to move. PowerPoint displays a red border around it.

3. Drag the slide to its new location.

Continued

TIP

Selecting Multiple Slides   To select multiple slides to delete, press **Ctrl**, select the slides, and then press the **Delete** key. ■

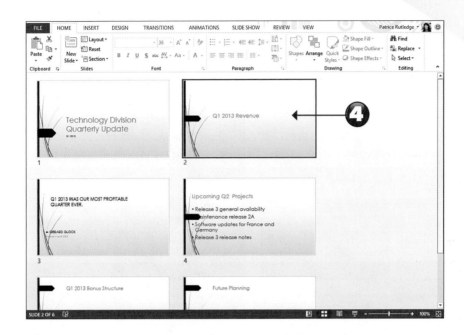

 PowerPoint displays the slide in its new location.

COPYING AND MOVING SLIDES FROM ONE PRESENTATION TO ANOTHER

Using Slide Sorter view, you can copy or move slides from one presentation to another.

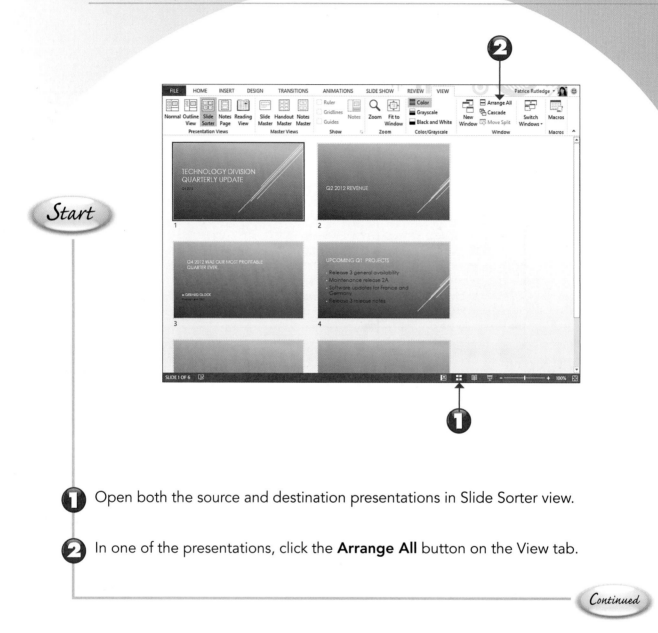

Start

1. Open both the source and destination presentations in Slide Sorter view.

2. In one of the presentations, click the **Arrange All** button on the View tab.

Continued

NOTE

Presentation Themes If each presentation uses a different theme, moving a slide changes its formatting to that of the new presentation, and the Paste Options button displays. To retain the formatting of the source presentation, click the down arrow to the right of the Paste Options button and choose **Keep Source Formatting**. Remember, however, that the best presentations use a consistent theme throughout. ■

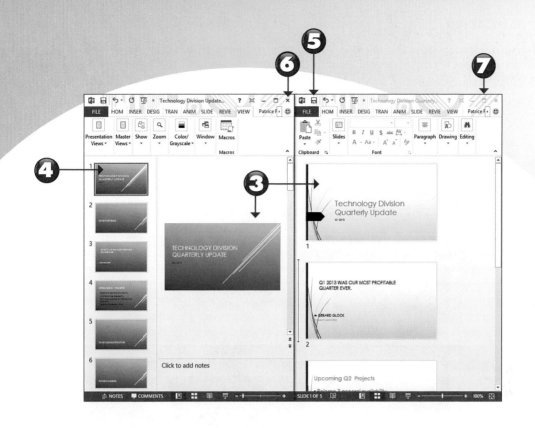

3 PowerPoint displays both presentations in different window panes in Slide Sorter view.

4 Drag and drop slides between presentations to copy them.

5 Click the **Save** button for any presentation you changed.

6 Click the **Close** button in the upper-right corner of the presentation you no longer want to view.

7 Click the **Maximize** button in the upper-right corner of the presentation you want to keep active.

End

TIP

Moving a Slide   To move a slide, select it, press **Ctrl+X** on your keyboard, position the mouse in the new destination location, and press **Ctrl+V**. The slide is removed from the source presentation and inserted in the destination presentation. ■

If you no longer need a slide or make a mistake and want to start again, you can delete it.

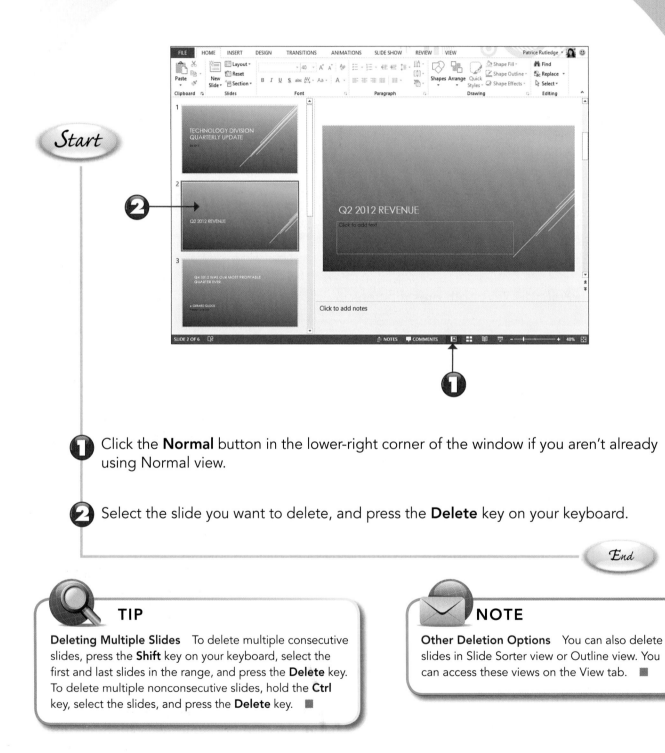

Start

2

1

Click to add notes

SLIDE 2 OF 6

1. Click the **Normal** button in the lower-right corner of the window if you aren't already using Normal view.

2. Select the slide you want to delete, and press the **Delete** key on your keyboard.

End

TIP

Deleting Multiple Slides   To delete multiple consecutive slides, press the **Shift** key on your keyboard, select the first and last slides in the range, and press the **Delete** key. To delete multiple nonconsecutive slides, hold the **Ctrl** key, select the slides, and press the **Delete** key. ■

NOTE

Other Deletion Options   You can also delete slides in Slide Sorter view or Outline view. You can access these views on the View tab. ■

Slide masters help you achieve uniformity by storing data about a presentation's theme and slide layouts, such as colors, fonts, effects, background, placeholders, and positioning—and applying it consistently throughout your presentation.

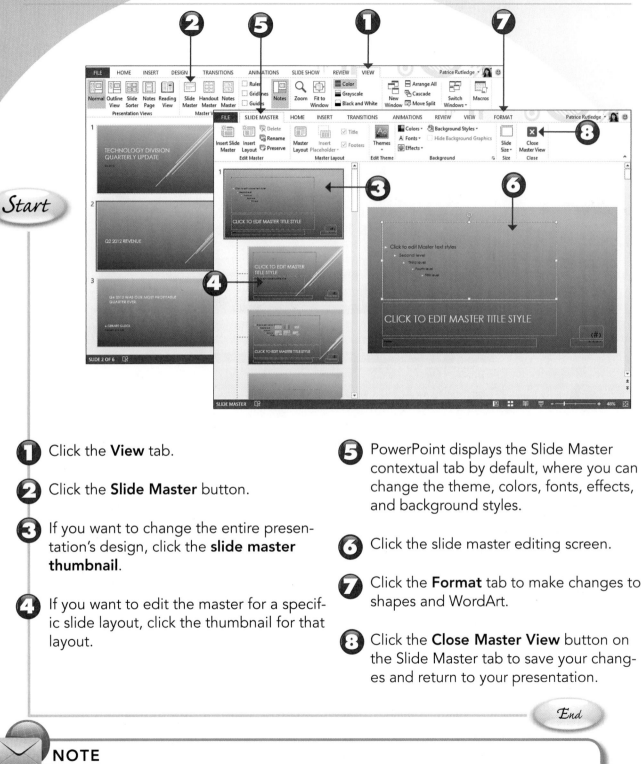

Start

1. Click the **View** tab.

2. Click the **Slide Master** button.

3. If you want to change the entire presentation's design, click the **slide master thumbnail**.

4. If you want to edit the master for a specific slide layout, click the thumbnail for that layout.

5. PowerPoint displays the Slide Master contextual tab by default, where you can change the theme, colors, fonts, effects, and background styles.

6. Click the slide master editing screen.

7. Click the **Format** tab to make changes to shapes and WordArt.

8. Click the **Close Master View** button on the Slide Master tab to save your changes and return to your presentation.

End

NOTE

Slide Masters Each presentation contains at least one slide master. Editing a slide master is optional and suited to experienced users. One popular reason to edit a slide master is to add your company logo to all slides. ■

INSERTING A HYPERLINK TO THE WEB

Inserting hyperlinks to external websites is a common use of PowerPoint's hyperlink feature. Inserting a hyperlink makes it easy to open a specific website or page during a presentation without having to manually enter its URL. You can add a hyperlink to text or to an object such as an image or shape.

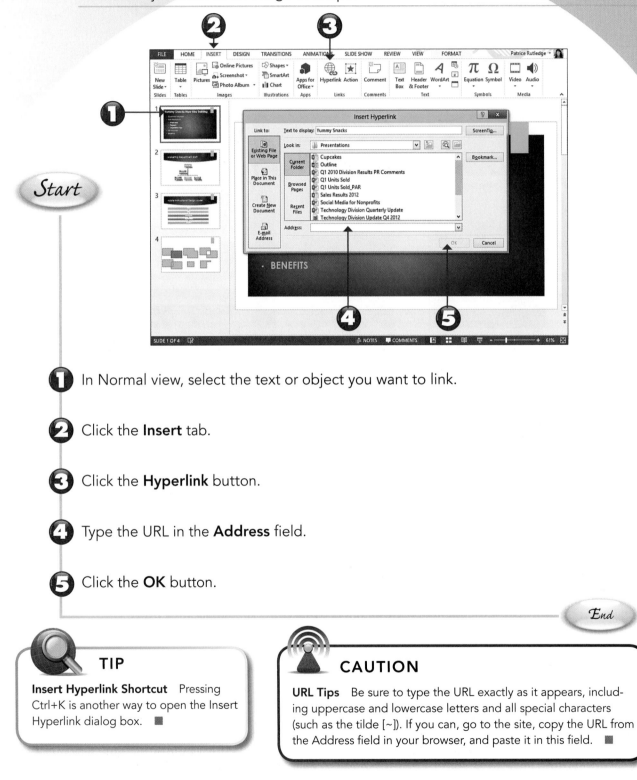

Start

1. In Normal view, select the text or object you want to link.

2. Click the **Insert** tab.

3. Click the **Hyperlink** button.

4. Type the URL in the **Address** field.

5. Click the **OK** button.

End

TIP

Insert Hyperlink Shortcut Pressing Ctrl+K is another way to open the Insert Hyperlink dialog box. ▪

CAUTION

URL Tips Be sure to type the URL exactly as it appears, including uppercase and lowercase letters and all special characters (such as the tilde [~]). If you can, go to the site, copy the URL from the Address field in your browser, and paste it in this field. ▪

In addition to linking to websites, you can also link to other slides in your presentation. Creating links to other slides helps you customize your slide show so that you can move quickly to the slides you need.

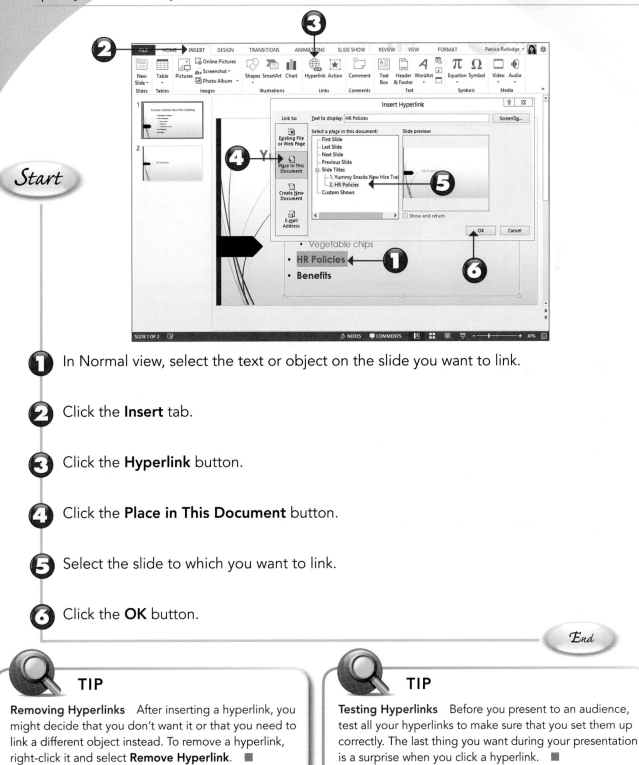

Start

1. In Normal view, select the text or object on the slide you want to link.

2. Click the **Insert** tab.

3. Click the **Hyperlink** button.

4. Click the **Place in This Document** button.

5. Select the slide to which you want to link.

6. Click the **OK** button.

End

TIP

Removing Hyperlinks After inserting a hyperlink, you might decide that you don't want it or that you need to link a different object instead. To remove a hyperlink, right-click it and select **Remove Hyperlink**. ■

TIP

Testing Hyperlinks Before you present to an audience, test all your hyperlinks to make sure that you set them up correctly. The last thing you want during your presentation is a surprise when you click a hyperlink. ■

If you plan to print your presentation—or create a PDF to distribute to participants—you can add headers and footers to your slides, notes, and handouts.

Start

1. Click the **Insert** tab.

2. Click the **Header & Footer** button.

3. Click the **Notes and Handouts** tab on the Header and Footer dialog box.

4. Click the **Date and Time** check box to print the date and/or time on each page, and select a formatting option from the drop-down list.

5. Click the **Page Number** check box to print a page number on the lower-right corner of each page.

6. Click the **Header** check box to print a header on the upper-left corner of the page.

7. Click the **Footer** check box to print a footer on the lower-left corner of the page.

8. Click the **Apply to All** button to close the dialog box.

End

TIP

Previewing You can preview your changes on the right side of the Headers and Footers dialog box. ■

You can export the slides and notes from your PowerPoint presentation to Microsoft Word, where you can use Word's formatting to create more sophisticated handouts.

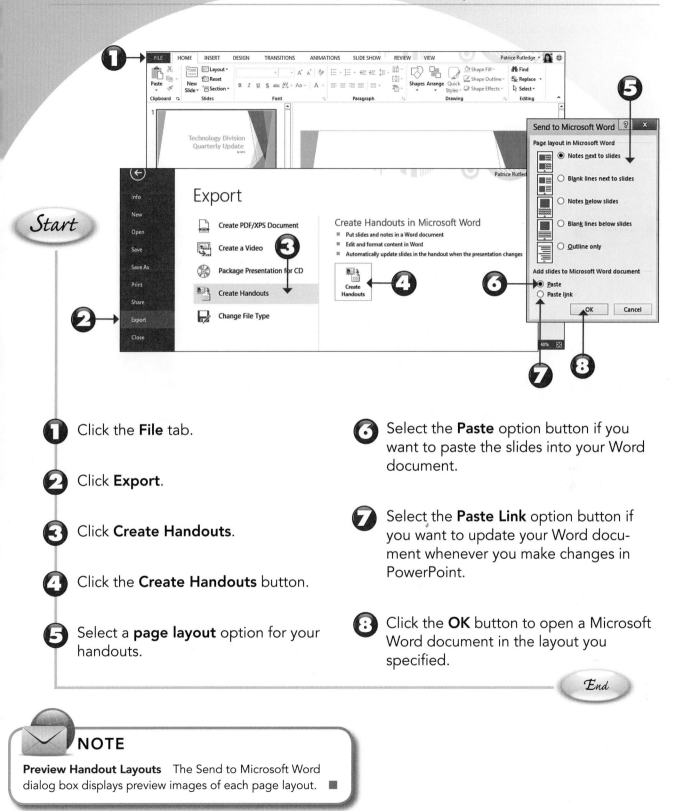

1. Click the **File** tab.

2. Click **Export**.

3. Click **Create Handouts**.

4. Click the **Create Handouts** button.

5. Select a **page layout** option for your handouts.

6. Select the **Paste** option button if you want to paste the slides into your Word document.

7. Select the **Paste Link** option button if you want to update your Word document whenever you make changes in PowerPoint.

8. Click the **OK** button to open a Microsoft Word document in the layout you specified.

NOTE

Preview Handout Layouts The Send to Microsoft Word dialog box displays preview images of each page layout. ■

PRINTING YOUR PRESENTATION

PowerPoint enables you to print more than just slides. You can also print notes to remind yourself of what you want to say while presenting, handouts to give to your audience, and outlines to help you proof your content. PowerPoint also includes numerous customization options for printing auxiliary materials.

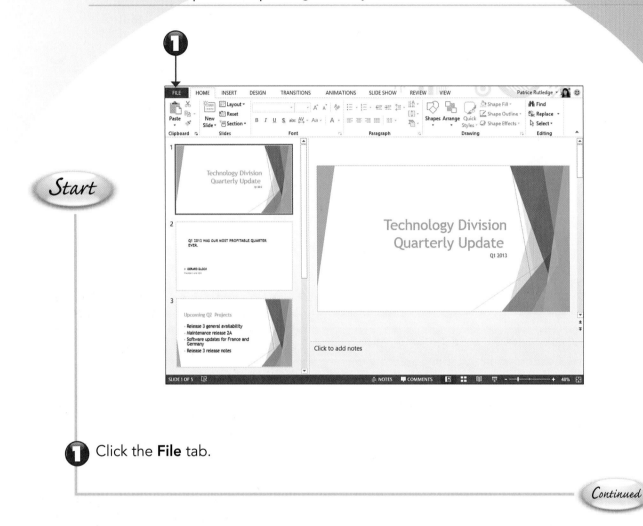

Start

1 Click the **File** tab.

Continued

TIP

Green Printing Alternatives   Consider a greener alternative to printing your presentation by saving it as a PDF and distributing it to your audience on the Web or on a company file-sharing site. Learn more at "Saving as a PDF" on page 22. That way, you need to print only for personal review, not wide distribution. ■

TIP

Scrolling and Zooming   Below the slide, you can click the left and right arrows to scroll through the presentation. You can also use the zoom control to reduce or enlarge the size of the slides. ■

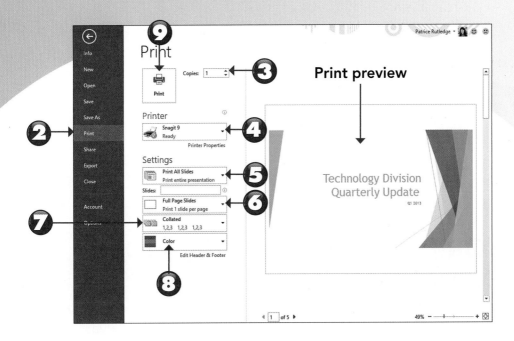

Print preview

2 Click **Print**.

3 Select the number of **Copies** you want to print.

4 Select your **Printer** from the drop-down list.

5 Select the slides you want to print. Your options include Print All Slides, Print Selection, Print Current Slide, or Custom Range.

6 Select the print layout you want to use. Options include Full Page Slides, Notes Pages, Outline, or nine different Handout layouts.

7 Specify whether you want to collate your printouts (print in consecutive order). This option is valid only if you choose to print more than one copy of your presentation.

8 Specify color options for your printed presentation. You can print in color, grayscale, or pure black and white.

9 Click the **Print** button to print your formatted presentation to the printer you selected.

End

NOTE

Print Preview Preview the way your presentation will display when printed on the right side of the Print window. Any changes you make to your presentation settings are reflected in this view, so you can verify before printing whether the choices you make work for you. ■

Chapter 17

WORKING WITH AUDIO, VIDEO, AND ANIMATION

PowerPoint offers a multitude of options to incorporate audio and video into your presentation, including several ways to insert clips and a vast array of formatting and playback options.

Animation and transitions can also enliven your presentation. You can animate the transition from one slide to another or animate how objects and text display on a slide.

Incorporating audio, video, transitions, and animation can give any presentation some pizzazz. Just remember that a little goes a long way, and focus on effects that truly enhance your presentation.

ANIMATIONS TAB AND PANE

Apply animation

Animations tab

Transitions tab

Animation Pane

Preview animation

Set timings

Apply effects

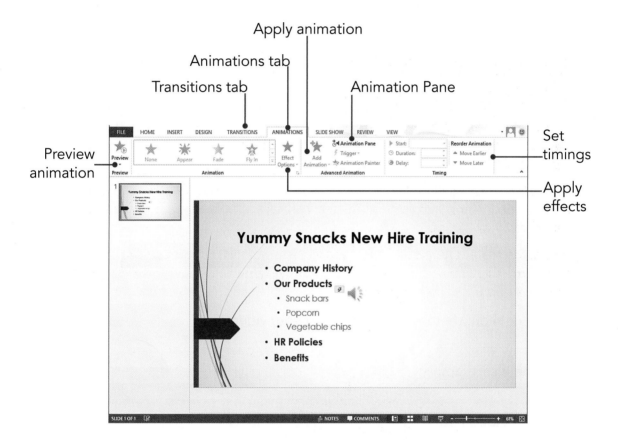

INSERTING ONLINE VIDEO

Inserting online video is an easy way to add a visual element to your presentation. PowerPoint enables you to insert video clips from an external website, such as YouTube. You can also search for videos on Bing, insert a video from one of your SkyDrive folders, or insert a video embed code.

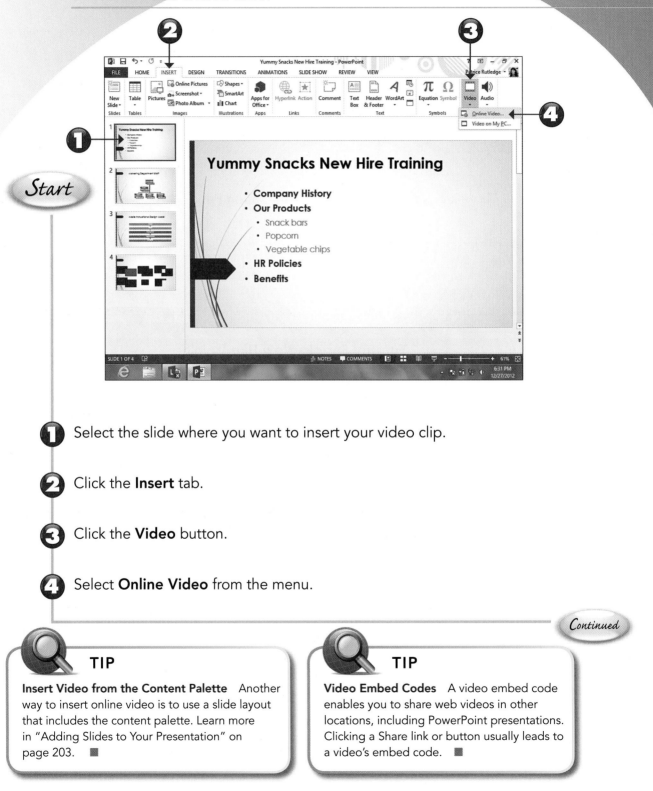

Start

Select the slide where you want to insert your video clip.

Click the **Insert** tab.

Click the **Video** button.

Select **Online Video** from the menu.

Continued

TIP

Insert Video from the Content Palette   Another way to insert online video is to use a slide layout that includes the content palette. Learn more in "Adding Slides to Your Presentation" on page 203. ∎

TIP

Video Embed Codes   A video embed code enables you to share web videos in other locations, including PowerPoint presentations. Clicking a Share link or button usually leads to a video's embed code. ∎

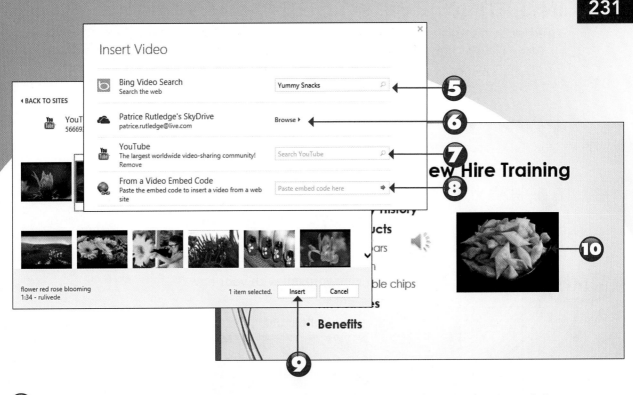

5 To search for a video on Bing, enter your search term, and press the **Search** button.

6 To insert a video from SkyDrive, click **Browse**.

7 To search for a video on YouTube, enter your search term, and press the **Search** button.

8 If you have an embed code from another website, paste it in the text box.

9 Follow the on-screen instructions to insert the video on your slide. For example, if you want to insert a YouTube video, select it and click the **Insert** button.

10 PowerPoint displays a thumbnail of the video on your slide.

End

TIP

Resize a Video Clip   You can resize and reposition a video by dragging the handles that surround it when it's selected. ■

TIP

Delete a Video Clip   To delete a video clip from a slide, select it and press the **Delete** key. ■

INSERTING A VIDEO CLIP FROM YOUR COMPUTER

Inserting a video clip from your computer or a network location is another easy way to incorporate video into your presentation. PowerPoint supports many video formats including the following: .ASF, .AVI, .MPEG, .WMV, .MOV, and Adobe Flash media.

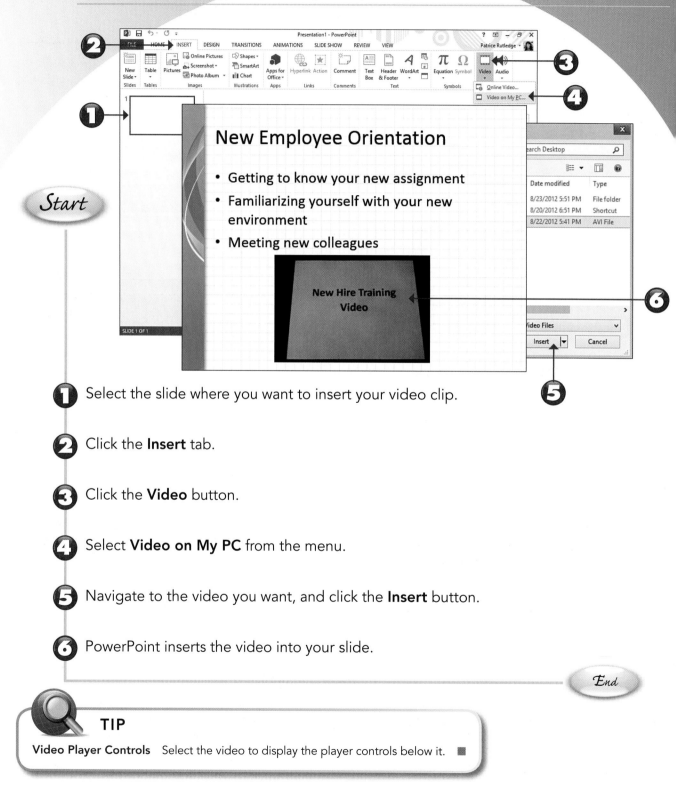

Select the slide where you want to insert your video clip.

Click the **Insert** tab.

Click the **Video** button.

Select **Video on My PC** from the menu.

Navigate to the video you want, and click the **Insert** button.

PowerPoint inserts the video into your slide.

TIP

Video Player Controls   Select the video to display the player controls below it. ■

FORMATTING VIDEO CLIPS

The Format tab displays when you select a video clip on a PowerPoint slide. Now explore some of the most popular formatting features available on this tab.

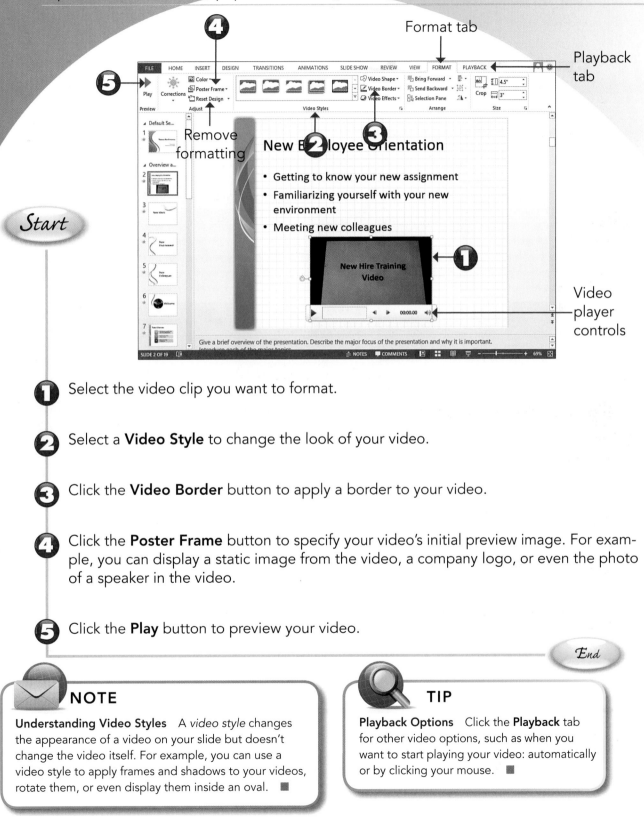

Format tab

Playback tab

Remove formatting

Video player controls

Start

1. Select the video clip you want to format.

2. Select a **Video Style** to change the look of your video.

3. Click the **Video Border** button to apply a border to your video.

4. Click the **Poster Frame** button to specify your video's initial preview image. For example, you can display a static image from the video, a company logo, or even the photo of a speaker in the video.

5. Click the **Play** button to preview your video.

End

NOTE

Understanding Video Styles A *video style* changes the appearance of a video on your slide but doesn't change the video itself. For example, you can use a video style to apply frames and shadows to your videos, rotate them, or even display them inside an oval. ■

TIP

Playback Options Click the **Playback** tab for other video options, such as when you want to start playing your video: automatically or by clicking your mouse. ■

INSERTING AN AUDIO CLIP FROM YOUR COMPUTER

You can insert an audio clip stored on your computer or a network location. PowerPoint supports the following audio file formats: .AIFF, .AU, .MIDI, .MP3, .WAV, .WMA, and .QT.

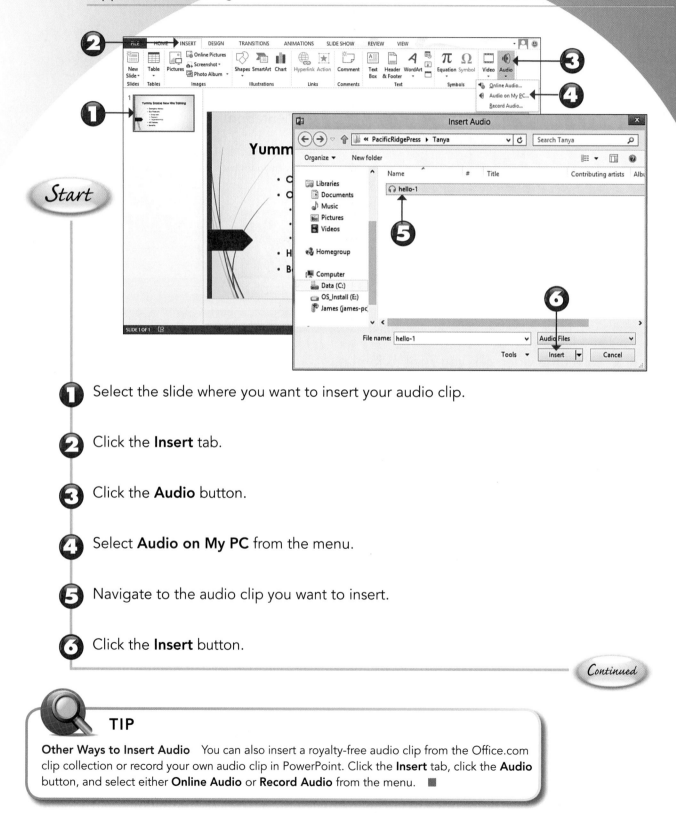

Select the slide where you want to insert your audio clip.

Click the **Insert** tab.

Click the **Audio** button.

Select **Audio on My PC** from the menu.

Navigate to the audio clip you want to insert.

Click the **Insert** button.

Continued

TIP

Other Ways to Insert Audio   You can also insert a royalty-free audio clip from the Office.com clip collection or record your own audio clip in PowerPoint. Click the **Insert** tab, click the **Audio** button, and select either **Online Audio** or **Record Audio** from the menu. ∎

7 PowerPoint inserts the audio into your slide in the form of an Audio Clip icon.

8 Select the audio clip to display the player control bar below it.

End

TIP

Reposition an Audio Clip   You can reposition and resize your audio clip if wanted. For example, you might want to drag this icon in the lower-right corner of your slide to keep the audience's focus on the slide content. ■

TIP

Delete an Audio Clip   To delete an audio clip from a slide, select it and press the **Delete** key. ■

SETTING SLIDE TRANSITIONS

Setting slide transitions is one of the most common animation effects. You can apply a slide transition to the entire presentation or just to the current slide.

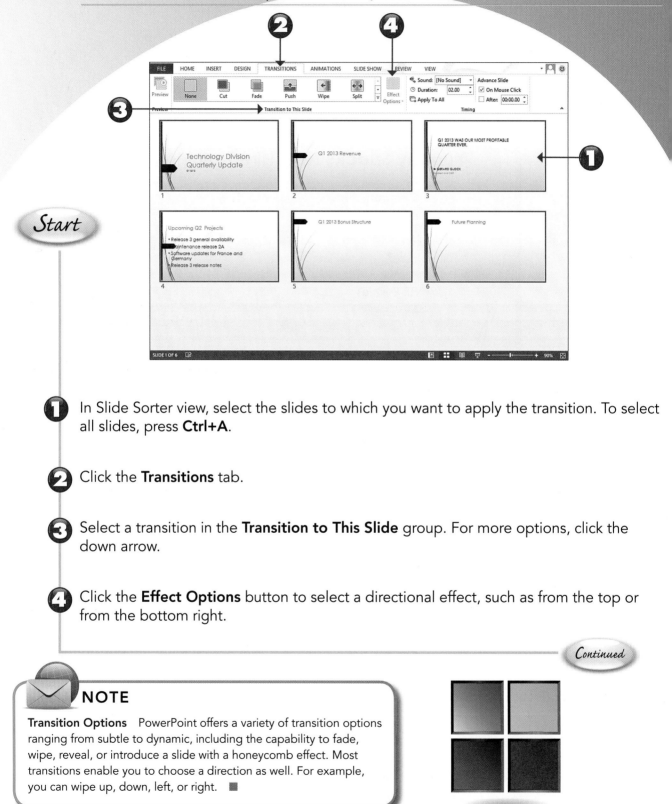

Start

1. In Slide Sorter view, select the slides to which you want to apply the transition. To select all slides, press **Ctrl+A**.

2. Click the **Transitions** tab.

3. Select a transition in the **Transition to This Slide** group. For more options, click the down arrow.

4. Click the **Effect Options** button to select a directional effect, such as from the top or from the bottom right.

Continued

NOTE

Transition Options   PowerPoint offers a variety of transition options ranging from subtle to dynamic, including the capability to fade, wipe, reveal, or introduce a slide with a honeycomb effect. Most transitions enable you to choose a direction as well. For example, you can wipe up, down, left, or right. ■

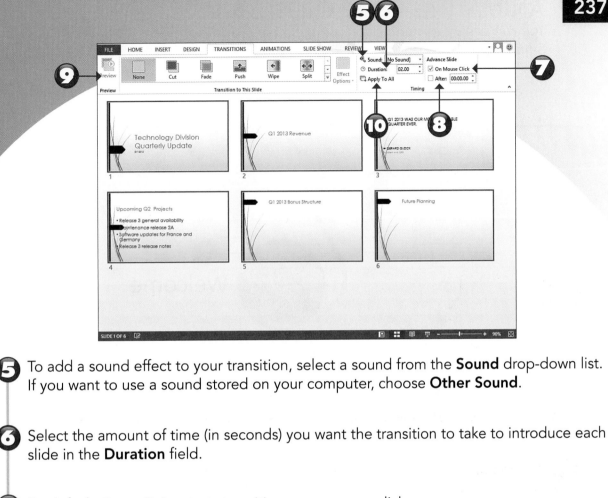

5 To add a sound effect to your transition, select a sound from the **Sound** drop-down list. If you want to use a sound stored on your computer, choose **Other Sound**.

6 Select the amount of time (in seconds) you want the transition to take to introduce each slide in the **Duration** field.

7 By default, PowerPoint starts transitions on a mouse-click.

8 If you would rather transition to the next slide after a specified amount of time, select the **After** check box and enter a time.

9 Click the **Preview** button on the left side of the Transitions tab.

10 Click the **Apply to All** button to apply the transitions to all slides in your presentation.

End

CAUTION

Don't Overdo Transitions As with so many PowerPoint features, use restraint with slide transitions. For the most professional results, choose one transition to use for every slide in a presentation. ■

NOTE

Advance Slides If you select the **On Mouse Click** check box, PowerPoint also advances to the next slide when you press a key such as the spacebar, Enter, or Page Up. ■

ANIMATING SLIDE OBJECTS

You can apply basic animation to objects such as shapes, text placeholders, text boxes, SmartArt graphics, and charts. For example, you can fly in text or make a shape spin.

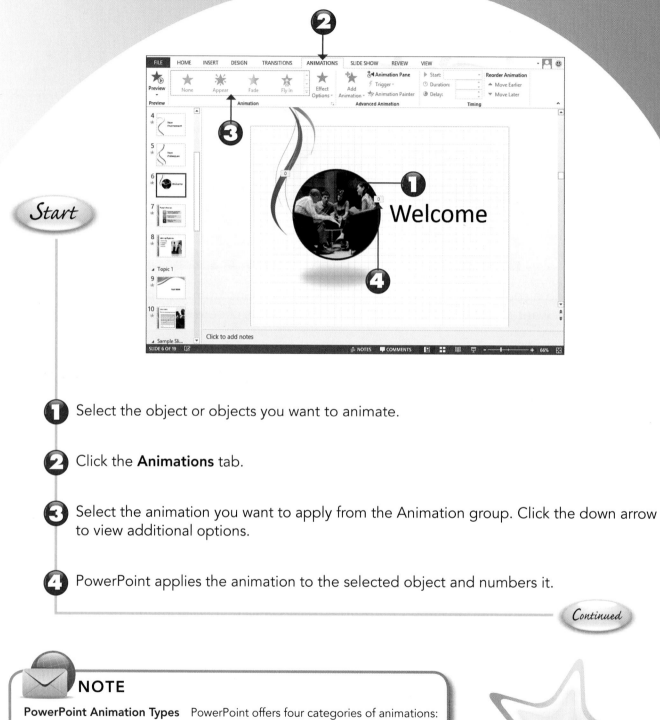

Start

1 Select the object or objects you want to animate.

2 Click the **Animations** tab.

3 Select the animation you want to apply from the Animation group. Click the down arrow to view additional options.

4 PowerPoint applies the animation to the selected object and numbers it.

Continued

NOTE

PowerPoint Animation Types PowerPoint offers four categories of animations: entrance animations that determine how the text or object enters the slide, emphasis animations that add emphasis to the text or object, exit animations that determine how the text or object exits the slide, and motion path animations that set a path that the selected text or object follows. ■

5 Click the **Effect Options** button to choose the direction to apply the animation, such as From Left or From Top-Right.

6 Click the **Trigger** button to specify what triggers this animation to start: the click of a specific object on the slide or a bookmark.

7 In the **Start** field, specify when to start the animation: with a mouse-click, with the previous animation, or after the previous animation.

8 Select a **Delay**, in seconds, between each animation. If you don't want a delay, select **00.00** in this field.

9 Select a **Duration**, in seconds, to determine how long the animation should last.

10 Click the **Preview** button to preview your animation choices.

End

NOTE

Animating Multiple Objects If you select more than one object, PowerPoint applies the animation to both objects at the same time. If you want the animations to occur in sequence, you must apply each animation separately. ■

CUSTOMIZING ANIMATIONS ON THE ANIMATION PANE

The tools available on the Animations tab should suit most of your animation needs. However, if you want to customize your animations even more, you can do so on the Animation pane. For example, you use this task pane to set animation effects for text, charts, SmartArt graphics, and media clips. Now explore this powerful tool.

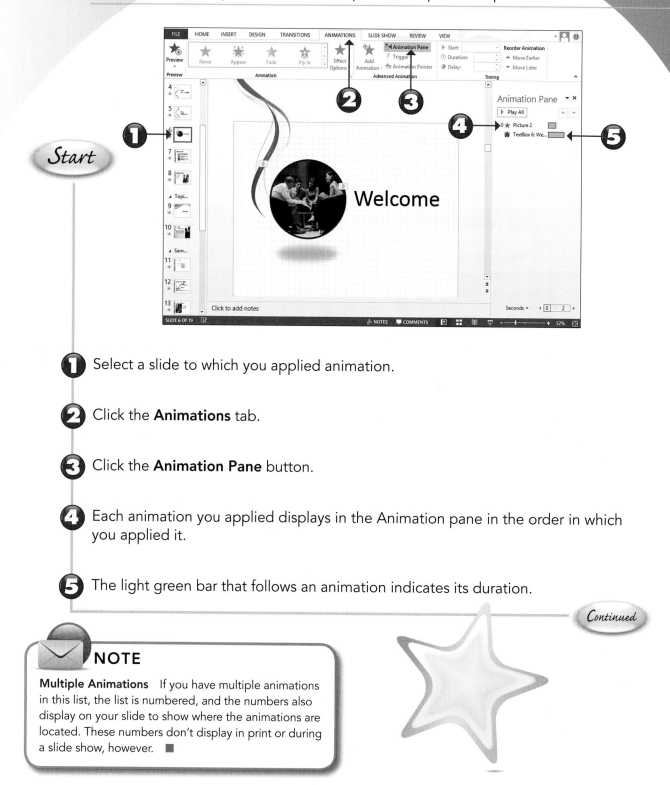

Start

1. Select a slide to which you applied animation.

2. Click the **Animations** tab.

3. Click the **Animation Pane** button.

4. Each animation you applied displays in the Animation pane in the order in which you applied it.

5. The light green bar that follows an animation indicates its duration.

Continued

NOTE

Multiple Animations   If you have multiple animations in this list, the list is numbered, and the numbers also display on your slide to show where the animations are located. These numbers don't display in print or during a slide show, however. ■

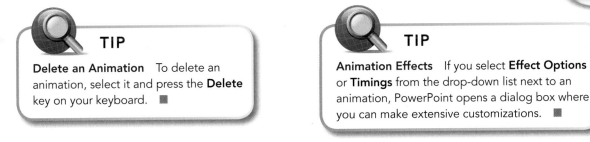

6 Pause the mouse over the animation in the list to display more information, such as the start option and effect type.

7 Select an animation in the list, and click the down arrow to its right to open a menu of additional options. For example, you can change the way an animation starts or its timing.

8 Reorder a selected animation by clicking the **up arrow** button or the **down arrow** button.

9 Click the **Play All** button to preview the animations in your current view.

End

TIP

Delete an Animation To delete an animation, select it and press the **Delete** key on your keyboard. ■

TIP

Animation Effects If you select **Effect Options** or **Timings** from the drop-down list next to an animation, PowerPoint opens a dialog box where you can make extensive customizations. ■

Chapter 18

REVIEWING AND MAKING PRESENTATIONS

After you create all the slides in your presentation, you might want to get some feedback on them and then plan how to present them in a slide show. Fortunately, PowerPoint makes it easy to review, set up, and rehearse a presentation.

When you're ready, you can present to people in the same room as you or to a worldwide audience on the Web. You can also create a video from your presentation for on-demand viewing.

SLIDE SHOW TAB

Create a custom show

Slide Show tab

Present online

Rehearse timings

Record slide show

Start slide show

Use Presenter View

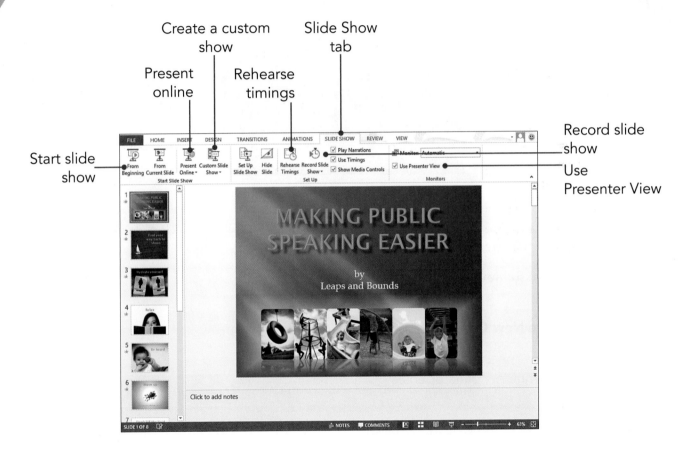

ADDING COMMENTS

Providing and incorporating feedback on PowerPoint presentations is an important part of the presentation design process in many organizations. One of the best ways to communicate your suggested changes to a presentation's author is to add a comment.

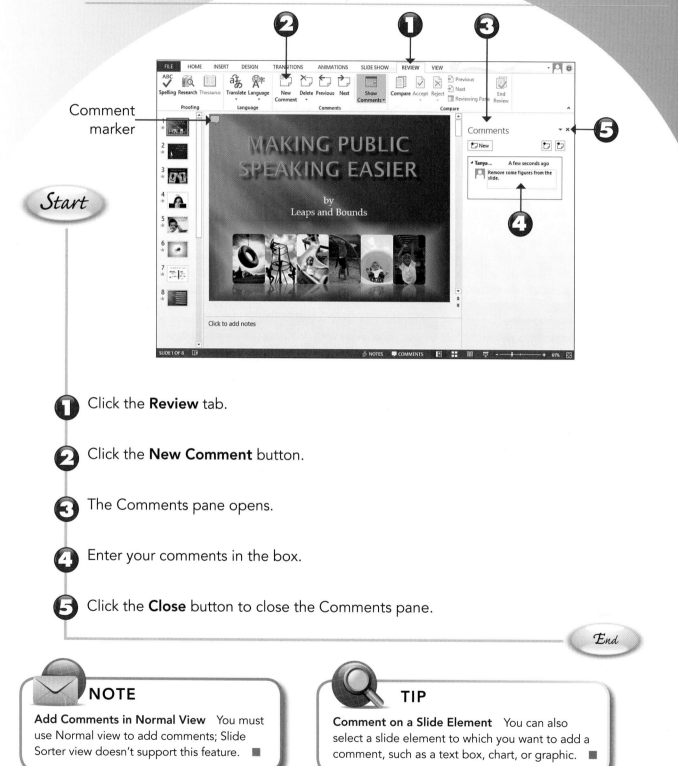

Comment marker

Start

1 Click the **Review** tab.

2 Click the **New Comment** button.

3 The Comments pane opens.

4 Enter your comments in the box.

5 Click the **Close** button to close the Comments pane.

End

NOTE

Add Comments in Normal View You must use Normal view to add comments; Slide Sorter view doesn't support this feature. ■

TIP

Comment on a Slide Element You can also select a slide element to which you want to add a comment, such as a text box, chart, or graphic. ■

MANAGING COMMENTS

After people comment on your presentation, you can review, edit, delete, and reply to their commentary.

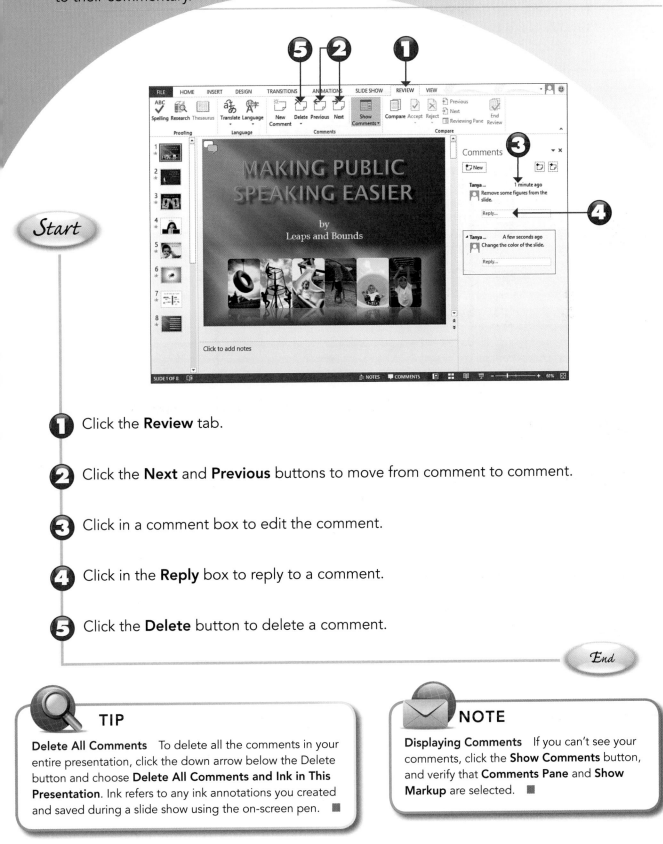

Start

1. Click the **Review** tab.

2. Click the **Next** and **Previous** buttons to move from comment to comment.

3. Click in a comment box to edit the comment.

4. Click in the **Reply** box to reply to a comment.

5. Click the **Delete** button to delete a comment.

End

TIP

Delete All Comments To delete all the comments in your entire presentation, click the down arrow below the Delete button and choose **Delete All Comments and Ink in This Presentation**. Ink refers to any ink annotations you created and saved during a slide show using the on-screen pen. ■

NOTE

Displaying Comments If you can't see your comments, click the **Show Comments** button, and verify that **Comments Pane** and **Show Markup** are selected. ■

COMPARING PRESENTATIONS

Although it's best if all reviewers comment on and edit the same version of a presentation, such as one stored in a central location, there are times when they will edit a separate version of your presentation. Fortunately, PowerPoint's Compare feature simplifies the process of analyzing and consolidating comments.

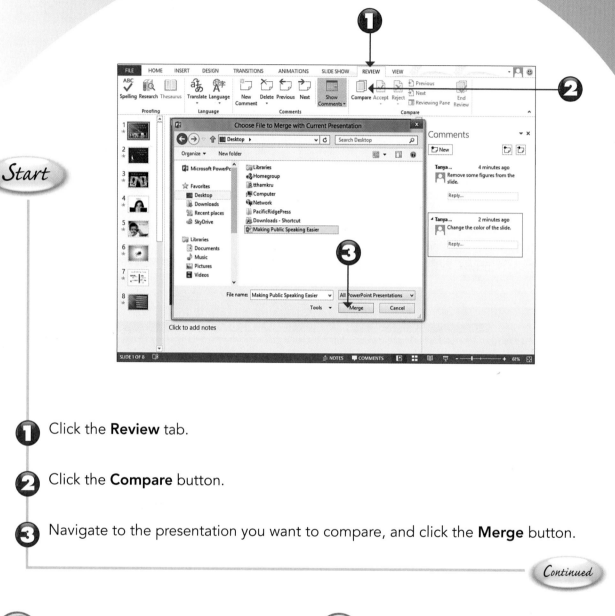

Start

① Click the **Review** tab.

② Click the **Compare** button.

③ Navigate to the presentation you want to compare, and click the **Merge** button.

Continued

TIP

Close the Revisions Pane To close the Revisions task pane, click the **Close** button (x) in the upper-right corner. Alternatively, on the Review tab, click the **Reviewing Pane** button, which serves as a toggle for this pane. ∎

TIP

Accept All Changes To accept all presentation changes, click the down arrow below the Accept button, and select **Accept All Changes to the Presentation** from the menu. ∎

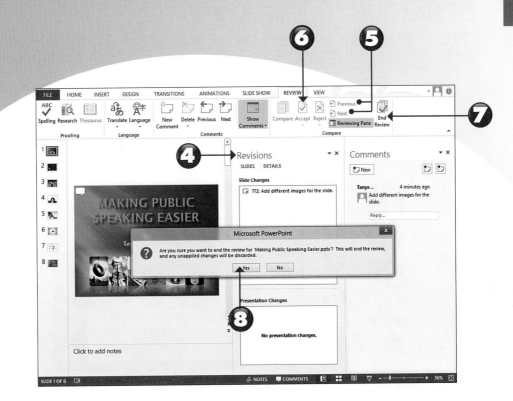

PowerPoint merges the two presentations and opens the Revisions task pane where you can view changes.

Use the **Next** and **Previous** buttons to scroll through changes.

Click the **Accept** button to accept a change.

When you finish comparing presentations, click the **End Review** button.

Click **Yes** to confirm that you want to end the review.

End

TIP

Rejecting Changes After you accept a change, the Reject button on the Review tab is now available. If you want to reject the active change, click the upper part of the **Reject** button. For more options, click the down arrow below the Reject button. ■

CAUTION

Ending Your Review When you end your review, all your accepted changes are applied to your original presentation; changes you didn't accept are discarded. You can't undo this action. ■

SETTING UP A SLIDE SHOW

Before delivering your slide show, you should set up all the show options you want to use.

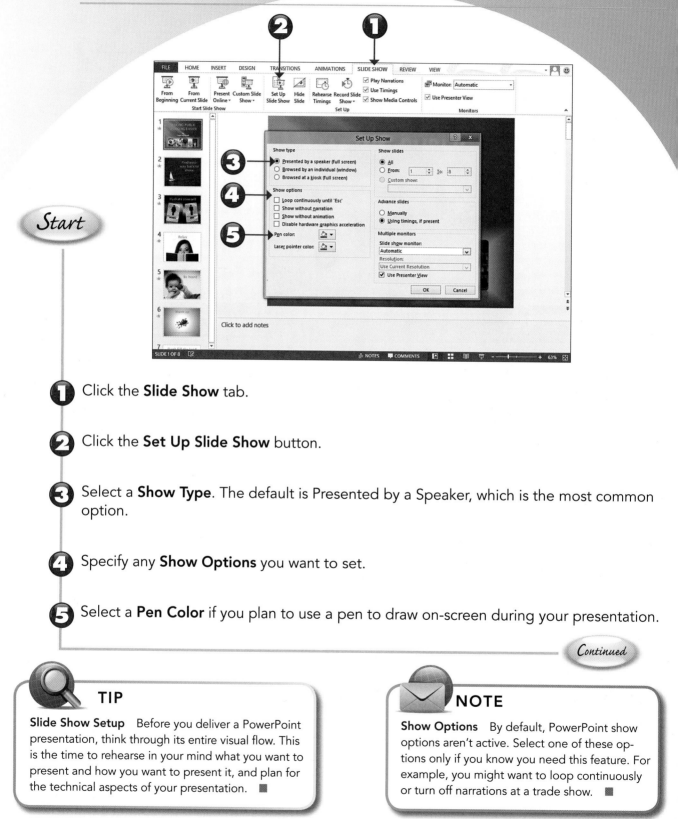

Start

1. Click the **Slide Show** tab.

2. Click the **Set Up Slide Show** button.

3. Select a **Show Type**. The default is Presented by a Speaker, which is the most common option.

4. Specify any **Show Options** you want to set.

5. Select a **Pen Color** if you plan to use a pen to draw on-screen during your presentation.

Continued

TIP

Slide Show Setup   Before you deliver a PowerPoint presentation, think through its entire visual flow. This is the time to rehearse in your mind what you want to present and how you want to present it, and plan for the technical aspects of your presentation. ■

NOTE

Show Options   By default, PowerPoint show options aren't active. Select one of these options only if you know you need this feature. For example, you might want to loop continuously or turn off narrations at a trade show. ■

6. Select a **Laser Pointer Color** if you plan to use a laser pointer during your presentation.

7. Choose the slides you want to include in your presentation.

8. Specify how you want to advance slides: **Manually** or **Using Timings, if Present**.

9. Select the **Use Presenter View** check box if you want to use this view.

10. Click the **OK** button.

End

TIP

Advancing Slides To advance a slide manually, you need to press a key or click the mouse. Choosing **Manually** in this field overrides any timings you previously set. See "Rehearsing Timings" later in this chapter. ■

NOTE

Presenter View Presenter View enables you to display speaker's notes, upcoming slides, the elapsed time of your presentation, and other useful information. See "Exploring Presenter View" later in this chapter. ■

REHEARSING TIMINGS

When you rehearse timings, PowerPoint keeps track of how long you spend on each slide. After you rehearse, you can use these timings to automate slide transitions or simply to help you adjust your presentation to fit into an allotted amount of time.

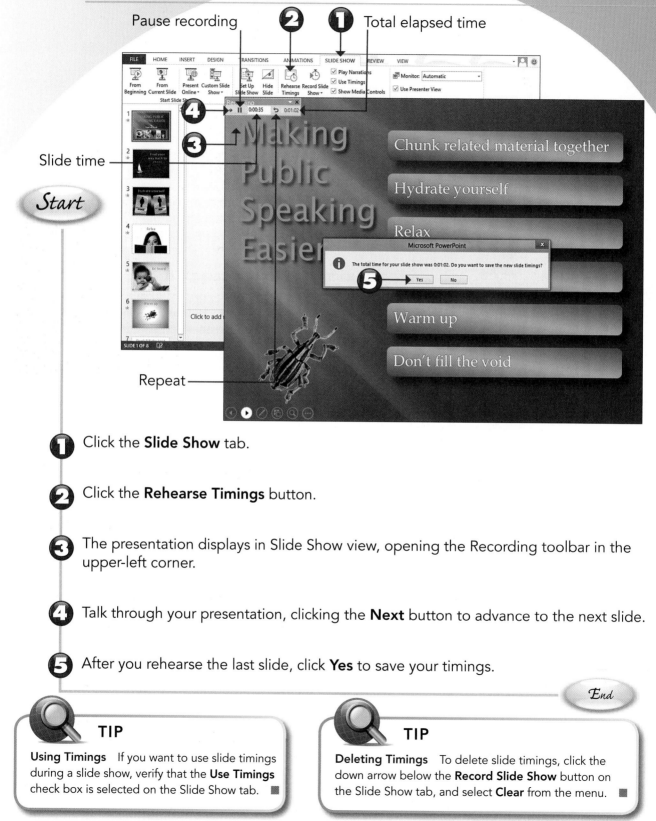

Pause recording

Total elapsed time

Slide time

Start

Repeat

1 Click the **Slide Show** tab.

2 Click the **Rehearse Timings** button.

3 The presentation displays in Slide Show view, opening the Recording toolbar in the upper-left corner.

4 Talk through your presentation, clicking the **Next** button to advance to the next slide.

5 After you rehearse the last slide, click **Yes** to save your timings.

End

TIP

Using Timings   If you want to use slide timings during a slide show, verify that the **Use Timings** check box is selected on the Slide Show tab. ■

TIP

Deleting Timings   To delete slide timings, click the down arrow below the **Record Slide Show** button on the Slide Show tab, and select **Clear** from the menu. ■

RECORDING VOICE NARRATIONS

You can record your own voiceover to accompany a web-based presentation or an automated presentation, such as one you run continuously at a trade show booth.

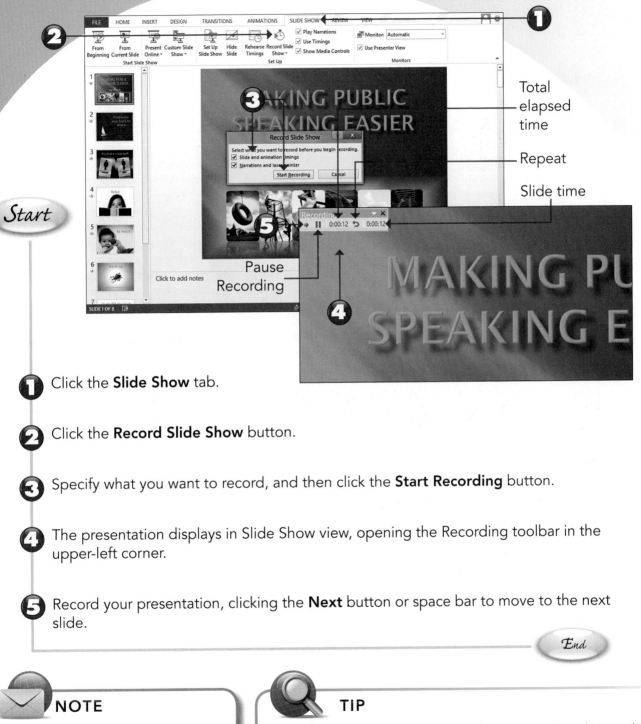

Total elapsed time

Repeat

Slide time

Pause Recording

Start

End

1. Click the **Slide Show** tab.

2. Click the **Record Slide Show** button.

3. Specify what you want to record, and then click the **Start Recording** button.

4. The presentation displays in Slide Show view, opening the Recording toolbar in the upper-left corner.

5. Record your presentation, clicking the **Next** button or space bar to move to the next slide.

NOTE

Preparing to Record   You need to have a microphone and a sound card to record a narration. And remember—the better the quality of the equipment you use, the more professional your narration will sound. ■

TIP

Playing and Deleting Narrations   To play voice narrations during a slide show, verify that the **Play Narrations** check box is selected on the Slide Show tab. To delete slide narrations, click the down arrow below the **Record Slide Show** button, and select **Clear**. From here, you can choose whether to clear timings or narrations on the current slide or all slides. ■

PRESENTING YOUR SHOW

After you set up your PowerPoint slide show, it's time to present it. When you present a show, PowerPoint uses the settings you entered in the Set Up Show dialog box and on the Slide Show tab.

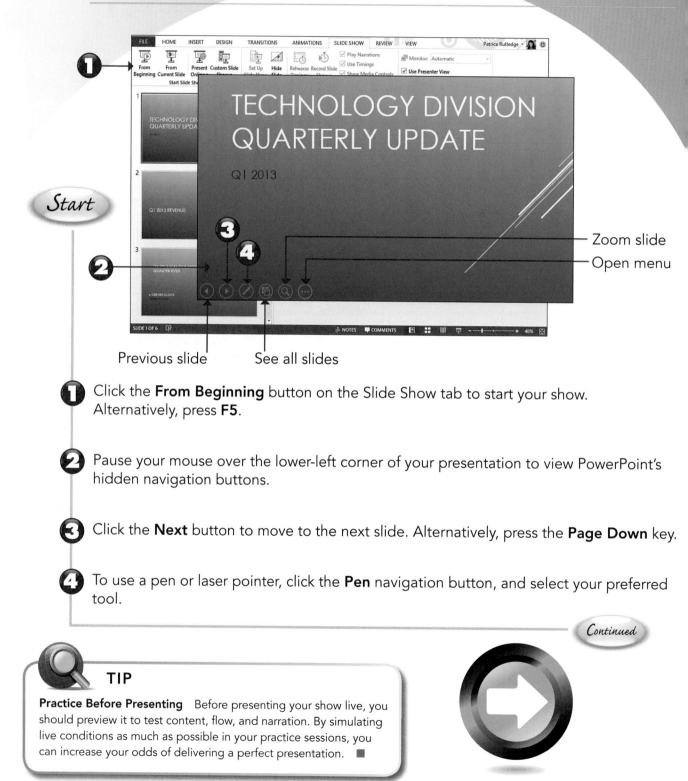

Zoom slide
Open menu

Previous slide
See all slides

Start

1 Click the **From Beginning** button on the Slide Show tab to start your show. Alternatively, press **F5**.

2 Pause your mouse over the lower-left corner of your presentation to view PowerPoint's hidden navigation buttons.

3 Click the **Next** button to move to the next slide. Alternatively, press the **Page Down** key.

4 To use a pen or laser pointer, click the **Pen** navigation button, and select your preferred tool.

Continued

TIP

Practice Before Presenting Before presenting your show live, you should preview it to test content, flow, and narration. By simulating live conditions as much as possible in your practice sessions, you can increase your odds of delivering a perfect presentation. ■

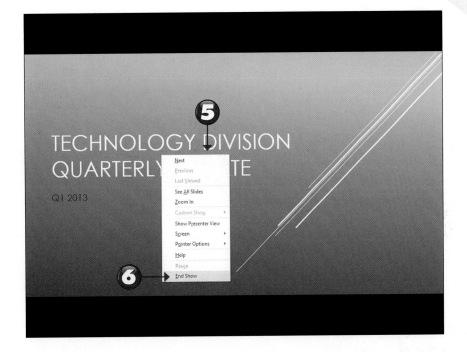

 Right-click to display a shortcut menu with options to show Presenter View, end your show, zoom, and more.

 Select **End Show** from the menu to end your show. Alternatively, press the **Esc** key.

End

TIP

Keyboard Commands Navigating your slide show with keyboard shortcut commands is another option. Right-click anywhere on the screen, and choose **Help** from the shortcut menu to display a list of shortcuts. ■

TIP

Arrow Pointer By default, PowerPoint displays an arrow pointer when you move your mouse and hides it after three seconds of inactivity. If you want to always or never display the arrow, right-click the slide, and choose **Pointer Options**, **Arrow Options** from the menu. ■

PRESENTING ONLINE

PowerPoint enables you to share your presentation in high fidelity with anyone on the Web, even if they don't have PowerPoint installed on their computer.

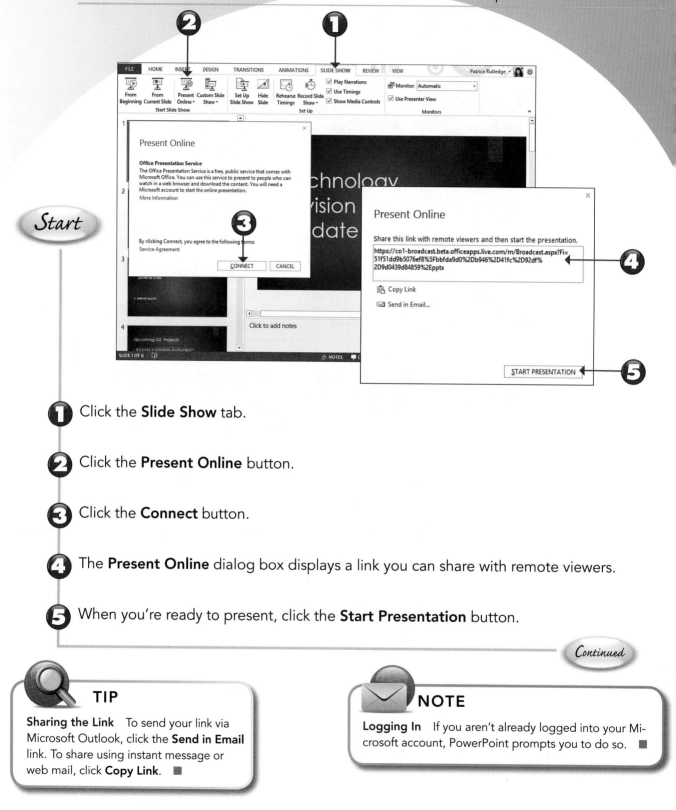

Start

1. Click the **Slide Show** tab.

2. Click the **Present Online** button.

3. Click the **Connect** button.

4. The **Present Online** dialog box displays a link you can share with remote viewers.

5. When you're ready to present, click the **Start Presentation** button.

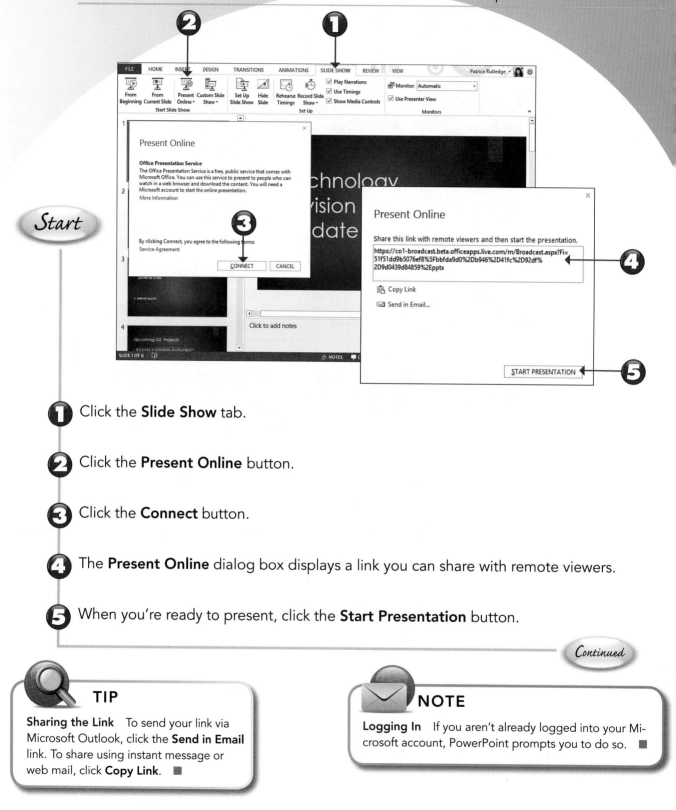

Continued

TIP

Sharing the Link To send your link via Microsoft Outlook, click the **Send in Email** link. To share using instant message or web mail, click **Copy Link**. ■

NOTE

Logging In If you aren't already logged into your Microsoft account, PowerPoint prompts you to do so. ■

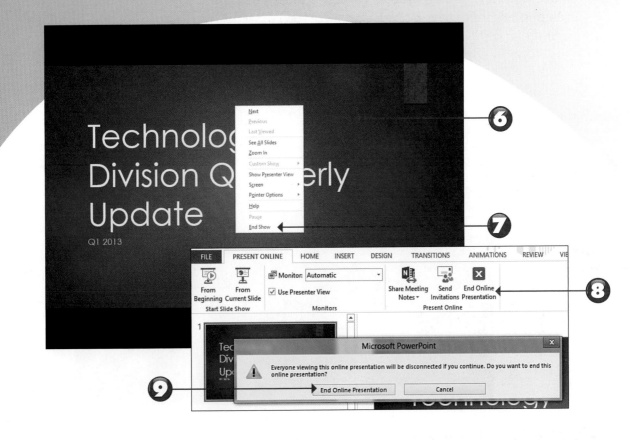

6 PowerPoint starts your slide show on the Web, where your viewers can see it.

7 When you finish your presentation, right-click and select **End Show**.

8 Click **End Online Presentation** on the Present Online tab to disconnect all your remote viewers.

9 Click **End Online Presentation** in the confirmation dialog box to confirm.

End

TIP

Present Online Tab Before broadcasting, review the options on the Present Online tab, where you can choose whether to start your show from the beginning or from the current slide, use Presenter View, share meeting notes, or send invitations. ■

TIP

Starting Manually To start Presenter View manually, right-click and select **Show Presenter View**. Learn more in the "Exploring Presenter View" section later in this chapter. ■

EXPLORING PRESENTER VIEW

Presenter View enables you to display a full-screen presentation that your audience can see and another view for you (the presenter) that includes slide previews, speaker notes, a timer, and more. Now explore some of the useful tools that Presenter View offers.

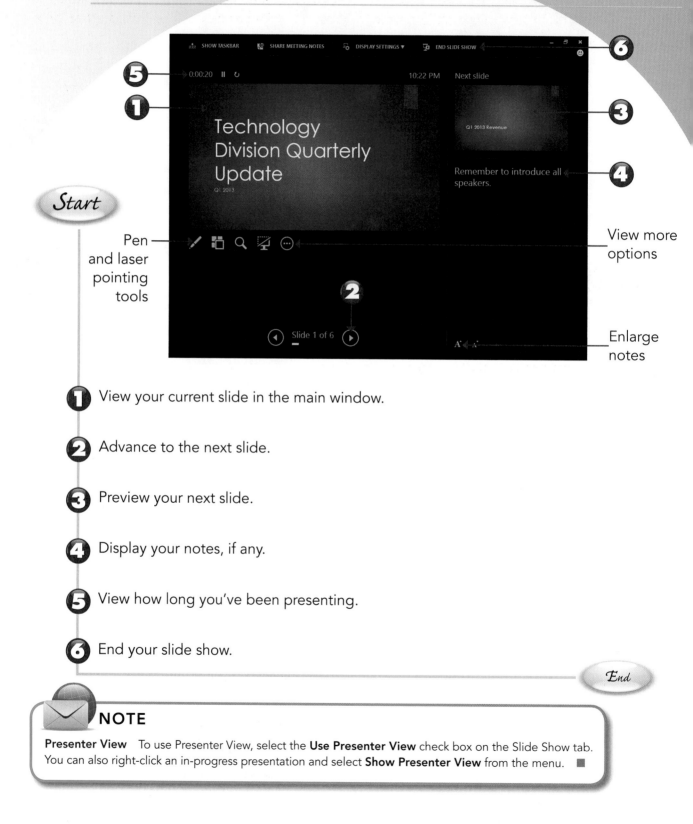

Pen and laser pointing tools

View more options

Enlarge notes

1 View your current slide in the main window.

2 Advance to the next slide.

3 Preview your next slide.

4 Display your notes, if any.

5 View how long you've been presenting.

6 End your slide show.

NOTE

Presenter View To use Presenter View, select the **Use Presenter View** check box on the Slide Show tab. You can also right-click an in-progress presentation and select **Show Presenter View** from the menu. ■

PowerPoint enables you to create full-fidelity video from your PowerPoint presentation in either a Windows Media Video (.wmv) or MPEG-4 Video (.mp4) format. You can distribute your video on the Web or mobile device, or through more traditional methods, such as on a DVD or through email.

Start

Export

Create PDF/XPS Document

Create a Video

Package Presentation for CD

Create Handouts

Change File Type

Create a Video

Save your presentation as a video that you can burn to a disc, upload to the web, or email

- Incorporates all recorded timings, narrations, and laser pointer gestures
- Preserves animations, transitions, and media

Get help burning your slide show video to DVD or uploading it to the web

Internet & DVD
For uploading to the Web and burning to standard DVD (Medium — 640 x 480)

Use Recorded Timings and Narrations
Slides that do not have timings will use the default duration set below. Any re...

Seconds spent on each slide: 05.00

Create Video

Desktop ▸

Organize ▾   New folder

Microsoft PowerPo

★ Favorites
  Desktop
  Downloads
  Recent places
  SkyDrive

Libraries
  Documents

Libraries
Homegroup
tthamkru
Computer
Network
PacificRidgePress
Downloads - Shortcut

File name: Making Public Speaking Easier

Save as type: MPEG-4 Video

Authors: Patrice   Tags: Add a tag

Hide Folders   Tools ▾   Save   Cancel

---

1 Click the **File** tab.

2 Select **Export** and then **Create a Video**.

3 Select your preferred video options.

4 Click the **Create Video** button.

5 Specify a filename, location, and video type.

6 Click the **Save** button.

End

TIP

Video Options Not sure which options to choose? PowerPoint offers explanations below each option that help you decide which is best for your presentation. ■

Chapter 19

SENDING AND RECEIVING MESSAGES

Microsoft Outlook is the perfect tool for communicating with others via email. You can use Outlook's Mail component to view, respond to, forward, and compose new emails, as well as create folders for organizing the emails you send and receive. You can use Outlook's many email features to attach files and open files you receive, as well as view information about contacts associated with the messages.

You can also set up Outlook to work with multiple email accounts and use a variety of tools to help you manage your messages. For example, you can set up a filter to weed out junk mail and spam. This chapter presents several key emailing features to get you up and running fast and communicating with the world at large.

NAVIGATING THE OUTLOOK PROGRAM SCREEN

Messages are
listed here

Use the
Folder Pane
to view email
accounts

The Reading
Pane lets you
read and reply
to messages

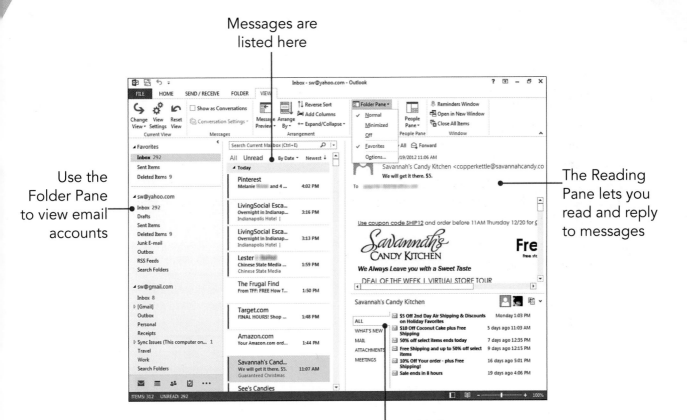

The People Pane displays
at-a-glance information
about a contact

ADD AN EMAIL ACCOUNT

You can set up Outlook to work with multiple email accounts from different services, such as Hotmail, Gmail, or Yahoo!. This enables you to check all your email from various services in one convenient spot.

Start

1. From the Outlook program window, click **File**.

2. The Info page appears by default; if not click **Info**.

3. Click **Add Account**.

4. Type your name.

5. Type your email address.

6. Type your password and then retype it.

7. Click **Next**.

Continued

NOTE

Manually Configuring Outlook attempts to automatically configure new email accounts you add. However, some email service providers might require additional setup steps. Be sure to contact your provider for help and then try the **Manual setup or additional server types** option in the Add Account dialog box to set up the account manually. ■

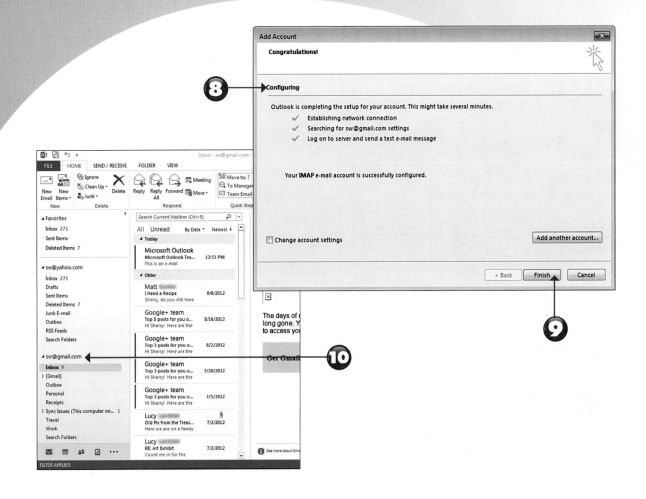

8 Outlook configures your account.

9 Click **Finish**.

10 Outlook displays your account.

End

TIP

Remove It! To remove an email account you no longer use, click **File**, **Info**, and then click the **Account Settings** button; choose **Account Settings**. This opens the Account Settings dialog box where you can change, repair, or remove accounts. Click the account you want to remove from the list, and click the **Remove** button. ■

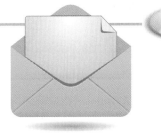

EXPLORING THE OUTLOOK LAYOUT

Outlook's program window is divided into panes that you can expand and collapse to change the view. You can use the View tab to change how panes display, or expand and collapse them using their icons.

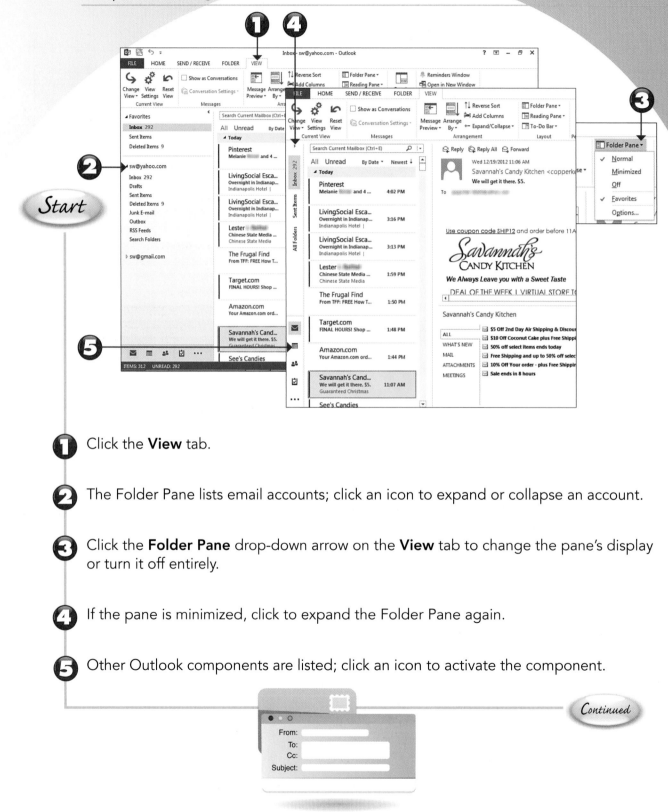

Start

1 Click the **View** tab.

2 The Folder Pane lists email accounts; click an icon to expand or collapse an account.

3 Click the **Folder Pane** drop-down arrow on the **View** tab to change the pane's display or turn it off entirely.

4 If the pane is minimized, click to expand the Folder Pane again.

5 Other Outlook components are listed; click an icon to activate the component.

Continued

From:

To:

Cc:

Subject:

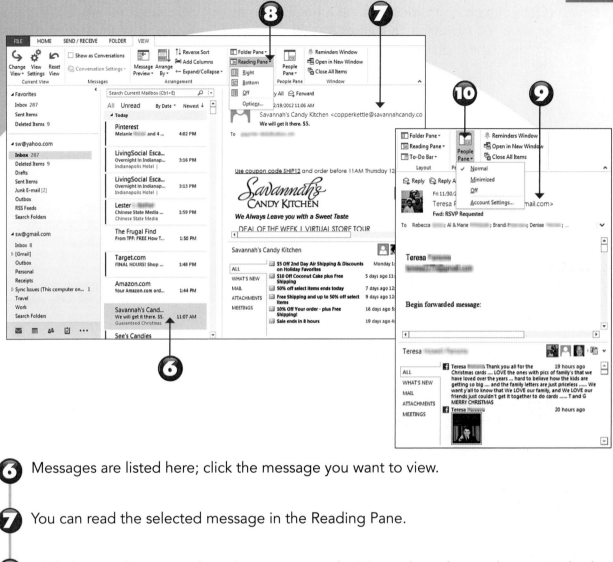

6 Messages are listed here; click the message you want to view.

7 You can read the selected message in the Reading Pane.

8 Click the **Reading Pane** drop-down arrow on the **View** tab to change the pane's display or turn it off entirely.

9 Read information about a particular contact in the People Pane.

10 Click **People Pane** to control its display.

End

TIP

Message Preview In addition to controlling the Reading Pane, you can also control how many lines from a message appear in the message list pane. By default, Outlook displays 1 line, but you can choose to view more or no message lines at all; click the **Message Preview** button on the **View** tab, and make a selection. ■

SENDING AN EMAIL MESSAGE

When composing a message in Outlook, you can use a message window. The message window includes tabs of options for formatting message text, attaching files, adding pictures, and more.

Start

New Hot Dog Recipes - Message (HTML)

FILE | MESSAGE | INSERT | OPTIONS | FORMAT TEXT | REVIEW

Calibri (Body) · 11 · A˚ A˚
B I U
Paste
Clipboard ⌐   Basic Text

Address Check
Book Names
Names

Attach File
Attach Item ·
Signature ·
Include

Follow Up ·
! High Importance
↓ Low Importance
Tags ⌐

Zoom
Zoom

From · | sw@yahoo.com
To... | ogredogs@yahoo.com
Cc...
Subject | New Hot Dog Recipes

Matt, I just heard about the new hot dog recipes and can't wait to try them! When are you open again?

ogredogs@yahoo.com

There are no items to show in this view.

FILE | MESSAGE | INSERT

Arial
Paste
Clipboard ⌐   Basic Text

Send

From · | sw@yah
To... | ogredogs
Cc...
Subject | New Hot

Matt, I just heard abo
are you open again?

ogredogs@yahoo.com

ALL
WHAT'S NEW
MAIL
ATTACHMENTS
MEETINGS

---

1 Click the **Home** tab.

2 Click **New Email**.

3 Type in the recipient's email address, or if it's already stored in your Address book, click the **To** button and choose the address.

4 Click in the **Subject** box and type in a message title.

5 Click here and type in your message text.

6 To change the formatting, such as a different font or size, choose from the **Message** tab's options, or click the **Format Text** tab for more formatting commands.

7 Click **Send** to send the message.

End

TIP

Send and Receive   To check for new email or send any messages waiting in your outbox, click the **Send/Receive** tab, and click **Send/Receive All Folders**. You can also click the **Send/Receive All Folders** button on the Quick Access toolbar. ■

Each email account you have set up in Outlook is listed in the Folder pane where you can choose which Inbox you want to view. You can read any message in your Inbox using the Reading pane, or you can open the message in its own window.

Start

1 Click **Send/Receive All Folders**.

2 From the Folder Pane, click the account **Inbox** you want to view.

3 Double-click the message you want to read.

4 Outlook opens the message in its own window.

5 Click here to close the window.

End

TIP

The Reading Pane You can also use the Reading Pane to read a selected message. If the pane is not visible, click the **View** tab, click **Reading Pane**, and then click **Right** or **Bottom** to turn on the pane. ■

TIP

New in Outlook 2013! You can now reply and forward messages you read in the Reading Pane. Simply click the **Reply**, **Reply All**, or **Forward** buttons at the top of the message and enter your new message. Click the **Pop Out** button to open the message in its own window. ■

REPLYING TO A MESSAGE

You can reply to a message from the Reading Pane or open the message window. The message window offers access to more commands and features for helping you format the message, proofread it, or insert pictures. When you reply to a message from the Reading Pane, an abbreviated group of commonly used formatting tools appears on the Message tab.

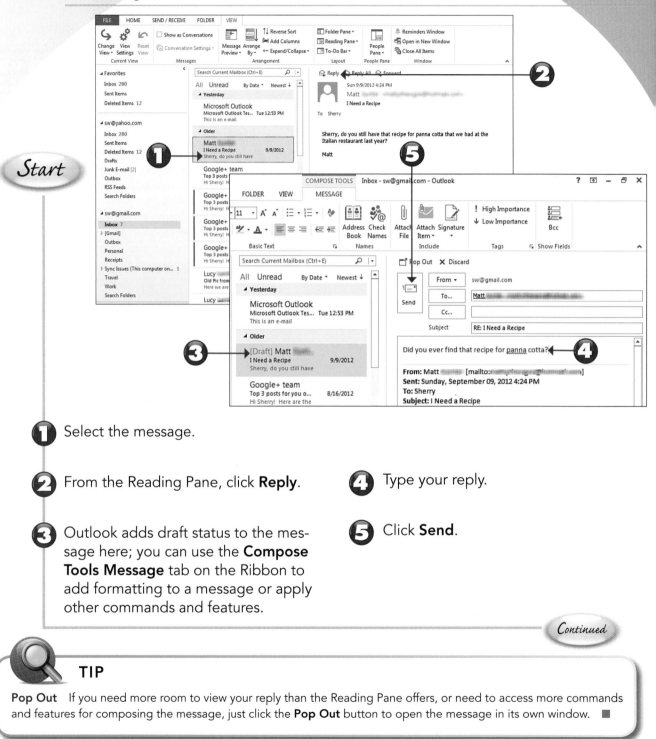

Start

1 Select the message.

2 From the Reading Pane, click **Reply**.

3 Outlook adds draft status to the message here; you can use the **Compose Tools Message** tab on the Ribbon to add formatting to a message or apply other commands and features.

4 Type your reply.

5 Click **Send**.

Continued

TIP

Pop Out If you need more room to view your reply than the Reading Pane offers, or need to access more commands and features for composing the message, just click the **Pop Out** button to open the message in its own window. ■

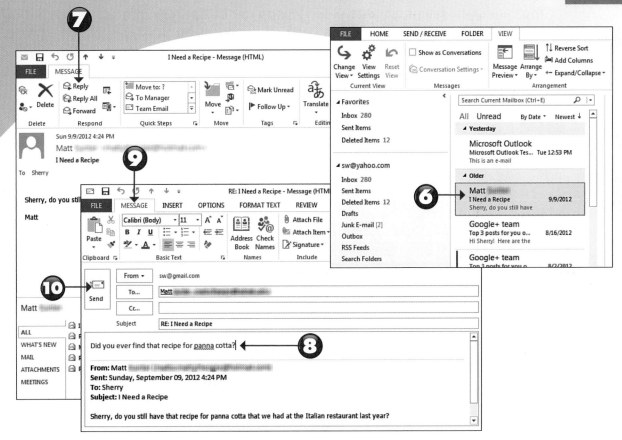

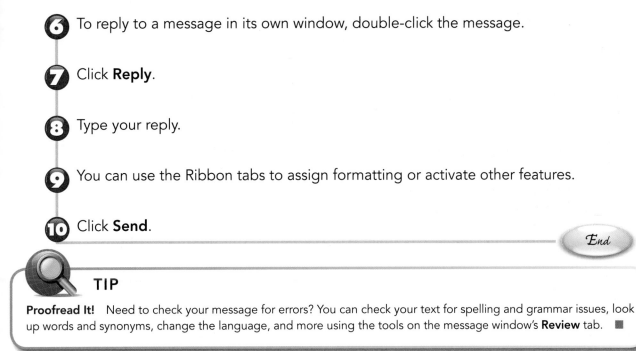

6 To reply to a message in its own window, double-click the message.

7 Click **Reply**.

8 Type your reply.

9 You can use the Ribbon tabs to assign formatting or activate other features.

10 Click **Send**.

End

TIP

Proofread It! Need to check your message for errors? You can check your text for spelling and grammar issues, look up words and synonyms, change the language, and more using the tools on the message window's **Review** tab. ■

FORWARDING A MESSAGE

You can forward a message to send it along to another recipient. Much like a reply, you can use the Forward option in the Reading Pane, or you can open the message in its own window and Forward it from there.

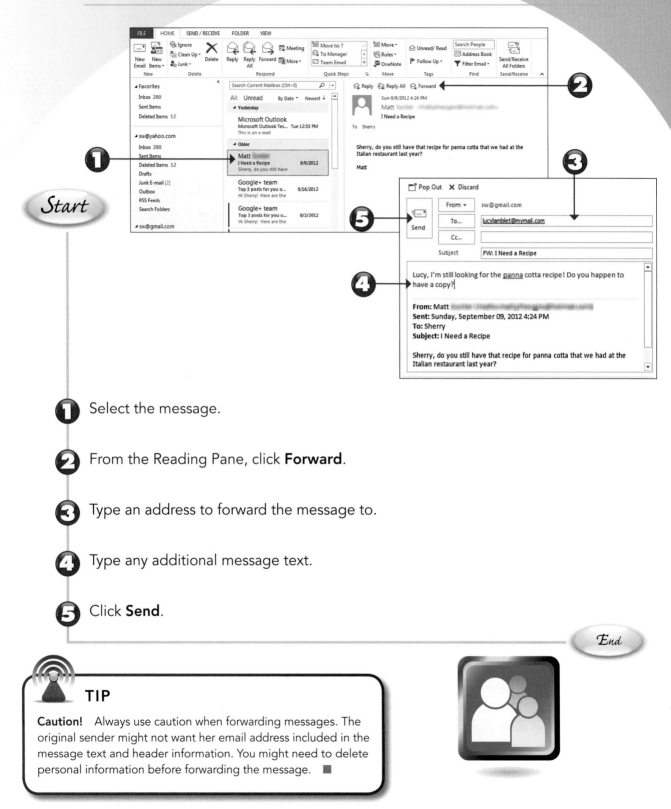

Start

1. Select the message.

2. From the Reading Pane, click **Forward**.

3. Type an address to forward the message to.

4. Type any additional message text.

5. Click **Send**.

End

TIP

Caution! Always use caution when forwarding messages. The original sender might not want her email address included in the message text and header information. You might need to delete personal information before forwarding the message. ■

You can send files stored on your computer to other email recipients. For example, if you need to send a document file to a colleague, you can attach it to your message.

Start

1. On the message window's Ribbon, click the **Message** tab.

2. Click **Attach File**. The Insert File dialog box opens.

3. Navigate to the file you want to attach and select the filename.

4. Click **Insert**.

5. Outlook attaches the file.

End

TIP

Attach Items You can use the **Attach Item** command on the **Message** tab to attach other Outlook items to the email, such as a business card, a calendar, another email, or a task. ∎

TIP

Open Attachments To open an attachment sent to you, double-click the attachment filename, and click **Open**. ∎

CREATING AN EMAIL SIGNATURE

A signature is a string of text that appears at the bottom of every email message you send. Signatures can include contact information, a personal quote or motto, or other special information.

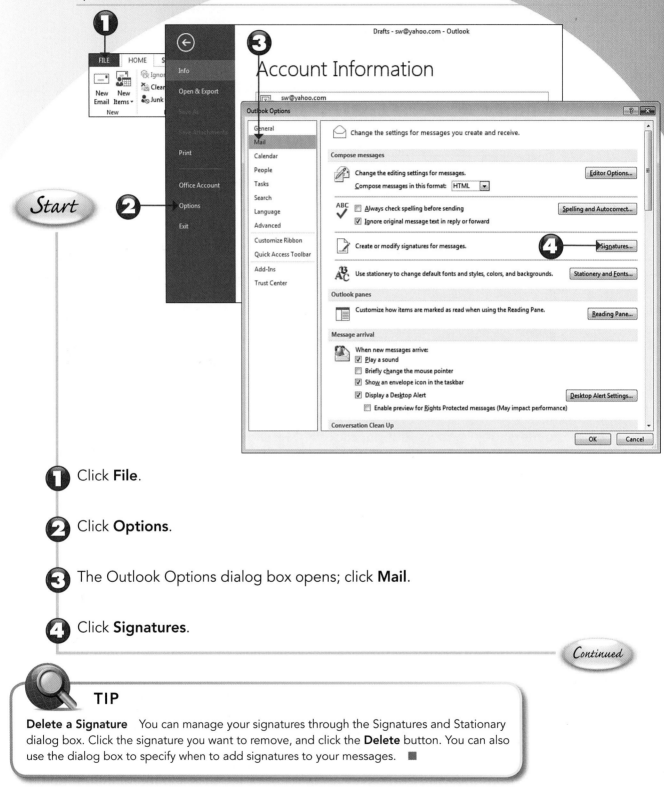

1 Click **File**.

2 Click **Options**.

3 The Outlook Options dialog box opens; click **Mail**.

4 Click **Signatures**.

Continued

TIP

Delete a Signature   You can manage your signatures through the Signatures and Stationary dialog box. Click the signature you want to remove, and click the **Delete** button. You can also use the dialog box to specify when to add signatures to your messages. ■

5 The Signatures and Stationary dialog box opens; click **New**.

6 Type a name for the signature.

7 Click **OK**.

8 Type your signature text and format it.

9 Click **OK**.

10 Click **OK**.

End

TIP

Choose One! If you create more than one signature, you can choose which one to add to a message. From the message window, click the **Signature** drop-down arrow and click the signature you want to apply. ■

You can set up rules that tell Outlook what to do with different messages you receive. For example, if you receive a spam email, you can identify it as spam with a rule and keep it from appearing in your Inbox again. You can also create rules to filter other types of unwanted emails.

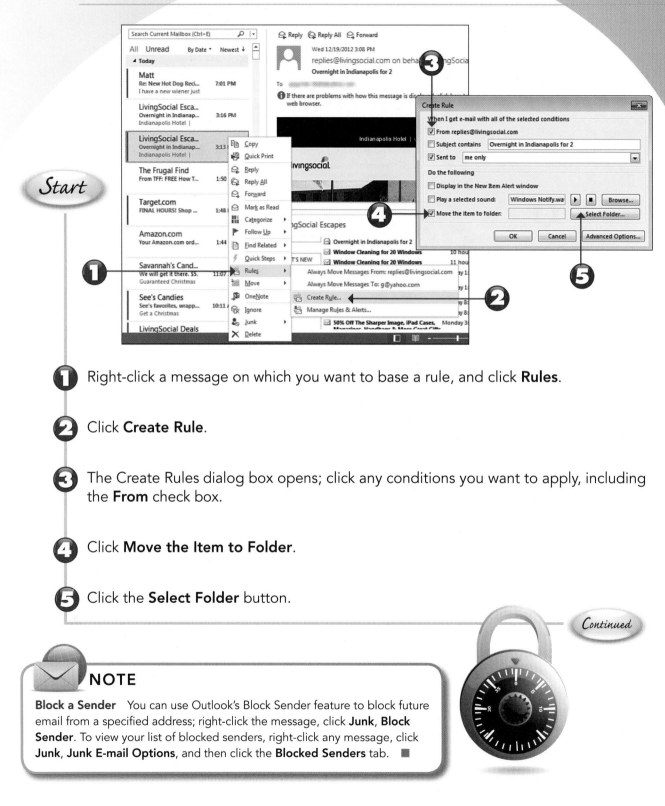

1 Right-click a message on which you want to base a rule, and click **Rules**.

2 Click **Create Rule**.

3 The Create Rules dialog box opens; click any conditions you want to apply, including the **From** check box.

4 Click **Move the Item to Folder**.

5 Click the **Select Folder** button.

Continued

NOTE

Block a Sender   You can use Outlook's Block Sender feature to block future email from a specified address; right-click the message, click **Junk**, **Block Sender**. To view your list of blocked senders, right-click any message, click **Junk**, **Junk E-mail Options**, and then click the **Blocked Senders** tab. ■

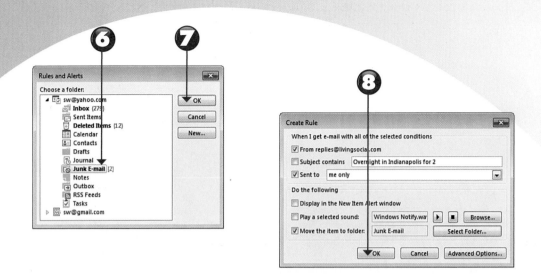

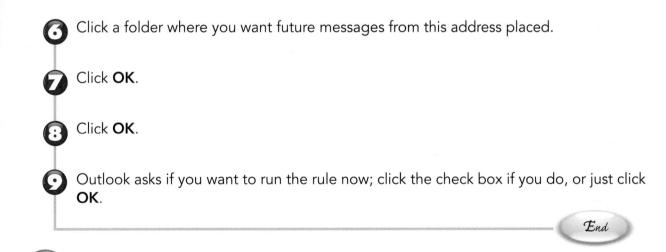

6 Click a folder where you want future messages from this address placed.

7 Click **OK**.

8 Click **OK**.

9 Outlook asks if you want to run the rule now; click the check box if you do, or just click **OK**.

End

TIP

Moving Messages You can organize your messages into folders and move messages around as needed. To create a new folder in the Folder Pane, right-click the **Inbox**, click **New Folder**, and then give it a distinct name. To move a message to the folder, right-click the message, click **Move**, and then click **Other Folder**. The Move Items dialog box opens; specify which one and click **OK**. ■

Chapter 20

ORGANIZING AND SCHEDULING IN OUTLOOK

Microsoft Outlook isn't just for email. You can use the program to stay organized, on track, and on schedule. Outlook's other components include Calendar, Contacts, and Tasks. You can use Calendar to keep track of your daily activities and set up appointments, meetings, and other calendar items. You can share your calendar with others, set up alarms to remind you about upcoming meetings, and publish your calendar online. You can use Contacts to manage your ever-growing list of contacts, including friends and family, business colleagues, and more. You can use Tasks to help you organize important things you need to tackle, whether it's an office project or just a shopping list to take with you and check off on the way home from work.

NAVIGATING THE OUTLOOK CALENDAR

The Calendar shows your schedule in daily, weekly, or monthly views

You can use the Date Navigator to view a specific date on the Calendar

You can click a component icon to switch between Mail, Contacts, Calendar, Tasks, and Notes

You can use Outlook's Contacts component, also called People, as a digital address book to manage all the people in your life, such as friends, work colleagues, clients, and such. You can keep relevant information, including phone numbers, email addresses, web pages, and more, just a glance away using the new People Cards. You can choose several ways to view your contacts.

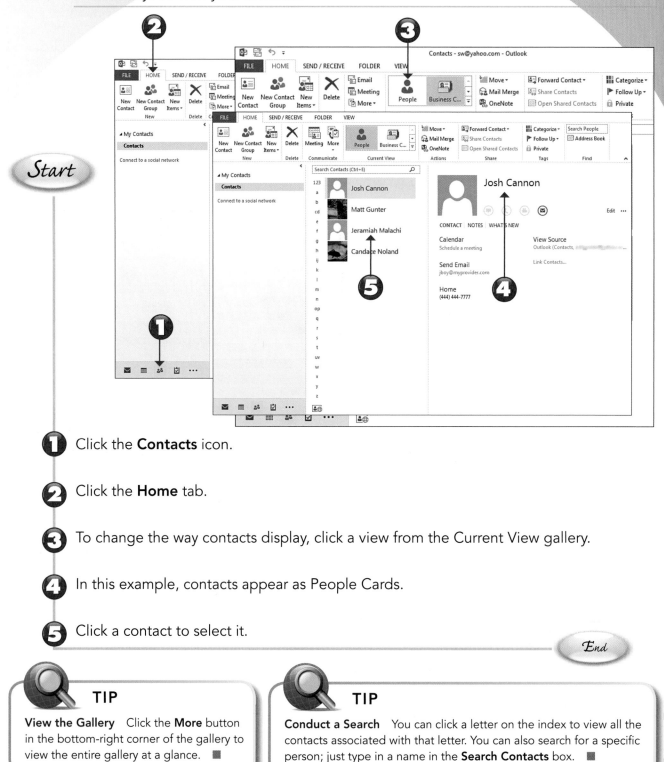

1 Click the **Contacts** icon.

2 Click the **Home** tab.

3 To change the way contacts display, click a view from the Current View gallery.

4 In this example, contacts appear as People Cards.

5 Click a contact to select it.

TIP

View the Gallery Click the **More** button in the bottom-right corner of the gallery to view the entire gallery at a glance. ■

TIP

Conduct a Search You can click a letter on the index to view all the contacts associated with that letter. You can also search for a specific person; just type in a name in the **Search Contacts** box. ■

EMAILING A CONTACT

Using Outlook's People Cards, you can quickly email a contact or schedule a meeting. Both options tap into Outlook's other components: Mail and Calendar. This task shows you how to email a contact.

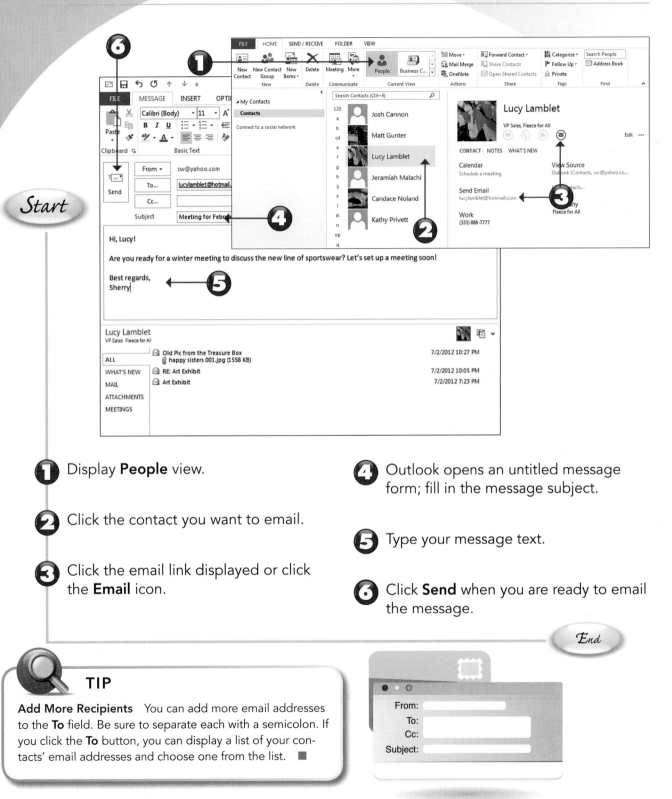

Start

End

1. Display **People** view.

2. Click the contact you want to email.

3. Click the email link displayed or click the **Email** icon.

4. Outlook opens an untitled message form; fill in the message subject.

5. Type your message text.

6. Click **Send** when you are ready to email the message.

TIP

Add More Recipients You can add more email addresses to the **To** field. Be sure to separate each with a semicolon. If you click the **To** button, you can display a list of your contacts' email addresses and choose one from the list. ■

ADDING A NEW CONTACT

You can easily add new contacts to your contacts list and choose exactly which types of information to include. The new contact form offers the most fields for filling in contact information.

1 Click the **Home** tab.

2 Click **New Contact**.

3 An untitled contact form opens.

4 Click to expand your view of the form's fields, if needed.

Continued

TIP

New Syncing With Outlook's new Exchange ActiveSync, you can use Outlook alongside other popular services (such as Hotmail or Gmail) and share access with contacts, calendars, and email. It's easy to add accounts; click the **File** tab, click **Info**, and then click the **Add Account** button. Choose to add or remove accounts or edit existing settings. ■

The contact form shows **Kathy Privett - Contact** with fields filled in:

- **Full Name...** Kathy Privett
- **Company**
- **Job title**
- **File as** Privett, Kathy

Internet
- **E-mail...** kp@skynet.com
- **Display as** Kathy Privett
- **Web page address**
- **IM address**

Phone numbers
- **Business...**
- **Home...** (555) 444-4444
- **Business Fax...**
- **Mobile...** (555) 444-5553

Addresses
- **Business...**
- ☐ This is the mailing address

Business card panel:
Kathy Privett
(555) 444-5553 Mobile
(555) 444-4444 Home
kp@skynet.com

⑤ Fill in the contact information you want to include.

⑥ Optionally, click to add a contact picture.

⑦ When finished, click **Save & Close**, and Word adds the new contact to your list.

End

TIP

Delete It! If you change your mind about adding a contact, click the **Delete** button to exit the form and discard any data you entered. To remove a contact already in your contacts list, select it and click the **Delete** button on the **Home** tab. ■

TIP

Editing Contacts You can make changes to contact information simply by clicking the **Edit Contact** link in People view and choosing fields to edit. If you prefer to use the original form used to create the contact, double-click a contact name in any other view. ■

You can use Outlook's Calendar component to keep track of your appointments, dates, and other scheduled events. Depending on how you want to view your information, Calendar offers several view modes you can switch between: Day, Week, and Month. You can also view just the work week or scheduled appointments.

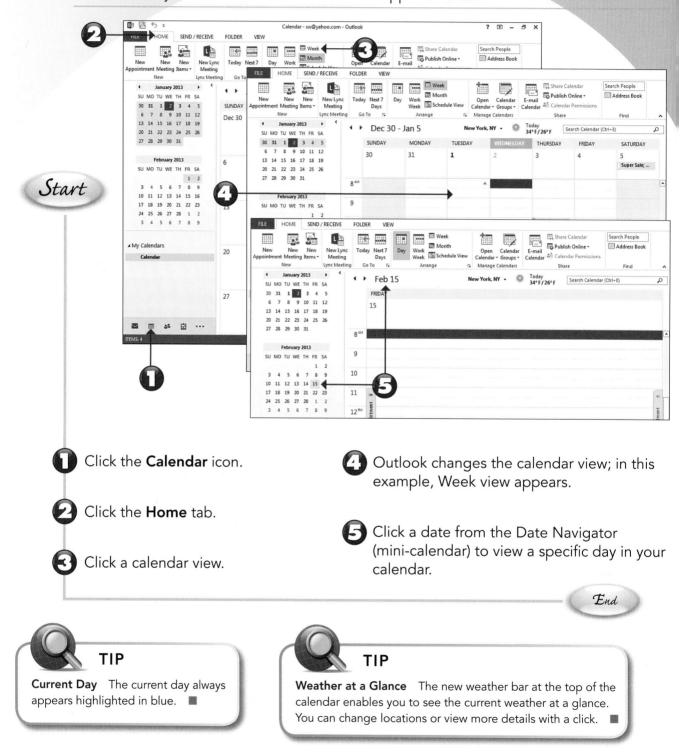

Start

1 Click the **Calendar** icon.

2 Click the **Home** tab.

3 Click a calendar view.

4 Outlook changes the calendar view; in this example, Week view appears.

5 Click a date from the Date Navigator (mini-calendar) to view a specific day in your calendar.

End

TIP

Current Day The current day always appears highlighted in blue. ■

TIP

Weather at a Glance The new weather bar at the top of the calendar enables you to see the current weather at a glance. You can change locations or view more details with a click. ■

You can schedule an appointment on your calendar using a form to fill out appointment details, such as setting a reminder alarm or specifying start and end times for the appointment.

Start

1 Click **New Appointment** on the **Home** tab.

2 An untitled appointment form opens; type a subject title for the appointment.

3 Optionally, you can specify a location if needed.

4 Set a start and end time using the drop-down menus and choosing specific times.

5 Optionally, type any notes you want to include about the appointment.

6 Click **Save & Close** to save the appointment and add it to the calendar.

End

TIP

Shortcut You can also double-click a date on the calendar to open the appointment form. When you do, be sure to unselect the **All Day Event** check box to create a regular appointment. ■

TIP

Appointment Options Click the **Options** drop-down arrow on the **Appointment** tab in the form to choose from display options for shared calendars, set a recurring appointment, or assign a reminder alarm. ■

SCHEDULING A MEETING

You can use Outlook's Calendar to set up meetings and email attendees. You can keep track of who is attending your meeting and check their calendars for availability as well.

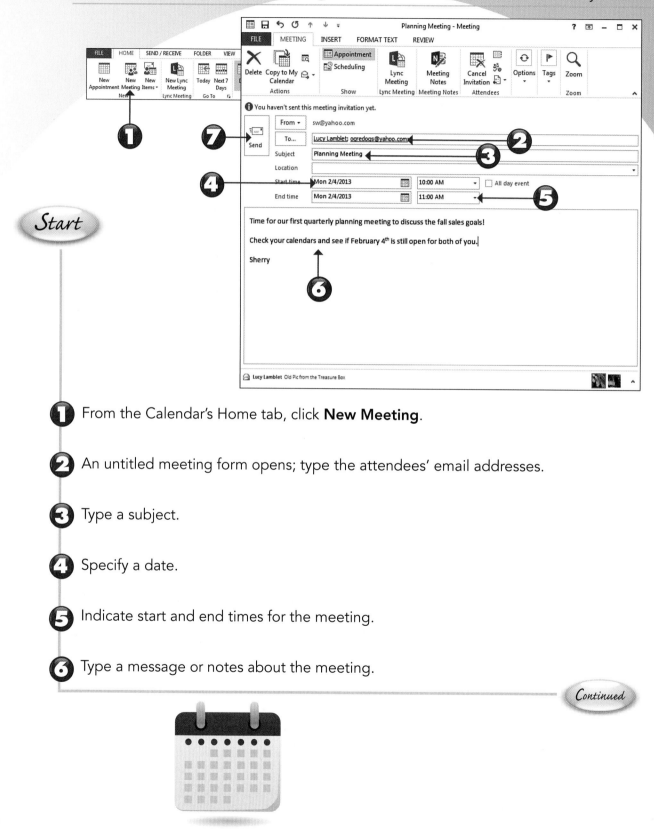

Start

1 From the Calendar's Home tab, click **New Meeting**.

2 An untitled meeting form opens; type the attendees' email addresses.

3 Type a subject.

4 Specify a date.

5 Indicate start and end times for the meeting.

6 Type a message or notes about the meeting.

Continued

7 Click **Send**.

8 Outlook adds the meeting to your calendar and sends a message to notify others.

End

TIP

Check Responses To see who is attending, double-click the appointment in the calendar to open the appointment form window. Expand the People pane at the bottom of the form to view who has accepted, declined, or not responded to your invitation. ▪

SHARING YOUR CALENDAR

You can share your calendar with others or online. One way to share it is to email it, which attaches the file as well as embeds it into the email message.

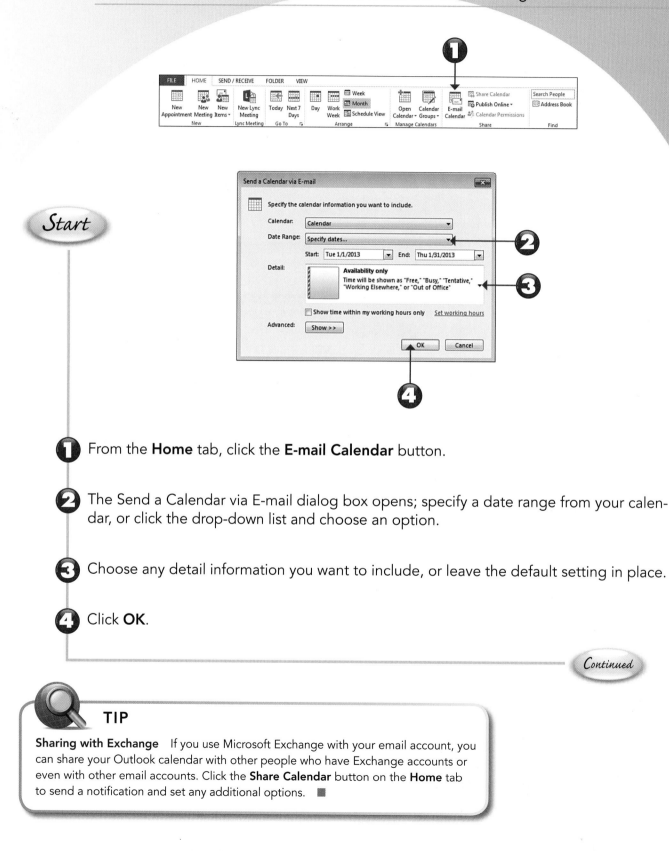

From the **Home** tab, click the **E-mail Calendar** button.

The Send a Calendar via E-mail dialog box opens; specify a date range from your calendar, or click the drop-down list and choose an option.

Choose any detail information you want to include, or leave the default setting in place.

Click **OK**.

Continued

TIP

Sharing with Exchange   If you use Microsoft Exchange with your email account, you can share your Outlook calendar with other people who have Exchange accounts or even with other email accounts. Click the **Share Calendar** button on the **Home** tab to send a notification and set any additional options. ■

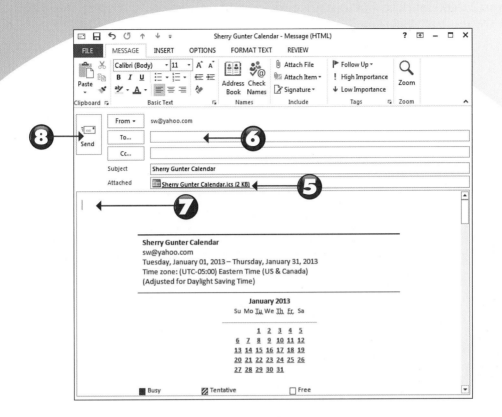

5 Outlook adds the calendar data as an attachment and embeds it in the message text.

6 Type the recipient's email address.

7 Type any additional message text you want to include.

8 Click **Send**.

End

NOTE

Publish It You can also publish your calendar online if you have space on a server using Microsoft's WebDAV feature. Click the **Publish Online** button on the **Home** tab, and choose **Publish to WebDAV Server** to start the process. ◼

From:
To:
Cc:
Subject:

CREATING A TASK

Use Outlook's tasking feature to create activity directives such as To-Do lists, projects, and more. Tasks can help you keep track of and manage project steps and other important things you need to accomplish.

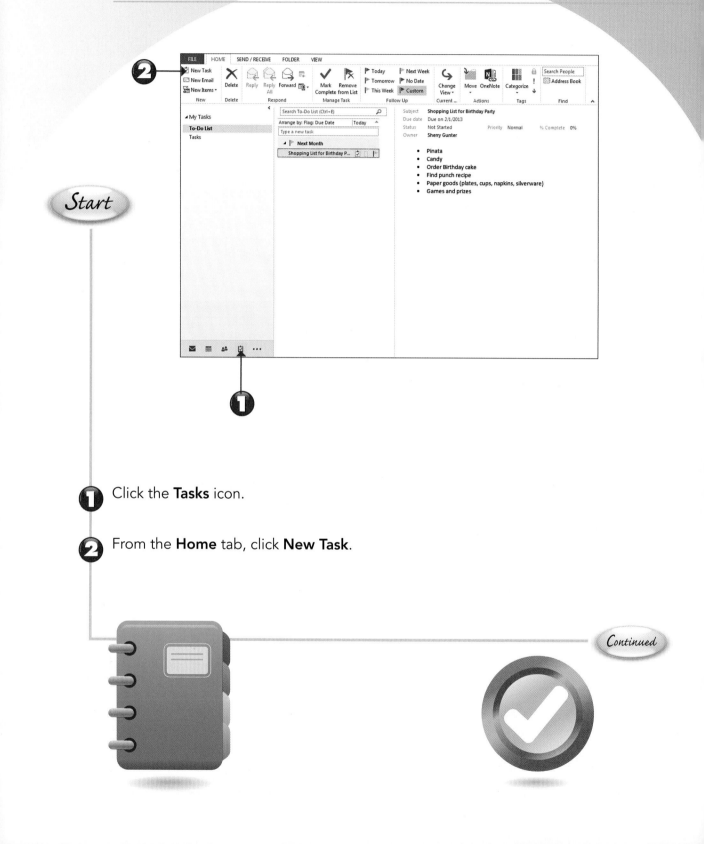

Start

1 Click the **Tasks** icon.

2 From the **Home** tab, click **New Task**.

Continued

3 An untitled task form opens; type a subject for the task.

4 Specify a start date and status, if needed.

5 Choose a due date for task completion.

6 Set any additional options, such as priority level or a reminder alarm.

7 Type your task information.

8 Click **Save & Close**.

9 Outlook adds the task view; this example shows the To-Do List view.

End

TIP

Change Task Views You can view your tasks in a variety of ways. The To-Do List view is the default when you first open Tasks. You can choose to view tasks by details, a simple list, priority, completion, and so on. To change views, click the **Change View** button on the **Home** tab, and choose another view. ■

MANAGING TASKS

You can manage your tasks by marking them when complete or removing them from the list when you no longer need to see them. You can edit tasks in any Tasks view. To see the tasks, even when complete, you must use another view besides the To-Do List view.

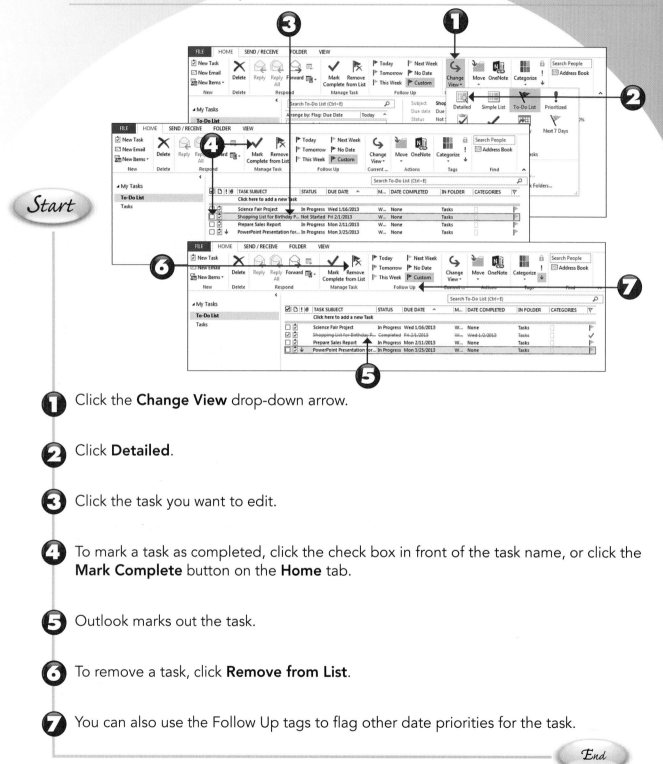

Start

1. Click the **Change View** drop-down arrow.

2. Click **Detailed**.

3. Click the task you want to edit.

4. To mark a task as completed, click the check box in front of the task name, or click the **Mark Complete** button on the **Home** tab.

5. Outlook marks out the task.

6. To remove a task, click **Remove from List**.

7. You can also use the Follow Up tags to flag other date priorities for the task.

End

CREATING NOTES

You can use Outlook's Notes feature to jot down notes for yourself. Notes resemble sticky notes that you can move around, even onto the Microsoft Windows desktop.

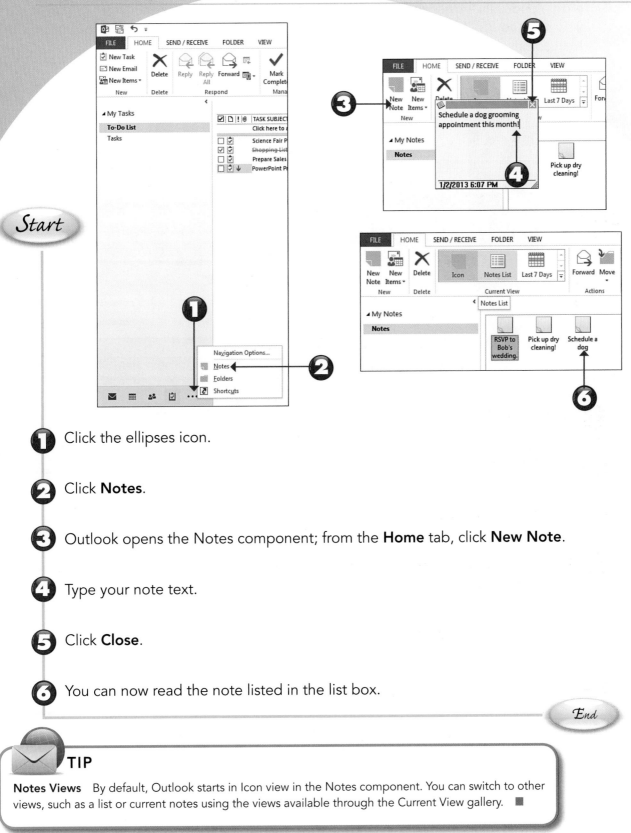

Start

1. Click the ellipses icon.

2. Click **Notes**.

3. Outlook opens the Notes component; from the **Home** tab, click **New Note**.

4. Type your note text.

5. Click **Close**.

6. You can now read the note listed in the list box.

End

TIP

Notes Views By default, Outlook starts in Icon view in the Notes component. You can switch to other views, such as a list or current notes using the views available through the Current View gallery. ■

SUBSCRIBING TO RSS FEEDS

RSS feeds, or Really Simple Syndication, is a technology that enables web content to be converted into a feed that is viewed as message posts. You can receive RSS feeds for blogs, podcasts, news, and more. You can use Outlook to check the latest updates of your favorite RSS feeds. Feeds you subscribe to appear in the RSS Feeds folder in the Mail component.

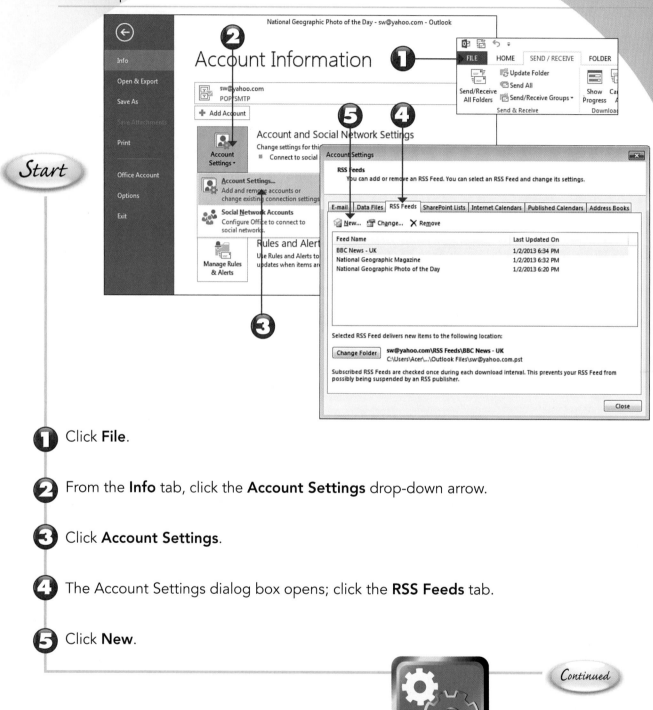

Start

1 Click **File**.

2 From the **Info** tab, click the **Account Settings** drop-down arrow.

3 Click **Account Settings**.

4 The Account Settings dialog box opens; click the **RSS Feeds** tab.

5 Click **New**.

Continued

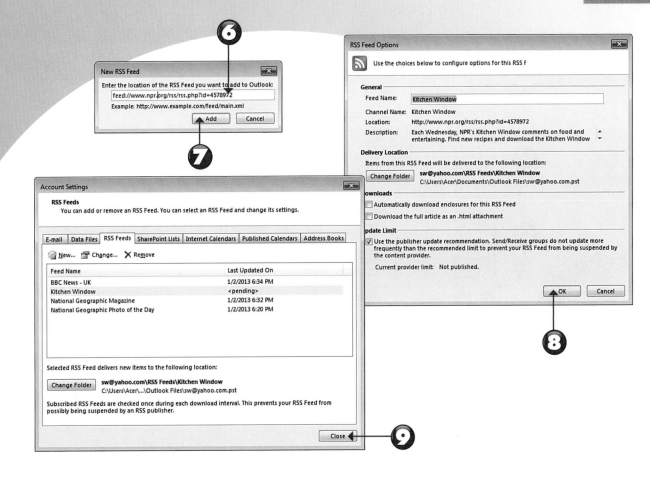

(6) Type the RSS Feed address.

(7) Click **Add**.

(8) The RSS Feed Options dialog box appears with a general name for the feed already assigned. Click **OK** to continue.

(9) The RSS Feed is added to the list box; click **Close**.

Continued

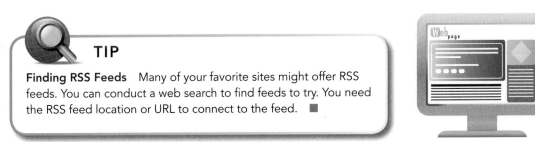

TIP

Finding RSS Feeds   Many of your favorite sites might offer RSS feeds. You can conduct a web search to find feeds to try. You need the RSS feed location or URL to connect to the feed. ■

10 Click the **Send/Receive** tab.

11 Click **Send/Receive All Folders** to update the latest posts.

12 Click the **RSS Feeds** folder to view your RSS feeds subfolders to which you are subscribed.

13 Click the folder you want to open.

14 Click the message you want to view.

15 You can read the message in the Preview Pane.

End

TIP

Unsubscribing If you no longer want to subscribe to an RSS Feed, reopen the **Account Settings** dialog box to the **RSS Feeds** tab, select the Feed Name, and then click the **Remove** button. ■

Chapter 21

CREATING NOTEBOOKS

OneNote is a handy organizing program you can use to help keep track of various pieces of information. Acting as a digital three-ring binder, you can use OneNote to store and organize clippings and text notes, as well as visual items such as digital photos and artwork, video clips, and more. You can move notes around and organize them into pages any way you want. You'll find plenty of uses for OneNote around the home, school, or the office. You can also print and share your digital notebooks and store them online in Microsoft's Cloud storage.

Notebooks are composed of pages and sections. You can add as many of each as you need. Sections display as tabs across the top of the page, whereas pages appear as tabs along the right side of the screen. Like all the other Office programs, OneNote displays commands, tools, and features on the Ribbon at the top of the program window. However, to give you plenty of space to work with your notebook pages, the Ribbon may be minimized until you need it. You never need to save your work in OneNote; the program saves things automatically for you as you go along.

ADDING NOTES IN NOTEBOOK

Text notes appear in their own moveable containers

Organize your notebook into sections

You can draw your own art-work, lines, and shapes

You can insert pictures of all kinds onto your notebook pages

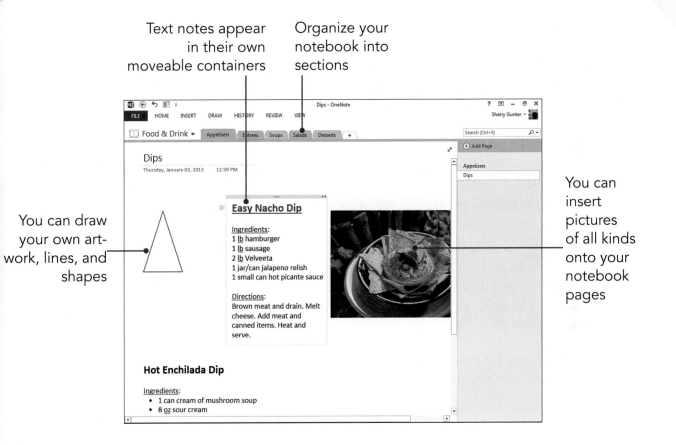

CREATING A NEW NOTEBOOK

Items you collect and store digitally with OneNote are placed into *notebooks*. Like a regular paper notebook, your digital notebooks are built page by page. When you create a notebook, OneNote starts with a single, blank page. You can start adding notes anywhere on the page.

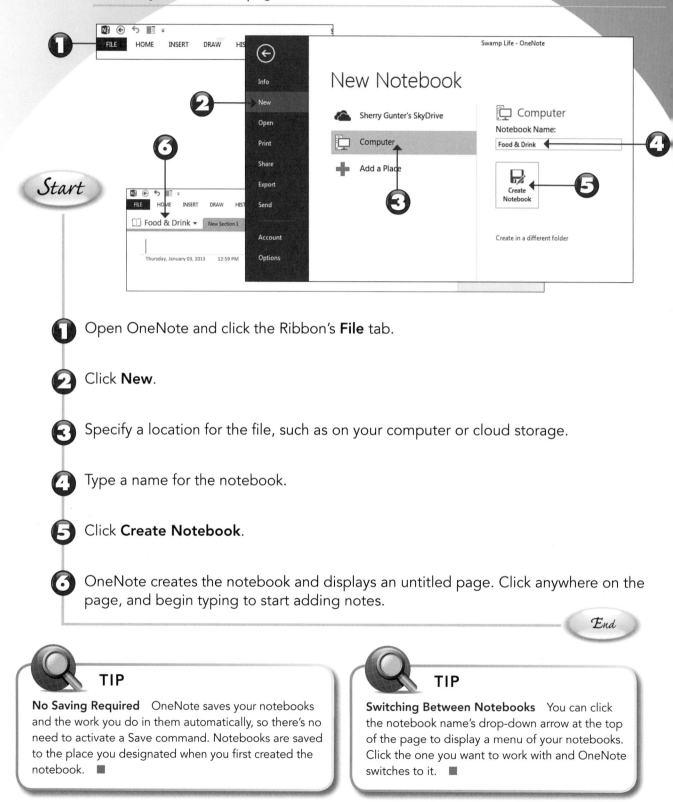

1 Open OneNote and click the Ribbon's **File** tab.

2 Click **New**.

3 Specify a location for the file, such as on your computer or cloud storage.

4 Type a name for the notebook.

5 Click **Create Notebook**.

6 OneNote creates the notebook and displays an untitled page. Click anywhere on the page, and begin typing to start adding notes.

End

TIP

No Saving Required OneNote saves your notebooks and the work you do in them automatically, so there's no need to activate a Save command. Notebooks are saved to the place you designated when you first created the notebook. ∎

TIP

Switching Between Notebooks You can click the notebook name's drop-down arrow at the top of the page to display a menu of your notebooks. Click the one you want to work with and OneNote switches to it. ∎

ADDING A PAGE TITLE

You can add titles to your notebook pages to help you keep your information organized and easy to identify. Titles appear at the top of the page and in the page tab area to the right.

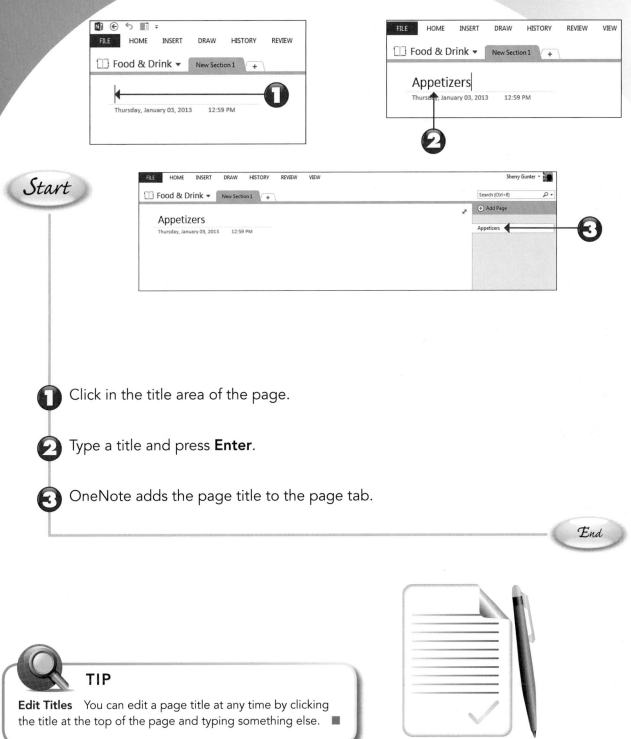

1 Click in the title area of the page.

2 Type a title and press **Enter**.

3 OneNote adds the page title to the page tab.

Start

End

TIP

Edit Titles You can edit a page title at any time by clicking the title at the top of the page and typing something else. ■

CREATING A SECTION

You can add sections to a notebook to create logical groups of pages. Sections are much like the color tabs in a binder notebook. Sections appear as tabs at the top of the page. You can add as many sections as you need to your digital notebook. To view a section, click the section tab.

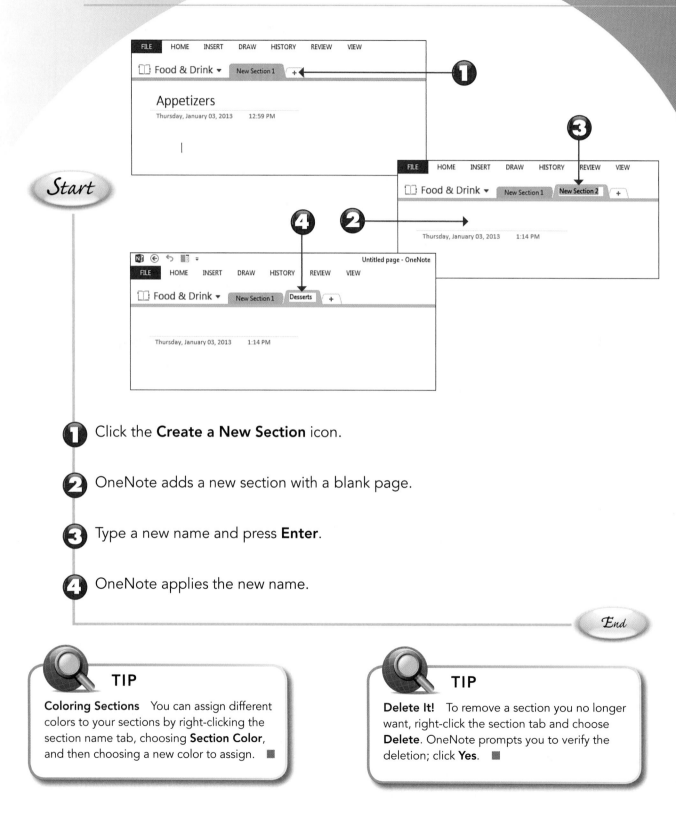

1 Click the **Create a New Section** icon.

2 OneNote adds a new section with a blank page.

3 Type a new name and press **Enter**.

4 OneNote applies the new name.

TIP

Coloring Sections You can assign different colors to your sections by right-clicking the section name tab, choosing **Section Color**, and then choosing a new color to assign. ■

TIP

Delete It! To remove a section you no longer want, right-click the section tab and choose **Delete**. OneNote prompts you to verify the deletion; click **Yes**. ■

You can easily move sections within your notebook. For example, you might want to move a section to the front of the notebook, or move another to the back.

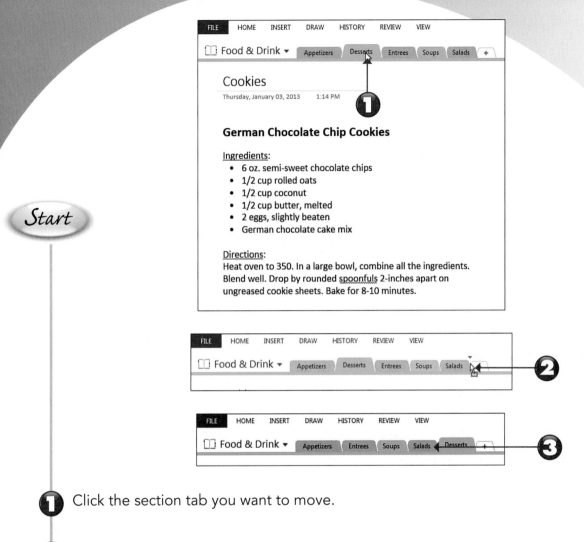

 Start

 End

1 Click the section tab you want to move.

2 Drag it to a new location and drop it into place; an indicator marker appears as you drag the section tab.

3 OneNote rearranges the existing tabs to fit the change in order.

TIP

Merging Sections You can merge sections, if needed, to create one large section. Right-click the section tab you want to merge and click **Merge into Another Section**. This opens the Merge Section dialog box. Select the section you want to merge into and click **Merge**. ■

TIP

Reset Colors You can change the colors of your section tabs. Right-click a tab, click **Section Color**, and then choose a different color from the menu list. ■

ADDING NOTES

You can add all kinds of notes to a page in a notebook simply by typing on the page. Although typing in notes is similar to typing text in Microsoft Word, notes are contained in their own boxes, which you can move around the page, resize, and format. Although boxed, no actual borders appear around the note text.

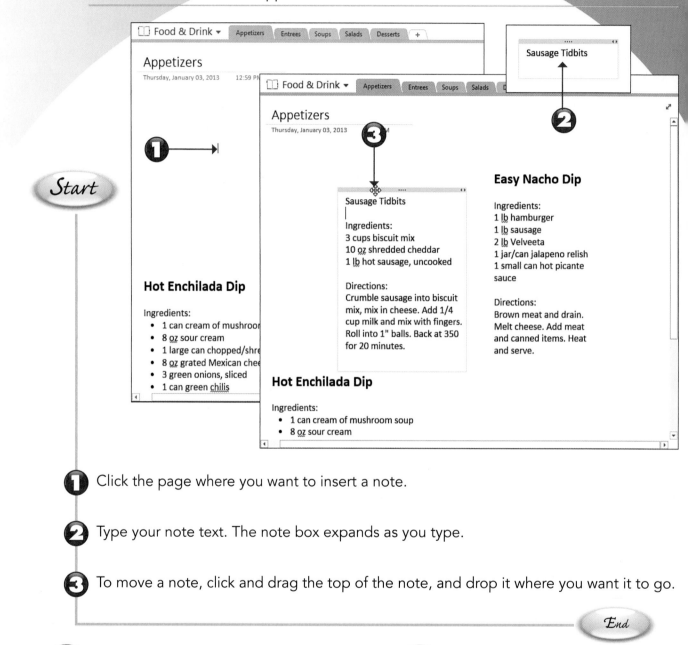

1 Click the page where you want to insert a note.

2 Type your note text. The note box expands as you type.

3 To move a note, click and drag the top of the note, and drop it where you want it to go.

Start

End

TIP

Formatting Text You can format your note text using the formatting commands on the Ribbon's **Home** tab or using the mini toolbar that appears when you select text. OneNote's basic formatting tools include fonts, sizes, font colors, and alignment settings, just to name a few. ■

TIP

Adding Other Elements You can also add other elements to your notebook, including artwork, video clips, sound files, and more. See Chapter 22, "Enhancing and Managing Notebooks," to learn more about including several of these elements in your notebooks. ■

ADDING PAGES

You can add pages to your notebook just as easily as you can add sections.

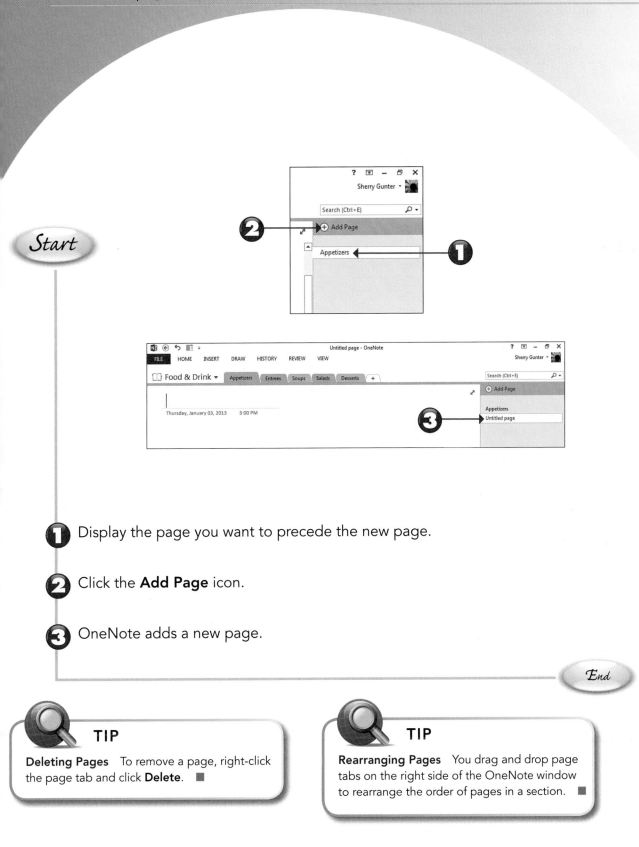

Start

Display the page you want to precede the new page.

Click the **Add Page** icon.

OneNote adds a new page.

End

TIP

Deleting Pages   To remove a page, right-click the page tab and click **Delete**. ■

TIP

Rearranging Pages   You drag and drop page tabs on the right side of the OneNote window to rearrange the order of pages in a section. ■

CREATING SUBPAGES

You can make a page subordinate to another page, which is handy when you want to group similar subjects together, yet keep them on separate pages.

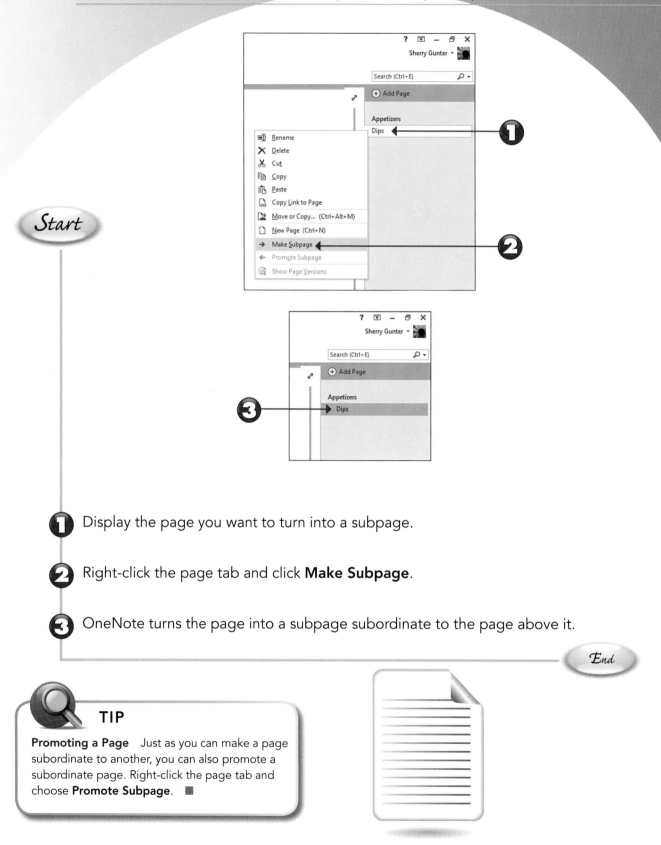

Start

1. Display the page you want to turn into a subpage.

2. Right-click the page tab and click **Make Subpage**.

3. OneNote turns the page into a subpage subordinate to the page above it.

End

TIP

Promoting a Page Just as you can make a page subordinate to another, you can also promote a subordinate page. Right-click the page tab and choose **Promote Subpage**. ■

ADDING A PICTURE

You can add pictures from your computer, the Web, a scanner, or a digital camera. In this task, you see how to add a picture stored on your computer. After you insert a picture, you can move it and resize it.

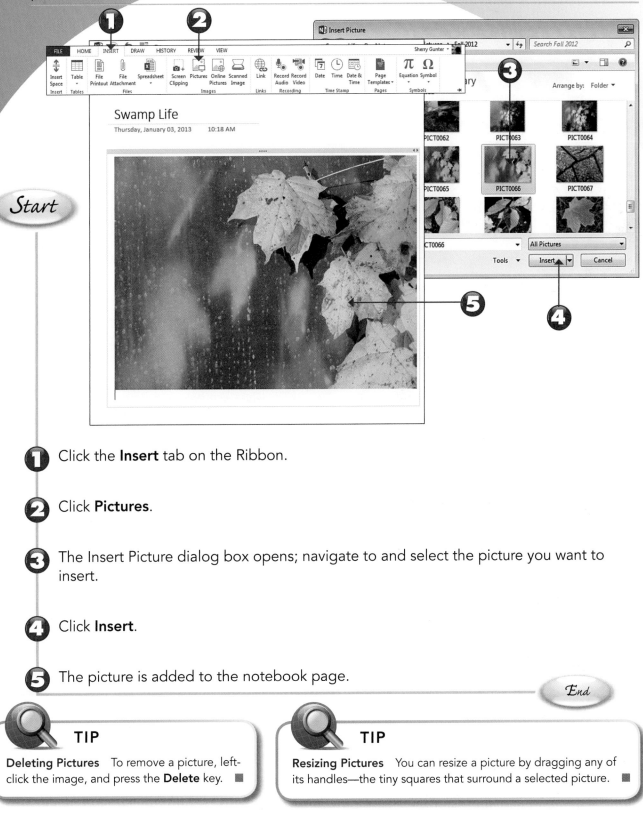

Start

1 Click the **Insert** tab on the Ribbon.

2 Click **Pictures**.

3 The Insert Picture dialog box opens; navigate to and select the picture you want to insert.

4 Click **Insert**.

5 The picture is added to the notebook page.

End

TIP

Deleting Pictures To remove a picture, left-click the image, and press the **Delete** key. ■

TIP

Resizing Pictures You can resize a picture by dragging any of its handles—the tiny squares that surround a selected picture. ■

APPLYING TAGS

You can use tags to help you remember important things or mark important notes in your notebooks. You can find a list of preset tags on the Ribbon's Home tab.

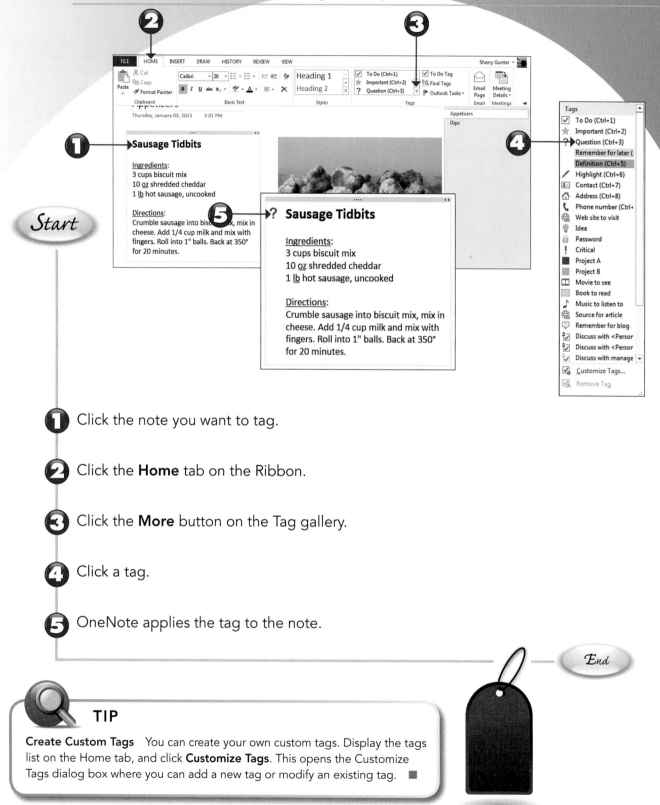

1. Click the note you want to tag.

2. Click the **Home** tab on the Ribbon.

3. Click the **More** button on the Tag gallery.

4. Click a tag.

5. OneNote applies the tag to the note.

TIP

Create Custom Tags   You can create your own custom tags. Display the tags list on the Home tab, and click **Customize Tags**. This opens the Customize Tags dialog box where you can add a new tag or modify an existing tag. ■

INSERTING LINKS

You can add links in your notes to other notebooks, pages, or websites. If you know a web address, you can type it or use your default browser program to navigate to a page.

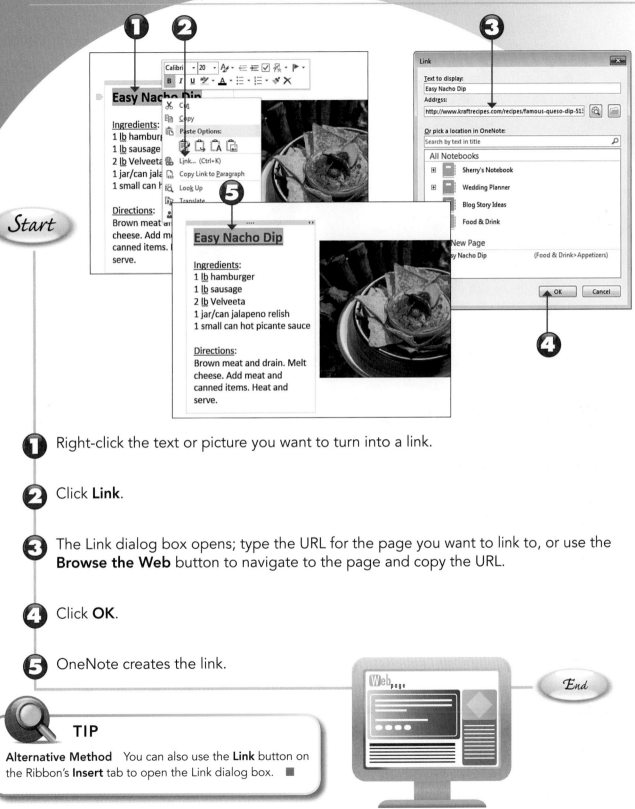

1 Right-click the text or picture you want to turn into a link.

2 Click **Link**.

3 The Link dialog box opens; type the URL for the page you want to link to, or use the **Browse the Web** button to navigate to the page and copy the URL.

4 Click **OK**.

5 OneNote creates the link.

TIP

Alternative Method   You can also use the **Link** button on the Ribbon's **Insert** tab to open the Link dialog box. ■

APPLYING A TEMPLATE

OneNote includes a variety of templates you can use to create all kinds of notebook pages. For example, you can apply templates for business meeting notes, lecture notes for classroom situations, to-do lists, and more.

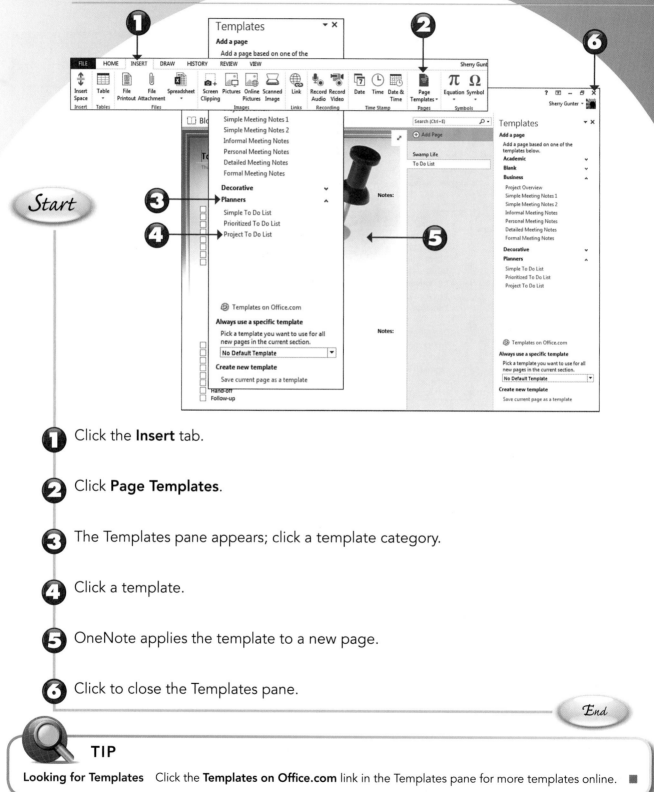

Click the **Insert** tab.

Click **Page Templates**.

The Templates pane appears; click a template category.

Click a template.

OneNote applies the template to a new page.

Click to close the Templates pane.

TIP

Looking for Templates Click the **Templates on Office.com** link in the Templates pane for more templates online. ■

CHANGE NOTEBOOK VIEWS

You can switch between Normal view (the default) and Full Page view, which enables you to view more of your notebook page onscreen.

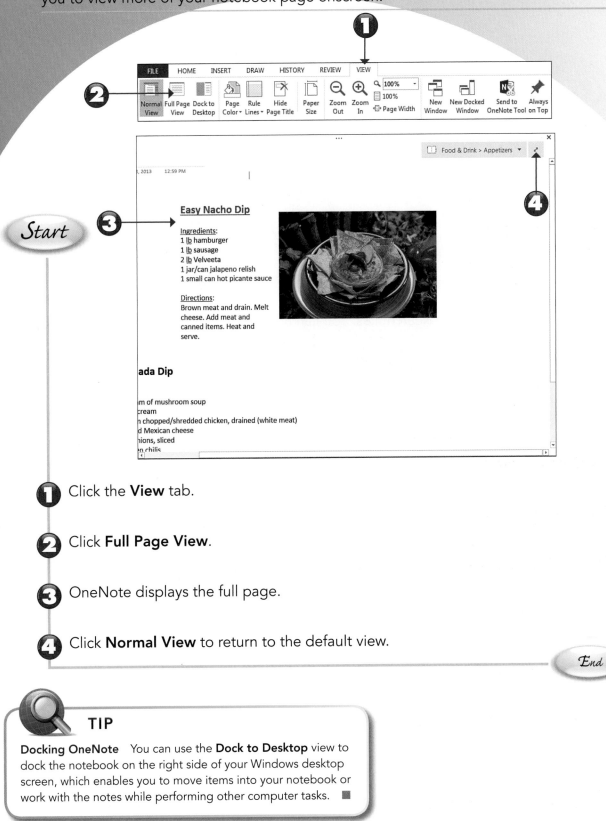

1 Click the **View** tab.

2 Click **Full Page View**.

3 OneNote displays the full page.

4 Click **Normal View** to return to the default view.

TIP

Docking OneNote You can use the **Dock to Desktop** view to dock the notebook on the right side of your Windows desktop screen, which enables you to move items into your notebook or work with the notes while performing other computer tasks.

Chapter 22

ENHANCING AND MANAGING NOTEBOOKS

Text notes and artwork aren't the only parts of building notebooks. You might need to collect other types of items for a project, such as video data or an entire folder of research files. You can add more than text notes and images inserted directly into your OneNote notebooks. You can also add the contents of files, create custom tables, record video and audio clips, and more.

OneNote also includes an entire tab of tools on the Ribbon to create drawings, shapes, and other freeform designs. For example, you can use the Highlighter Pen to highlight text in your notes, or you can use the shapes tools to draw arrows and circles on your pages.

In addition to other types of information you can add, you can also tap into OneNote's other powers to quickly swap tasks with Microsoft Outlook and import files into your notebook pages.

ADDING VIDEO TO A NOTEBOOK

The playback tools help you work with video and audio clips

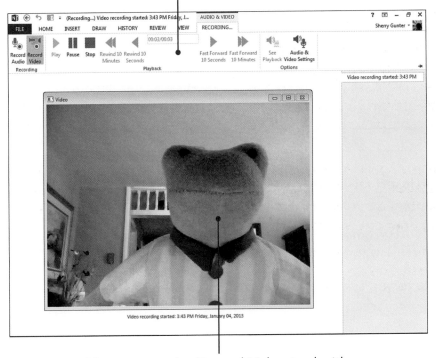

You can use the Record Video tool with your computer's built-in camera to record video clips

ATTACHING FILES

OneNote is a great place to organize information about a particular project or subject, including keeping copies of files. You can add file attachments of all kinds. You can choose to attach files as icons, which can be clicked to open the original file, or you can attach files as printouts, which insert a copy of their content as a note on the page.

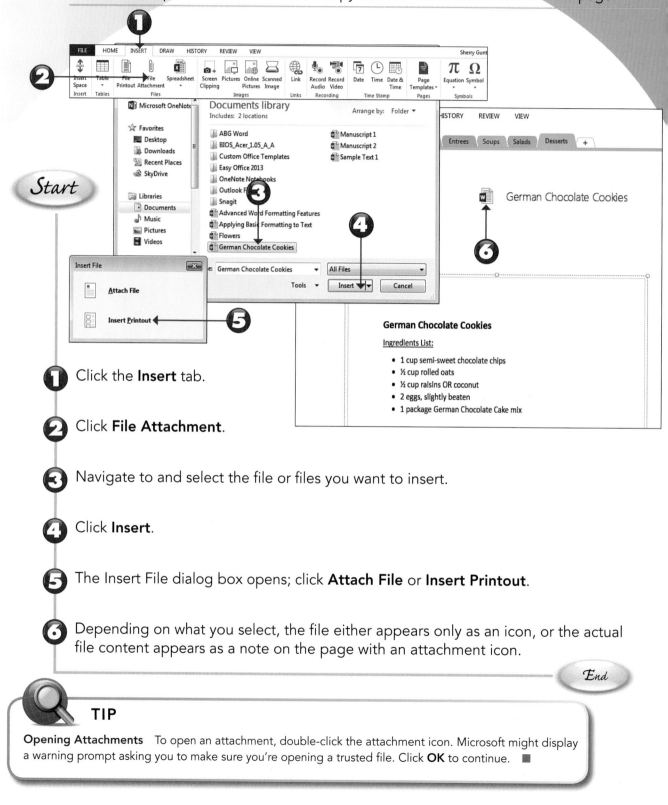

Click the **Insert** tab.

Click **File Attachment**.

Navigate to and select the file or files you want to insert.

Click **Insert**.

The Insert File dialog box opens; click **Attach File** or **Insert Printout**.

Depending on what you select, the file either appears only as an icon, or the actual file content appears as a note on the page with an attachment icon.

End

TIP

Opening Attachments To open an attachment, double-click the attachment icon. Microsoft might display a warning prompt asking you to make sure you're opening a trusted file. Click **OK** to continue. ■

INSERTING TABLES

You can insert basic tables as notes on a page. You can specify how many rows and columns you want and populate the cells with data. When you add a table, a special tab appears on the Ribbon with tools for working with the table.

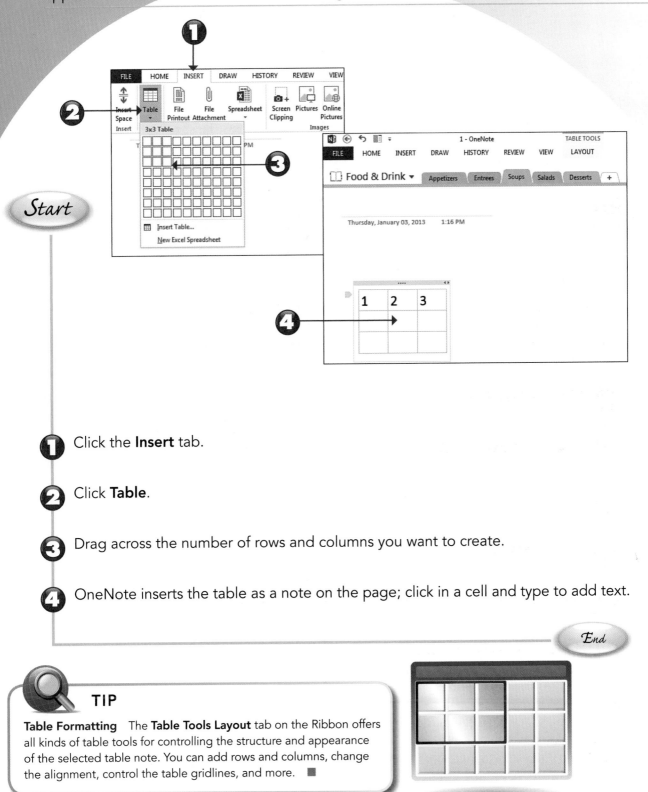

Start

1 Click the **Insert** tab.

2 Click **Table**.

3 Drag across the number of rows and columns you want to create.

4 OneNote inserts the table as a note on the page; click in a cell and type to add text.

End

TIP

Table Formatting The **Table Tools Layout** tab on the Ribbon offers all kinds of table tools for controlling the structure and appearance of the selected table note. You can add rows and columns, change the alignment, control the table gridlines, and more. ■

If your computer has a built-in microphone, which most computers do, you can record audio to a notebook page. This is handy if you need to record a lecture or presentation.

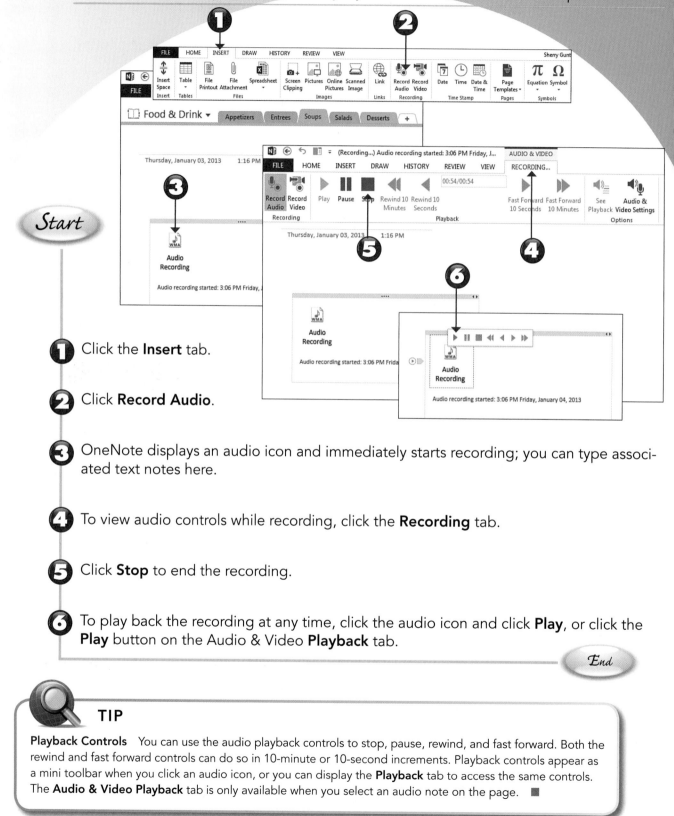

Start

1. Click the **Insert** tab.

2. Click **Record Audio**.

3. OneNote displays an audio icon and immediately starts recording; you can type associated text notes here.

4. To view audio controls while recording, click the **Recording** tab.

5. Click **Stop** to end the recording.

6. To play back the recording at any time, click the audio icon and click **Play**, or click the **Play** button on the Audio & Video **Playback** tab.

End

TIP

Playback Controls   You can use the audio playback controls to stop, pause, rewind, and fast forward. Both the rewind and fast forward controls can do so in 10-minute or 10-second increments. Playback controls appear as a mini toolbar when you click an audio icon, or you can display the **Playback** tab to access the same controls. The **Audio & Video Playback** tab is only available when you select an audio note on the page. ■

You can use your computer's built-in video camera to record video clips as notes on your notebook page.

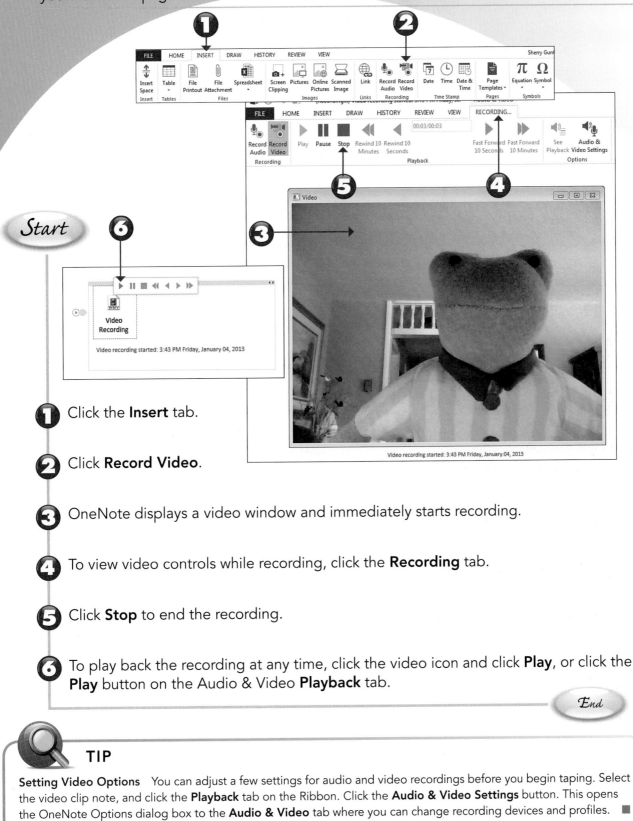

① Click the **Insert** tab.

② Click **Record Video**.

③ OneNote displays a video window and immediately starts recording.

④ To view video controls while recording, click the **Recording** tab.

⑤ Click **Stop** to end the recording.

⑥ To play back the recording at any time, click the video icon and click **Play**, or click the **Play** button on the Audio & Video **Playback** tab.

End

TIP

Setting Video Options   You can adjust a few settings for audio and video recordings before you begin taping. Select the video clip note, and click the **Playback** tab on the Ribbon. Click the **Audio & Video Settings** button. This opens the OneNote Options dialog box to the **Audio & Video** tab where you can change recording devices and profiles. ■

ADDING A TIMESTAMP

Some of the notes and pages you create might need a date or time added so that you can keep track of when you made the note. You can use OneNote's Timestamp tools to instantly add a note containing the date or the time, or both.

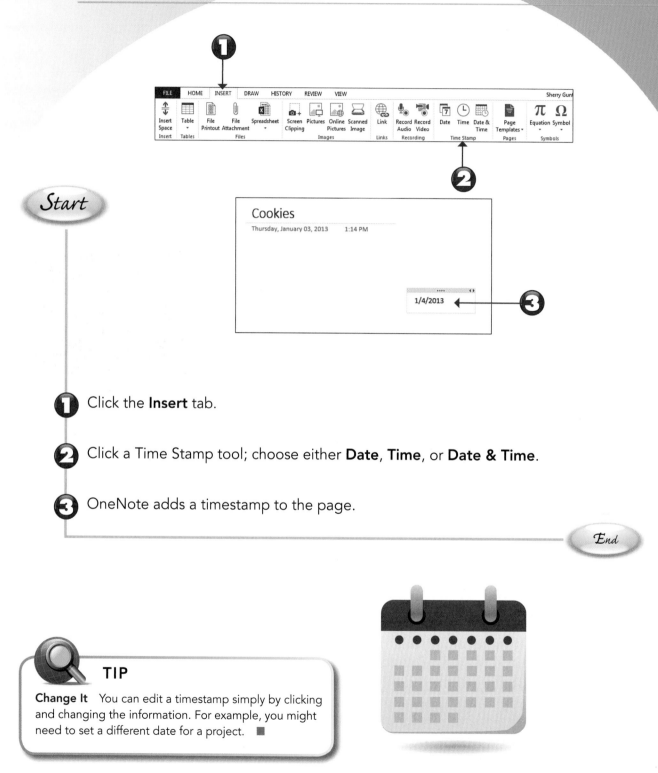

Click the **Insert** tab.

Click a Time Stamp tool; choose either **Date**, **Time**, or **Date & Time**.

OneNote adds a timestamp to the page.

TIP

Change It   You can edit a timestamp simply by clicking and changing the information. For example, you might need to set a different date for a project. ■

EMAILING A PAGE

You can use OneNote with Microsoft Outlook to email a notebook page.

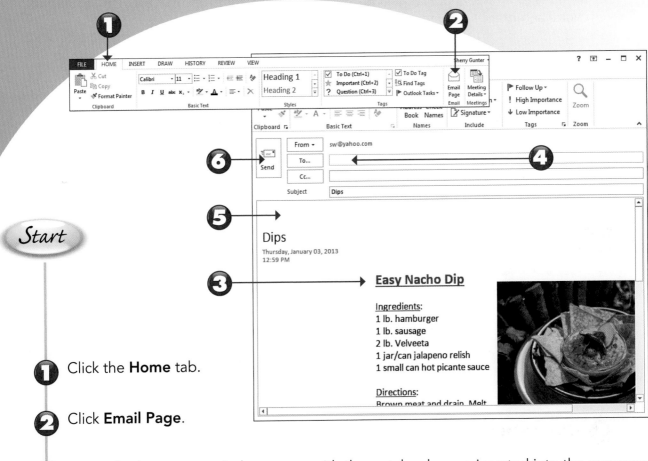

Start

1. Click the **Home** tab.

2. Click **Email Page**.

3. An Outlook message window opens with the notebook page inserted into the message body and the page title as the subject heading.

4. Type the recipient's email address.

5. Type any additional message text, as needed.

6. Click **Send**.

End

TIP

Sending You can also send an entire notebook as an attachment, PDF file, Word file, or blog. Click the **File** tab and choose **Send** to view your options. ■

From:
To:
Cc:
Subject:

The Draw tab on OneNote's Ribbon has an array of drawing tools and controls for adding all kinds of freehand drawings and shapes to your pages. You can use the tools to create charts and graphs, pointer arrows, and more.

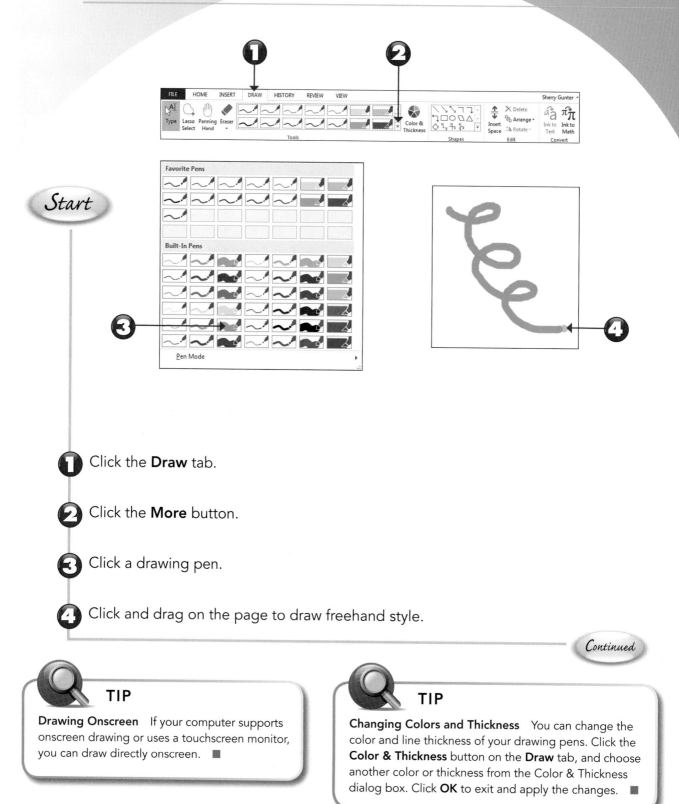

Start

1. Click the **Draw** tab.

2. Click the **More** button.

3. Click a drawing pen.

4. Click and drag on the page to draw freehand style.

Continued

TIP

Drawing Onscreen   If your computer supports onscreen drawing or uses a touchscreen monitor, you can draw directly onscreen. ■

TIP

Changing Colors and Thickness   You can change the color and line thickness of your drawing pens. Click the **Color & Thickness** button on the **Draw** tab, and choose another color or thickness from the Color & Thickness dialog box. Click **OK** to exit and apply the changes. ■

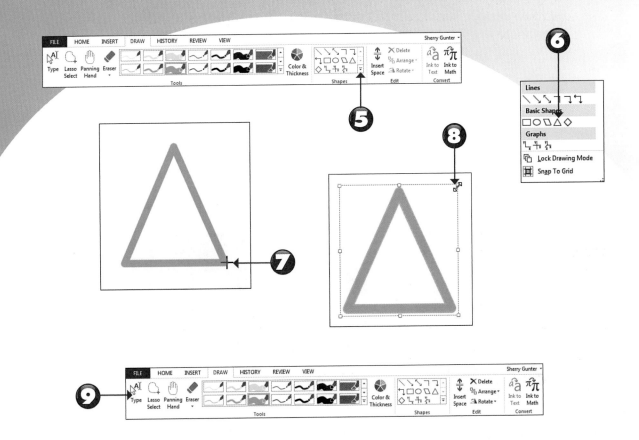

5 To draw a shape with your selected pen, click the Shapes palette's **More** button.

6 Click a shape.

7 Click and drag on the page to draw.

8 To resize a shape, click and drag a handle.

9 To turn off the drawing tool, click the **Type** button on the Draw tab.

End

TIP

Highlight It You can use the highlighter pens to highlight in your text notes. You might find this useful when taking notes in class or in meetings, or when reviewing information later. ■

TIP

Undo It You can use the **Undo** button on the Quick Access toolbar to undo a drawing. You can also erase parts of a drawing using the Eraser tool on the **Draw** tab. ■

SENDING A TASK TO OUTLOOK

You can turn a note into an Outlook task. For example, you might want to take a to-do list in a notebook and use it as a to-do list in Outlook to assign it to a co-worker or coordinate it with calendar dates.

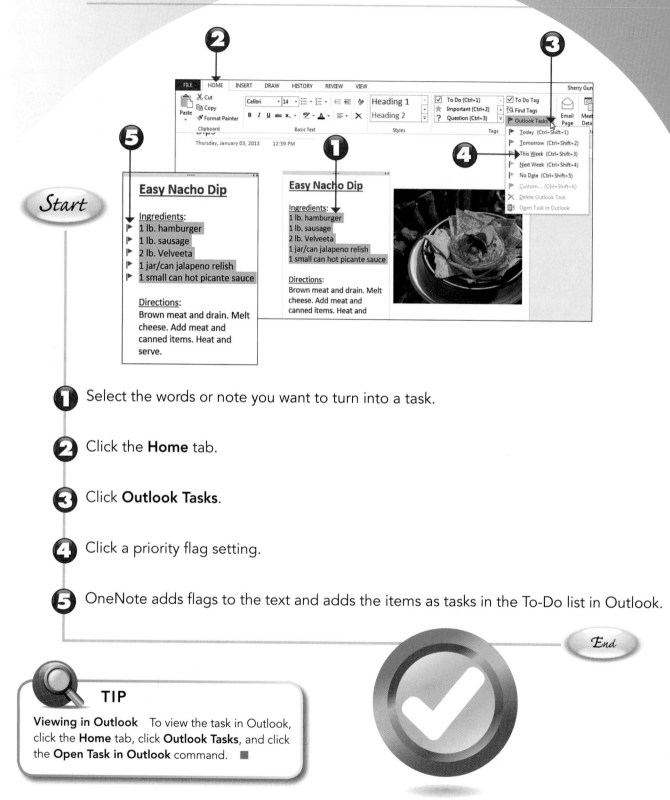

Start

Select the words or note you want to turn into a task.

Click the **Home** tab.

Click **Outlook Tasks**.

Click a priority flag setting.

OneNote adds flags to the text and adds the items as tasks in the To-Do list in Outlook.

End

TIP

Viewing in Outlook   To view the task in Outlook, click the **Home** tab, click **Outlook Tasks**, and click the **Open Task in Outlook** command. ∎

SENDING A FILE TO ONENOTE

Using OneNote's handy Send to OneNote Tool, you can quickly clip items on your Windows desktop screen and send to a notebook. You can also send other Microsoft Office files or web pages. The Send to OneNote Tool sits on the desktop ready to use when you start the OneNote program.

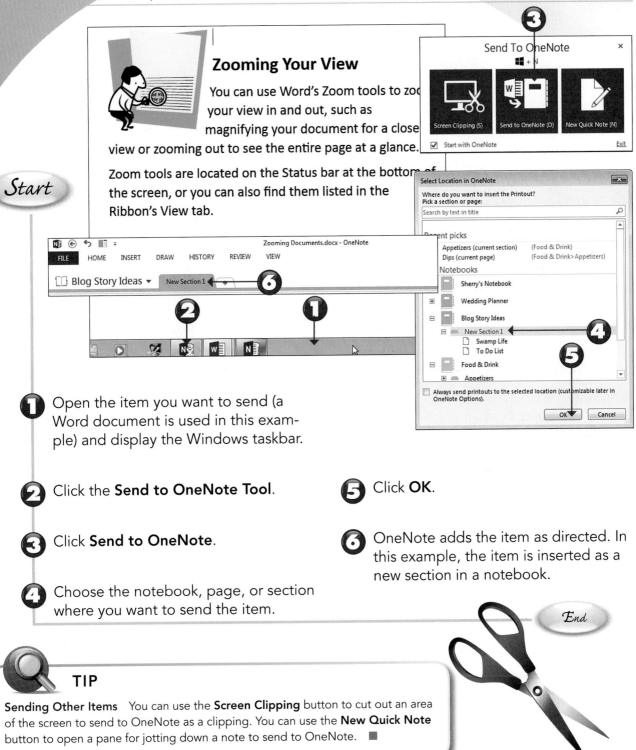

Zooming Your View

You can use Word's Zoom tools to zoom your view in and out, such as magnifying your document for a close view or zooming out to see the entire page at a glance.

Zoom tools are located on the Status bar at the bottom of the screen, or you can also find them listed in the Ribbon's View tab.

Start

1. Open the item you want to send (a Word document is used in this example) and display the Windows taskbar.

2. Click the **Send to OneNote Tool**.

3. Click **Send to OneNote**.

4. Choose the notebook, page, or section where you want to send the item.

5. Click **OK**.

6. OneNote adds the item as directed. In this example, the item is inserted as a new section in a notebook.

End

TIP

Sending Other Items   You can use the **Screen Clipping** button to cut out an area of the screen to send to OneNote as a clipping. You can use the **New Quick Note** button to open a pane for jotting down a note to send to OneNote. ■

Glossary

A

active cell   The selected cell in Excel, highlighted with a border.

animation   A PowerPoint design tool that makes objects move. You can apply basic animation to objects such as shapes, text placeholders, text boxes, SmartArt graphics, and charts.

appointment   A specified date and time on an Outlook calendar.

AutoSum   An Excel button that sums a series of numbers in a row or column automatically.

B

Backstage view   Area of Office, accessed by clicking the File tab, in which you can perform common file-related tasks in one place.

Bcc   Abbreviation for blind carbon copy. In Outlook, using the bcc box sends a copy of the message to listed recipients without notifying other recipients.

bitmap   A picture type composed of pixels (tiny dots of color), such as photos from a digital camera. Common bitmap file formats include .bmp, .gif, .jpg, .png, and .tif.

bookmark   An identification of a section or place in a Word document. You can add bookmarks to lengthy documents that jump you to another location within the document.

C

Cc   Abbreviation for carbon copy. In Outlook, using the cc box sends a copy of the message to the listed recipients and notifies other recipients of the copy.

cell   A box in an Excel worksheet where you can enter data and perform calculations. Each cell identifies the intersection of a row and column, such as A1.

cell address   The intersection of an Excel column letter and row number, such as cell A1 or cell D8. The name box in the upper-left corner of the screen displays the cell address of the selected cell.

chart   A graphical representation of data displaying numbers as shapes that can be compared to one another. Common chart types include column, pie, line, and bar.

Clipboard   A pane that stores cut, copied, and pasted objects.

content palette   A group of six buttons that displays on selected PowerPoint slide layouts, enabling you to add a table, chart, SmartArt graphic, picture, online picture, or video to your slide.

contextual tab   A tab that displays only when you perform a specific task. For example, the Drawing Tools–Format tab displays only when you select a shape.

crop   A tool that removes excess content in a picture.

D

dialog box launcher   A diagonal arrow in the lower-right corner of selected groups on the Ribbon that opens a related dialog box.

E

email signature   Text or graphics that display at the bottom of Outlook email messages.

event   An all-day occurrence in an Outlook calendar, such as a birthday, anniversary, or conference.

F-G

footer   Text that repeats at the bottom of every page in a Word, Excel, or PowerPoint document, such as a page number.

Format Painter   A button on the Home tab to reuse formatting you applied to an existing object.

formula   An Excel calculation that adds, subtracts, multiplies, or divides two or more numbers.

H

header   Text that repeats at the top of every page in a Word, Excel, or PowerPoint document, such as a title or date.

I-L

ink   An annotation you create and save during a PowerPoint slide show using the on-screen pen.

M

Microsoft account   A free online account required to access Microsoft applications, such as SkyDrive, Hotmail, or Messenger. Formerly, this was called a Windows Live ID.

mini toolbar   A small contextual toolbar that displays only when you perform a specific task. For example, when you select text, this toolbar displays with options related to text formatting.

N

notebook   A OneNote electronic document for collecting and storing data.

O

object   A component you include in an Office document, such as text, shapes, pictures, text boxes, placeholders, SmartArt, charts, WordArt, and so forth.

Office theme   A theme that controls the appearance of the Office interface rather than the appearance of any documents you create.

operator   An indicator of an action to perform in Excel: plus (+), minus (–), multiply (*), or divide (/).

P

pane   A window in which you can perform common tasks; it differs from a dialog box because a pane does not cover your screen.

PDF   Abbreviation for Portable Document Format, a file format that makes your Office documents readable by anyone who has the free Adobe Reader software.

PivotTable   A table that summarizes and analyzes Excel data.

placeholder   Container on a PowerPoint slide layout in which you can insert and position content.

Presenter view   A PowerPoint view that displays a full-screen presentation your audience can see and another view for you (the presenter) that includes slide previews, speaker notes, a timer, and more.

Q

Quick Access toolbar   A small toolbar that displays in the upper-left corner of your screen and is available no matter which Ribbon tab you select.

R

Ribbon   A navigation tool divided into tabs that displays across the top of all Office applications and provides an easy way to access common commands and buttons.

RSS feed   Abbreviation for Really Simple Syndication feed, a technology that enables web content to be converted into a feed that you can view as message posts. In Outlook, you can receive RSS feeds for blogs, podcasts, news, and more.

S

shape   An object, such as a line, arrow, rectangle, circle, square, or callout.

SkyDrive   Microsoft's online storage and file-sharing solution, available at http://skydrive.com.

slide layout   A PowerPoint tool for adding specific types of content to your slides, such as text, tables, charts, and pictures.

slide master   A PowerPoint design tool that helps you achieve uniformity by storing data about a presentation's theme and slide layouts, such as colors, fonts, effects, background, placeholders, and positioning—and applying it consistently throughout your presentation. Each presentation contains at least one slide master.

Slide Sorter view   A PowerPoint view that displays smaller versions of slides in several rows and columns.

slide transition   A PowerPoint animation effect between two slides, such as a fade, wipe, or reveal.

SmartArt   A design tool for combining shapes and text to create informative lists, matrixes, pyramids, and more.

sparkline   An Excel mini chart that graphically represents the data in adjacent cells.

T-U

template   The underlying structure for a document; a fill-in-the-blanks skeleton to help you build files.

theme   A standalone file with coordinated colors, fonts, and effects that you apply to an Office document.

V

vector   A picture type composed of points, lines, and curves. Common vector file formats include .eps and .wmf.

video embed code   A string of HTML code that enables you to share web videos in PowerPoint presentations. For example, YouTube and Vimeo offer video embed codes for embedding their videos.

W

Web App   An abbreviated version of a Microsoft Office application that you can access online via SkyDrive. Web apps are available for Word, Excel, PowerPoint, and OneNote.

WordArt   A design tool for creating special text effects such as shadowed, rotated, stretched, and multicolored text.

workbook   An Excel file, identified with the extension .xls.

worksheet An individual "page" in an Excel workbook consisting of a series of rows and columns. Each Excel workbook contains one or more worksheets, identified with a unique tab at the bottom of the screen.

X-Z

XPS Abbreviation for XML Paper Specification, a format that enables you to create documents readable with the XPS Viewer.

Index

E

P

T

W

X-Y-Z

MAKE THE MOST OF YOUR SMARTPHONE, TABLET, COMPUTER, AND MORE! CHECK OUT THE MY…BOOK SERIES

ISBN 13: 9780133371727   ISBN 13: 9780789750334   ISBN 13: 9780789748515   ISBN 13: 9780789749482

Full-Color, Step-by-Step Guides

The "My…" series is a visually rich, task-based series to help you get up and running with your new device and technology, and tap into some of the hidden, or less obvious, features. The organized, task-based format allows you to quickly and easily find exactly the task you want to accomplish, and then shows you how to achieve it with minimal text and plenty of visual cues.

Visit quepublishing.com/mybooks to learn more about the My… book series from Que.

Your purchase of *Easy Office 2013* includes access to a free online edition for 45 days through the **Safari Books Online** subscription service. Nearly every Que book is available online through **Safari Books Online**, along with thousands of books and videos from publishers such as Addison-Wesley Professional, Cisco Press, Exam Cram, IBM Press, O'Reilly Media, Prentice Hall, Sams, and VMware Press.

Safari Books Online is a digital library providing searchable, on-demand access to thousands of technology, digital media, and professional development books and videos from leading publishers. With one monthly or yearly subscription price, you get unlimited access to learning tools and information on topics including mobile app and software development, tips and tricks on using your favorite gadgets, networking, project management, graphic design, and much more.

Activate your FREE Online Edition at
informit.com/safarifree

STEP 1: Enter the coupon code: TVCXEBI.

STEP 2: New Safari users, complete the brief registration form.
Safari subscribers, just log in.

If you have difficulty registering on Safari or accessing the online edition,
please e-mail customer-service@safaribooksonline.com

igloobooks

Published in 2013
by Igloo Books Ltd
Cottage Farm
Sywell
NN6 0BJ
www.igloobooks.com

Copyright© 2013 Igloo Books Ltd

FIR003 0513
2 4 6 8 10 9 7 5 3 1
ISBN 978-1-78197-467-4

Illustrated by Natalie Hinrichsen

Printed and manufactured in China

Old MacDonald had a Farm

Old MacDonald had a farm, E-I-E-I-O,
and on that farm he had some hens, E-I-E-I-O.

With a cluck-cluck here and a cluck-cluck there,
here a cluck, there a cluck, everywhere a cluck-cluck.
Old MacDonald had a farm, E-I-E-I-O.

Old MacDonald had a farm, E-I-E-I-O,
and on that farm he had some chicks, E-I-E-I-O.

With a cheep-cheep here and a cheep-cheep there,
here a cheep, there a cheep, everywhere a cheep-cheep.
Old MacDonald had a farm, E-I-E-I-O.

Old MacDonald had a farm, E-I-E-I-O,
and on that farm he had some cows, E-I-E-I-O.

With a moo-moo here and a moo-moo there,
here a moo, there a moo, everywhere a moo-moo.
Old MacDonald had a farm, E-I-E-I-O.

Old MacDonald had a farm, E-I-E-I-O,
and on that farm he had a horse, E-I-E-I-O.

With a neigh-neigh here and a neigh-neigh there,
here a neigh, there a neigh, everywhere a neigh-neigh.
Old MacDonald had a farm, E-I-E-I-O.

Old MacDonald had a farm, E-I-E-I-O,
and on that farm he had some pigs, E-I-E-I-O.

With an oink-oink here and an oink-oink there,
here an oink, there an oink, everywhere an oink-oink.
Old MacDonald had a farm, E-I-E-I-O.

Old MacDonald had a farm, E-I-E-I-O,
and on that farm he had some ducks, E-I-E-I-O.

With a quack-quack here and a quack-quack there,
here a quack, there a quack, everywhere a quack-quack.
Old MacDonald had a farm, E-I-E-I-O.

Old MacDonald had a farm, E-I-E-I-O,
and on that farm he had a dog, E-I-E-I-O.

With a woof-woof here and a woof-woof there,
here a woof, there a woof, everywhere a woof-woof.
Old MacDonald had a farm, E-I-E-I-O.

Old MacDonald had a farm, E-I-E-I-O,
and on that farm he had some sheep, E-I-E-I-O.

With a baa-baa here and a baa-baa there,
here a baa, there a baa, everywhere a baa-baa.
Old MacDonald had a farm, E-I-E-I-O.

Old MacDonald had a farm, E-I-E-I-O,
and on that farm he had some mice, E-I-E-I-O.

With a squeak-squeak here and a squeak-squeak there,
here a squeak, there a squeak, everywhere a squeak-squeak.
Old MacDonald had a farm, E-I-E-I-O.

Old MacDonald had a farm, E-I-E-I-O,
and on that farm he had a cat E-I-E-I-O.

With a miaow-miaow here and a miaow-miaow there,
here a miaow, there a miaow, everywhere a miaow-miaow.
Old MacDonald had a farm, E-I-E-I-O.

Old MacDonald had a farm, E-I-E-I-O,
and on that farm he had some animals, E-I-E-I-O.

With a cluck, cheep, neigh and a moo, oink, quack,
here a woof, there a baa, everywhere a miaow, squeak!
Old MacDonald had a farm, E-I-E-I-O.